GROUNDWORK

GROUNDWORK

The Inside Story Behind
Jim Smith's
Derby County

RYAN HILLS

First published by Pitch Publishing, 2022

Pitch Publishing
9 Donnington Park,
85 Birdham Road,
Chichester,
West Sussex,
PO20 7AJ
www.pitchpublishing.co.uk
info@pitchpublishing.co.uk

A CIP catalogue record is available for this book
from the British Library.

ISBN 978 1 80150 088 3

Typesetting and origination by Pitch Publishing
Printed and bound in Great Britain by TJ Books, Padstow

CONTENTS

THE BALD EAGLE

The Bald Eagle landed
then conquered
armed with the tactics
the players responded
switched the narrative
to change the story
from years in the shadows
to top-flight glory
restored our Pride
before we moved to the park
the Baseball Ground
that Sunday
one mighty roar
the limbs were flying
as Van Der Laan scored
a next-level squad
those players we saw
from Igor Štimac
to Paul McGrath
thrashing the Arsenal
against all odds
he led us to victory
as underdogs
to hear you've sung
your final swansong
has hit this fanbase
like a bullet
through the heart
never forgotten
always revered
gave those that remember
some of our best years
as you take your final flight
Bald Eagle
you'll always be here
from our hearts Jim Smith
you'll never disappear

Poem by Jamie Thrasivoulou

FOREWORD BY STEVE McCLAREN

DERBY COUNTY is a very special football club for me. When I look at my career, I've been there as a player, an assistant, a manager (twice) and in a consultancy role as well. But for everything I have achieved in my career, it wouldn't have followed the same path if I had never met Jim Smith. My time as a player had come to an end when I first became acquainted with Jim at Oxford United. I'll never forget that when he came to visit the club, I would essentially be his waiter. I'd ask for his order and without fail it would be "whisky and water, three ice cubes." I never knew where that simple act would take me, nor did I know how quickly it would lead to success that neither of us envisaged when we stepped foot onto Raynesway for the first time.

Myself and Jim came to Derby with a remit of rebuilding on a budget. The ask was never to achieve promotion, but it became clear to us quite early on that the squad we had built was something special. The mercurial Igor at the back with Dean Yates and Gary Rowett. Robin van der Laan alongside Darryl Powell, Gabbiadini and Dean Sturridge at the top. We couldn't believe what we had stumbled upon with that formation at the back. I remember we did one session on the field where we used it. We played just a little practice, worked on some things and... oh my God, we've got it.

Jim was just ahead of the game and everywhere he went, he was loved. That was the beauty of working with him. I went everywhere and saw the love and the affection that everybody gave him. Others will say the same for themselves, but Jim was like a second dad to me.

What we achieved in those years at the Baseball Ground and then Pride Park is something I will forever be proud of.

FOREWORD BY IGOR ŠTIMAC

DERBY IS my home, it's my home. When you mention Derby County, the first word which comes to my mind is home. That's my home. I'm not there but it's my home. Simple as that. My time at Derby County was something I didn't really expect to happen. When I first arrived at the Baseball Ground, I knew very little of the club – I didn't even know the division they were in. But from the moment I arrived, I felt like I was in the right place for me.

What we managed to achieve in a short space of time was incredible and I will forever be proud to be a part of a side managed by Jim Smith. He trusted me, and I loved him as a human being. I considered him as a father. But above this, the main memory I will always have is with the supporters of Derby County. You made me feel welcome from the first day and it was a privilege to captain The Rams. You can win fans hearts only in two ways – giving your heart on the pitch or playing amazing football. I think that I combined both.

A DISCLAIMER

I'M WRITING this introduction at the end of January 2022. We've just received the news that we are not going out of business, at least yet. It's the most harrowing time in the history of Derby County Football Club and, come the end of writing, this could be about a club that used to exist.

Derby County to me is everything. It's the one thing that can put a smile on my face when everything else can fail. In among darkness, the one thing I know can bring a sparkle back is visiting Pride Park. Admittedly when I get there it soon reminds me why over the years I've felt glum in the first place, but football has just a wonderful way of reminding you of the person you have been at different points in your life. That's what I hope this book can do for you.

The 1990s was one of the best decades in the history of Derby County, and it wasn't due to successes in terms of trophies. First Division promotion aside, the club didn't collect any silverware. Not a European trophy, nor a qualification. Not a domestic cup. Not even an Anglo-Italian sparkler. But what those years, and in particular from 1995–1999, brought to the city of Derby is indescribable.

Led by the Bald Eagle and ably supported by a coaching staff who would go on to every height imaginable in the game, Derby County became something more than the club of a city; they became world leaders. At the forefront of technology, formations and new ways of looking at the game, other clubs would follow the lead of Jim Smith and co. And masterminded and financed by a devoted chairman in Lionel Pickering, it was a perfect case of everything falling into place.

A wave of mesmerising talents would descend on Derbyshire. Igor, Stefano, Ciccio, Ace. They don't even need surnames to evoke a warm feeling somewhere deep inside. Then there was the move from the historic yet dilapidated Baseball Ground to Pride Park, marking what looked like a new era.

This is what Derby County is, but to a greater extent it is what a football club is. Because a football club is about building these memories and looking back with the fondness you don't get from anything else in life. While I loved working on my last book, *Pride: The Inside Story of Derby County*, it was about a 20-year spell mired in turmoil and ultimately disaster. This period is neither of those things. It was one of hope, of genuine delight among the fanbase and of the ability to dream. And that's what supporting a football club should be about. It's more than 90 minutes, it's a lifestyle. It's a family, a bond you can never break. Yes, it can be tough, it can be horrible and it can infuriate. But life without it is not worth considering right now.

I hope that we can have those days again. I hope we have survived.

ACKNOWLEDGEMENTS

THIS BOOK could not have been completed without the time, help and, ultimately, the kindness of all of those who contributed to it. Thank you to all of those who were involved in the club who I spoke with as part of this: Andy Croft, Andy Dawson, Bill Beswick, Branko Strupar, Chris Powell, Craig Burley, Damon Parkin, Dane Farrell, Danny Higginbotham, Dean Sturridge, Diane Wootton, Deon Burton, Don Amott, Gary Rowett, Igor Štimac, Jacob Laursen, the late Keith Loring, Kerry Ganly, Kevin Harper, Lars Bohinen, Lee Morris, Malcolm Christie, Marian McMinn, Mark Robinson, Mark Smith, Mart Poom, Marvin Robinson, Neil Sillett, Paul Simpson (and apologies once again for not thanking you in Pride), Paulo Wanchope, Peter Gadsby, Ramm Mylvaganam, Robin Van Der Laan, Ross Fletcher, Seth Johnson, Spencer Prior, Stefano Eranio, Steve Elliot, Steve McClaren, Steve Round, Steve Taylor and Youl Mawéné.

Thank you also to those close friends of Jim who gave up their time to go down memory lane: Harry Redknapp and Howard Wilkinson. I'd like to thank the Smith family for their support as well. To Colin Gibson and Graham Richards, it was an honour to sit down and hear your stories from those wonderful years. And Matija Grebenić, thank you for enlightening me on the War of Independence as part of the Igor chapter.

And thank you to those supporters who reminisced about the good times at the Baseball Ground and Pride Park with me: Andrew Beckett, Andy Margett, Dan Walls, George Glover,

Jamie Allen, Jimmy McLoughlin, Kelly Dreuitt, Ross Lowe, Stephen Newman and Tim Coxon.

This book could not have been done without the support of Jane at Pitch Publishing, so thank you again for taking a chance on me with *Pride* and *Groundwork*. Thanks also to Duncan Olner for the fantastic design of both. And a huge thank you to Gareth Davis, who is not only the wonderful editor of this book, but also an encyclopaedic devourer of Derby content.

Lastly, I would like to dedicate this book to every person who was a part of those fantastic years. There would be no book without those phenomenal days. I hope I've been able to do your work justice. Thank you to everyone who has supported and paid an interest in *Groundwork* as well. I won't list people (you know who you are) but I would like to just again thank my mum. You're great.

1

THE EAGLE HAS LANDED

'I AM not too sure I was flavour of the month with every Derby supporter,' wrote Jim Smith in his wonderfully nostalgia-driven memoir, *It's Only a Game*. 'I would say it was about 50-50.' Not one to accuse the great man of being wrong, but his maths may have been a little off. The camp of support was considerably below that 50.

By the time Roy McFarland had been moved on from the club following the disappointing 1994/95 campaign, Lionel Pickering was at a quandary. Spending hadn't worked, and now Arthur Cox and McFarland hadn't got the results separately either. A pair of play-off failures, followed by an abject ninth-placed finish was not the upturn in form expected by the Rams owner, and needing to re-evaluate, cost-cutting became the new focus. Therefore, any incoming manager had to have that factored in.

The still new-look Derby board had tried experienced and inexperienced to get to the Premier League for the first time, yet neither had worked. So when it came to the interview process they went for a blend. 'Sometimes you can say it was all sophisticated, but it was people sitting down and putting names together, aided and bettered by the fans. Selecting a manager was very methodical, not like nowadays with computers and stats. And there was no social media, no John Percy or *The Sun*,' admits Peter Gadsby who was the vice-chairman at the time. 'We had a lovely warm day in

Ednaston Manor [the home of Lionel Pickering], sitting around outside in Lionel's mansion. There was [Stuart] Webb, there was myself, the late John Kirkland and one other. And we interviewed three people that day: Neil Warnock, Martin O'Neill and Steve Bruce.' All three have in the years since been repeatedly rumoured for the Rams' managerial hotseat at various times, yet they remain in a select group of football managers in England who have not taken the job. Stuart Webb wrote in his autobiography *Clough, Maxwell and Me* that two other names were also considered: Ossie Ardiles and Mike Walker.

Gadsby said, 'Neil Warnock had made his name then at Huddersfield. He breezed in and talked through, and you could see people were thinking, "Yeah, looks a man."' And then he suddenly said, "I tell you what guys … you're lovely people, but I'm going to say no. I left my missus a week ago and I want to be as far away from Sheffield as I can. I've got Dan McCluskey at Plymouth who wants me to go down there, so I'm going there for a couple of years."' Warnock would be close to the Derby job many more times over the following 27 years but would never take charge.

'Then Steve Bruce came, all smart, perfect. Would have been player-manager so we'd got two for the price of one and Lionel liked that. He looked the man. Then he went away, subsequently to find out as soon as he got back that Alex Ferguson was at his house, telling him he was going nowhere and he wanted him there for another year,' Gadsby continued. Bruce would be close to the Derby job many more times over the following 27 years but would never take charge.

'Then we interviewed Martin O'Neill. [He was] doing a good job at Wycombe, been at Gainsborough before or somewhere, sat down and talked eloquently. Lionel sat there and said, "If I said to you I want to go back to the old Wolves formation, the W, attacking play and attacking football, what do you think you'd do?" He said, "Chairman, I'd look at it, I'd talk to you and then I'd do it my way." And Lionel went, "Hmm, big head, I don't like him." O'Neill would be close … you get the picture.'

With the three options seemingly out, attentions turned from inexperience to over-experience. Brian Horton was the first name debated. Recently departed from Manchester City after Francis Lee had taken charge as chairman, Horton had pedigree in the game and was – after that initial round of interviews – left with the job as his to lose. Gadsby remembers, 'Colin Gibson [of BBC Radio Derby] got to know that Brian Horton was coming to the Manor for an interview with Lionel. And he caught up with me and said, "[its] All over the radio, the fans don't want Brian Horton." It was quite vociferous, and he was very persuasive. Colin was Colin. I went into Lionel and told him that we can't have Brian, which Lionel was very upset by, but just said "you do you".'

As is the case, a search for a successor to McFarland was growing long and tedious, not aided by the head-rearing presence of Barry Fry, then of Birmingham City. 'I got a phone call when we used to do the live sports desk on a Sunday morning,' interjects Colin Gibson. 'I went in and I got a phone call from a director of the club saying, "Barry Fry is going to be our next manager. You can speculate on it this morning if you want to." So, we go on and "BBC Radio Derby understands Barry Fry is being lined up". And we did the sports desk, left at half past ten and an hour later my phone rings. "Is your name Colin Gibson?" And I can't remember whether it was Gold or Sullivan who were the owners of Birmingham at the time, one of the two. "Have you just said on the radio that our manager is going to be the manager of Derby County? How do you know this? I can tell you he's not going to be your next manager, he's our manager." Barry Fry was out of contract at Birmingham and was after a new one, and he played Birmingham an absolute blinder and the next day he got a new contract at Birmingham.'

Three managers had been interviewed. Two more were in the running. Yet Gadsby and his fellow directors were as far away from finding someone to lead Derby County into a new season as they had been weeks earlier. An impasse of days turned into weeks, with a decision still no closer to being agreed upon.

* * *

'Jim Smith? Eh?' That was the less than impressed consensus across the fanbase. For all the managerial experience Smith had, he would have been 'the last on that list' according to Gibson. Smith's record in football management was fine, to do him a slight disservice. Managing eight different clubs in 26 years, Smith was far from a newcomer to the managerial game like the three candidates interviewed in Ednaston Manor were. But so far removed was he from the early stages of management that he had seemingly gone completely out of the other side. Employed as the chief executive at the League Managers' Association (LMA), Smith had opted for a steer away from the grind of the training pitch and looked to have settled for life after management.

As his long-time friend and the then manager of recent First Division champions Leeds United, Howard Wilkinson, recalls, Jim and a desk job were not a match made in heaven. 'We started it [the LMA] in 1992/93, Graham Taylor and I started it. And that weren't a job for Jim; we both knew it. The main thing in regards to that was that I knew him and could trust him.' The duo had built up a mutual respect and strong bond since first meeting at local Sheffield football levels decades earlier. A joint stint together at Boston United followed, and the pair met time and again on the touchlines. But Wilkinson knew that if an opportunity was to come back up in management, it would be snatched at, as Smith himself admitted. 'As I feared, it did not take long for the doubts to be realised. To me management is like a drug and four months of cold turkey [Smith had left previous club Portsmouth after a defeat at Derby in January 1995] was more than enough. By the end of that season, I realised it was not for me.'

As the timeline turns out, it was a case of either/or between Smith and Horton, and when Gadsby and the media ensured that the latter wouldn't take the reins, the path was clear for Smith to swoop into place. And as Smith recalled a later conversation with Lionel Pickering, 'He [Pickering] took it upon himself to go out and give "Nobby" [Brian Horton] the bad news before telling Stuart [Webb] to call me and tell me the job was mine.' Smith, who claimed to have eight possible roles on his desk, was only intrigued by two: Derby County and Sheffield Wednesday. Ultimately, he opted for the sleeping giant of Derby and Pickering would assure Smith in the process that he had been his first choice. For Pickering himself, that may well have been true, notwithstanding the previous interviews. Years earlier the duo had met following a victory for Smith's then Portsmouth side at the Baseball Ground, finding a mutual appreciation for each other over post-match drinks, in a theme which would play a heavy part in their ability to maintain a relationship when working together.

Writing insightfully and with an honesty now alien in the modern game, Pickering's programme notes in the Arsenal edition of *The Ram* in 1997, the final game at the Baseball Ground, stated, 'By the time the Derby vacancy came up, Jimmy would have been first choice on my list and I told the board so. But we believed he had a pretty cushy number ... and we thought no one in his right mind would leave that job! Despite reports to the contrary, plenty of managers – some available, some already with clubs – would have jumped at the chance to manage Derby County. We were accused of dithering – not so. Eventually it came down to Jimmy and one other – and the board's unanimous decision was Jimmy – the **only** person to be offered the job!' Pickering would add, in a lovely sense of Alan Partridge-like 'Needless to say, I had the last laugh' one-upmanship, 'Jimmy has earned the respect of all those Doubting Thomases who wrote in or phoned us. One guy had the shock of his life. His letter to the board was so nasty, so vicious – suggesting we were all stark, raving mad setting on Jim – that I phoned him immediately and gave him a mouthful! Late in the season he had the grace to write again – this time apologising for what he had said. He even offered to buy us a meal.'

A master of the boardroom and management of senior directors, Smith's instantly likeable persona only built on Pickering's already positive impression of the man. And weeks after the search had begun, Derby opted to appoint the 54-year-old as the 19th manager in the history of the club.

It seems the right time to run through just who Jim Smith was, for those who need it. A confident midfielder who made his progression through the Sheffield leagues as a player, the man who would become known as the Bald Eagle plied his trade primarily in the lower divisions of the Football League, appearing over 100 times for both Halifax and Boston. But it was' to 'in management is where he would become part of the footballing furniture. Heading up Boston and Colchester in his formative years, it was with Oxford, Blackburn, Birmingham, Newcastle, QPR and Portsmouth where Jim became synonymous with the gruff style of coaching that matched the 1970s and '80s in England.

Often overlooked and unappreciated by supporters in equal measure, Smith's tenures had a common theme of coming to an abrupt close after a certain level of disappointment. Even in a time where managers could expect a longer shelf life, his longest continuous run at a single club was barely four years.

With a new man in place, the immediate inquest would begin with Rams supporters. Gibson immediately thought to Smith's career thus far. 'You look at the other clubs he was at. He got near with Portsmouth, nearly got them promoted. Newcastle, he didn't really do anything. Oxford, he worked wonders with but he'd gone by the time they won the League Cup in the mid-'80s. So it was when Stuart Webb phoned me and said, "The new Derby manager is … Jim Smith." And I went, "Oh … OK."' Legendary BBC Radio Derby announcer Graham Richards, adding, 'I remember being sat down on the chairs with you [Gibson] at Radio Derby and going, "Oh God, Jim Smith."' A hastily arranged episode of the Monday night *Sportscene Talk-In* show drew dismay from fans that felt they had missed any opportunity for Derby to progress. Supporter Jamie Allen remembers, 'It was so unexpected with Jim because when he was appointed, he wasn't even a manager at the time. He was a chairman at the League Managers' [Association].

We knew about him obviously, but he came in and it was "Jim Smith?"'

* * *

The latter days of Arthur Cox and the tenure of McFarland had flattered to deceive, the collective play-off failures and subsequent mid-table finish meaning Lionel Pickering's early days of investment had failed. That was an awareness Smith would come in with, and the summer of 1995 was always destined to see him need to arrange a squad in the knowledge that many of those at the club would be moving on shortly. Writing in *It's Only a Game* that his brief was simply to cut costs and achieve a mid-table finish, Smith would soon meet a selection of first-teamers disgruntled with life in Derbyshire. Craig Short, the man who had epitomised Pickering's initial carefree attitude to squad spending, 'was the first to knock on the door and announce, "I'm leaving. I'm going to Everton"'. The next player to present himself was Paul Williams, who was equally belligerent, declaring, 'I don't care who came [sic] in as manager – Alf Ramsey or Joe Bloggs. I'm on my way' The duo would leave, Mark Pembridge too as nearly £5m was raised in exchange for two part-exchange arrivals: Gary Rowett and Sean Flynn. Dean Sturridge would also look set for a departure to Torquay where he had spent previous months on loan, but they couldn't raise the £75,000 asking fee.

And while neither of the new faces were known particularly in the game, Smith knew what he was looking for in arrivals: fight. That was evidenced throughout his first transfer foray, with a succession of new players entering Raynesway who had endeavour over individual ability. Darryl Powell, a stalwart of his Portsmouth side, would arrive for £750,000. Exciting forward Ron Willems joined from Swiss side Grasshoppers for less than half of that. Then there was just enough time to bring in a new skipper.

Robin Van Der Laan wasn't your typical mid-1990s Football League signing. The Dutchman arrived in Britain after serving a long suspension in his native Netherlands, and his first port of call in England was the sunny streets of Port Vale. Now a coach for Manchester United's academy, Van Der Laan has made the UK absolutely his home from home, with Derby his second stop. 'I was out of contract,' he remembers, 'so we went on holiday to America, and my sister-in-law was housesitting for us. I said, "Listen, if anyone comes into contact or any clubs when I'm out, just let me know." And I got a new offer from Port Vale but I thought, professionally, if I want to achieve things and play as high as possible, I would have to move to a bigger club. The first two weeks we were on holiday and nobody contacted me, and in them days it was a little bit different because most managers signed players at the end of the holidays so they don't have to pay them all the way through the summer. And then we had Portsmouth, West Brom, and I ended up provisionally signing for West Bromwich Albion and that was going to end up going to a tribunal. The deal was made with West Brom, which was a player exchange plus cash, and I trained there for a week before getting the call that John Rudge had spoken to Jim Smith with a better deal for Port Vale, and was I willing to go and speak to Derby. Derby had been trying for the last few years at that time to get up into the First Division, they spent a lot of money and didn't really get there, so I knew they were very ambitious and it was a great opportunity to come on board at that time. I spoke to Jim and we made a deal with Lee Mills going the other way.'

In actuality, when considering the incomings across the summer months, it was relatively serene for the contract-makers. Powell, Rowett, Flynn, Van Der Laan and Willems. Steady footballers, some of whom had been proven at various levels and some who were striving for their first real breakthroughs. Just like another man who arrived: Steve McClaren. It's known what became of McClaren, but turn the clock back to the very beginning of his coaching career. Semi-retired after injuries at Oxford United, it was there that McClaren first began to plant the seeds of a career which would take him to the pinnacle of European football. Speaking in the midst of the liquidation threat,

McClaren proudly joined a Zoom call sporting his Derby County club jacket. Recently departed to Manchester United after his fifth spell in various capacities, and even opting to work unpaid in 2022, he is a man who has been one of few (almost) constants across 35 years of the club.

McClaren said, 'I'd almost finished playing and I was injured, when I had an opportunity to take a coaching role at Oxford. I was youth coach and reserve coach for maybe four years and it was a great grounding, and I loved it. The connection with Jim is quite interesting because Denis Smith was manager at the time, but because Jim had an affinity with Oxford and he lived in Woodstock, at games he used to come to the Manor Ground. We'd call the manager's office "The Bunker" because there were no windows and, after every game, managers would come in and Denis would invite any manager who was at the game to come on in. So, Jim always used to come for a drink. And at that time, I was, well, I was the drinks man. So I was kind of like the water boy. Jim used to come in, I used to do the rounds of, "What do you want to drink? Jim, what do you want to drink?" "Oh whisky, water and three ice cubes." And I used to say, "OK, no problem." So every time, whisky, water, three ice cubes were delivered to him. And eventually I got to know when he was coming in and instead of him asking as soon as he sat down, there was a whisky, water and three cubes of ice. So that's how we got to know each other.

'He knew Maurice Evans very well and Maurice was the chief scout at Oxford and kind of my mentor in my early coaching days. So they knew each other, Maurice gave me good references and Jim always kept an eye on me, when Maurice said, "If you ever get a job again, you want to take Steve." So I said to Jim, "Why did you take me?" and he did laugh and said, "Well I liked your smile when you delivered the whisky, water and three cubes of ice. And then Maurice gave you a good reference. So, I thought you were a good lad and apparently a good coach." And that's how I hooked up with Jim initially.'

Fresh from a seeming retirement, Smith returned to the training field alongside a man 30 years his junior, a relatively unproven coach and one who the board almost refused to sanction at a time when assistants were still frowned upon by some. Gadsby adds, 'He brought along Steve McClaren and his words were, "He's a great pourer of red wine," in a mischievous way. Anybody who knew Jim knew that, after the game, it was always red wine. It's what he presented young McClaren as, who was his coach at Oxford, but a nice capable lad. They came in and started quite gingerly and they had to move and shake people out because our wages were too high, players were in there who weren't really devoted and Jim wanted to get together his side.'

Arriving almost in conjunction with Smith was another man who would help to shape the look, feel and immediate prosperity of the club, Keith Loring. Loring, who arrived as chief executive off the back of almost ten years with Brentford, was installed prior to the managerial unveiling and would bridge the gap between board and manager. Together, the duo would build a working relationship that would take Derby County levels beyond their own expectations and would, in time, put the eyes of world football on them. Spearheaded by Lionel Pickering, ably supported by the likes of Gadsby and Webb, a core of management was being built which hadn't been in place for several years. The long run would see manager and board members intertwine. In the short run, there were three aims: build a side, finish comfortably, consolidate.

As things tend to occur with Derby County, it didn't go *exactly* to plan.

* * *

An opening day in front of just under 11,000 was what greeted Jim Smith's new-look side in August 1995. Growing disgruntlement since the play-off failures, along with a cap on the Baseball Ground's capacity following the 1990 publication of the Taylor Report, had driven casual supporters to new hobbies for their Saturday afternoons. Considering the first outing of Smith's side, it looked like he'd have a job to convince them to return from perusing market stalls at the Eagle Centre. In fact, things would get worse before they would get better.

That opening on 13 August produced little in the way of excitement, a goalless draw against Port Vale. To follow that up with two away defeats – one of which saw Derby fall to a 3-0 hammering at Wolverhampton Wanderers – did little to endear the already disappointing new management team to supporters. Attendances would fall further, dropping to a less-than-impressive four figures by mid-September. Only eight goals were scored in the opening nine games, and 15 fixtures had produced a paltry four victories, nailing down an early expectation that the season would be more about anxiously picking up points for consolidation than anything else. Smith was struggling to find the right personnel for his system, evident by the bold choice to replace his goalkeeper Steve Sutton at half-time of a 2-0 victory over Sheffield United, bringing Russell Hoult on in his place. That result was a rare bright moment though. With little in the way of hope and a squad failing to gel on the field, it all culminated in one of the most important fixtures in the history of Derby County: a 5-1 defeat to Tranmere Rovers.

'The first few games were a bit of a nightmare really,' admits McClaren. 'At one stage I do know Jim was very concerned. He was making signings and they were good signings, but we just couldn't find the right formula, the right personnel, the right system and the right identity or way of playing. We were a bit in between everything. We lost 5-1 and most people would think, well that's the end of us because we were under severe pressure anyway.' As Jim's son-in-law Andy Dawson puts simply, 'He was getting a lot of abuse wherever we went for those first games.'

For many managers – especially one as unpopular as Smith in those early months – four wins in the first third of the season would have spelled the end, and both McClaren and Smith could sense that the discontent in the stands was beginning to seep through to the boardroom, including to Gadsby: 'That night we had Bonfire Night at Markeaton Park down in Derby. Jim and all the family were there, and he and McClaren must have absolutely hated me because I just moaned and groaned about what the bloody hell is going on.'

From trying to understand how their side had been beaten quite so easily to being heavily quizzed on his direction by one of the men who had opted to appoint him, it was a painful Saturday for the duo. And they knew that with fan opinion plummeting, media attention would not provide a respite for them either. Returning from his first journey to Prenton Park, Graham Richards had an expectation that he would be discussing a side with a new man at the helm a week later: 'We came back in the car from the Wirral that evening convinced we were heading for relegation. We were talking about chances of going down. We thought there was a very fair chance we were going to be relegated under this bloke who we considered a very nice chap, but a nothing manager.'

2

BOW DOWN

'EVERYTHING WAS falling apart. It was not a question of if I was going to become successful, we were just thinking about surviving and how to defend the country from aggressors from Serbia, and how to survive.'

It's a paragraph that wouldn't normally be needed in any book about a fairly sub-par First Division English football side of the 1990s. But to understand the premise and reason behind why this book has been written, it's imperative. Croatia's history is long and complex, and sadly like many countries which have had to push for their own independence, it's a history covered in bloodshed. Far from being an expert in the field, to understand the situation from a Croatian perspective I spoke with Matija Grebenić, a Zagreb-born Paralympian who grew up during what is commonly referred to in the country as the War of Independence.

'It all started with Zvonimir Boban,' begins Grebenić. Boban, a Croatian icon not for his political work but for his majesty on the football pitch, would go on to represent AC Milan for a decade, but it was what happened on a pitch in Belgrade, at the heart of Yugoslavia, in 1990 that would be the biggest impact he made on the world. Grebenić continued, 'Dinamo Zagreb vs Red Star Belgrade is considered by football fans as the start of the war, even though it wasn't. Dinamo played Red Star, and the war started in 1991. But there was a huge riot because Red Star fans were throwing things at Dinamo fans and Dinamo fans were rounded in a huge fence. They broke out, started fighting and one of the police officers started beating a Dinamo fan. There is an iconic shot of Boban doing a high jump-kick to the police officer to save the fan. With the fans of Belgrade, there was a war criminal [Željko Ražnatović] who wasn't a football fan, but he was strictly there as a Serbian ambassador to start riots and start problems. That is what football fans call the start of the war between Serbia and Croatia.'

Far from acting as the beginning of the war, it was perhaps the most notable moment from years of turmoil. Croatia, one of several states within Yugoslavia, saw 94 per cent of its people vote in favour of independence from the federation in 1991. Grebenić said, 'Yugoslavia was the federation and Croatian parliament voted that they wanted to get out of the federation. But Yugoslavian forces and army were not letting it happen, even though Slovenia also wanted out. Everyone wanted out, Macedonia as well. Afterwards it was still Yugoslavia but they changed their name to Serbia and Montenegro, then it was Serbia alone and Montenegro alone. In Croatia, Serbians were held highly in some positions. If you had a police station, the chief would be Serbian in smaller cities. The south, now Kosovo, they had problems, they had no money and worked for nothing basically. I don't want to go too hard on Serbia, but nobody liked them. They had Slobodan Milošević who basically had a plan to take half of the coast which was always Croatia and turn it to Serbia. They had a saying that, "Wherever a Serbian man lives, that's Serbia." Milošević had party gatherings all around Yugoslavia claiming that every piece of land a Serbian was living on was Serbia. They were toying with that rhetoric and uneducated people started eating it up.'

Among the battle of fighting for independence, war began. Over four years, an estimated 20,000 people lost their lives, 13,500 of whom were from Croatia. It came amid the bloodiest years in Europe since the Second World War. Approximately 25 per cent of the Croatian economy was decimated and cities were ruined. And within this, life as it was known came to a standstill. In amongst the time, the first Croatian league was formed, albeit one that was played in turmoil. 'We did have a championship in Croatia, but it was strange. Hajduk Split didn't play in Split, they played on an island because Serbia couldn't reach there. In 1992 they had a league but, because of war, in four cities they couldn't play any games. Clubs near Serbia didn't play in their cities. So, football wasn't very regular and people were terrified, and some of the players stopped playing because they went to fight in the war, but they somehow managed to find the will to keep the sport alive,' said Grebenić.

Without this battle to keep football going in Croatia, Derby County would likely never have welcomed a man who would go on to be seen by many as one of the greatest players in the history of the football club. In the above-mentioned Split vs Belgrade tie, there was another player at the heart of it, dismissed for brawling. That match, and the subsequent freedom which Croatia gained, elevated the nation into a world of footballing independence that it had not yet experienced, revealing a country ready to leave its shackles behind. It was a nation with ambition and drive to succeed outside of their newly independent country.

There was one man who had those two qualities like few others. It was the same man who received that red card in the Split vs Belgrade encounter. The same man who gave the quote at the top of this chapter. A man who was as imposing off the field as he was on it. A man who would be referred to simply as God in certain quarters. Igor Štimac: The Man.

* * *

'Without high dreams, nothing good will happen in the future. That is how I live my life.' Igor Štimac clicks on to the Zoom link sent days previously and one thing is immediately apparent: he's not changed. Endearing and terrifying in equal measure, over the course of two hours Igor would go through an amount of cigarettes so high in volume that it was frankly remarkable we managed to converse between them. Sitting in his living area, behind Igor is a picture of God. To look at him, you might not picture him as a natural caresser of a football, with his intimidating size and look making him more akin to a warrior. Or, to put it in a slightly clearer context, he exudes the power of a man who could do considerable damage to most mere mortals on this earth. From exchanging pleasantries and hearing his dismay at the way Mel Morris has destroyed the football club he still loves in recent years, memory lane is firmly journeyed down.

'It was very difficult because I was still in Croatia in the Croatian league, which nobody was coming to see or watch or follow. But the good thing for me is I was still part of the national side, playing regularly from the very beginning. And that gave me the chance to get out and try to find my place in the football world. I need to say that my dream was always England because I felt that the Premier League would suit me well, I could find myself and adapt to the style of play there, and I was just waiting for my chance.'

Štimac was at that point an established international footballer, though relatively unknown to the English supporter. Capped 53 times across the course of his entire international career and progressing through the Yugoslavia youth systems, it was at champions Hajduk Split where he would begin to garner significant interest. 'We won the double with the Croatian Cup and domestic league, and this gave us the chance to promote ourselves, our qualities and Hajduk and the country. As champions we also participated in the pre-qualifying round for the next Champions League as well, where we faced Panathinaikos in what I think was September. We didn't go through because our stadium was suspended in Split for, well, unknown reasons to be honest. It was UEFA's decision and we assumed that Panathinaikos at the time had a lot of strong influence, they had a great influence on UEFA's decisions. Throughout 1994/95 we were in our stadium, and then the following year when everything was settling down with the war, we were not allowed to host our games at our home ground.

So, we played one game at a neutral ground, another in Greece but we lost on away goals. And it was very difficult for the club to keep us more experienced and more expensive players for that season. That was the time that Derby approached me.'

The significance in the detail of the War of Independence is crucial to the understanding of how the man who had captained his nation would come to Derby, and it would all come through the shrewd understanding of Jim Smith. Throughout a long managerial career, Smith had formed a network of trusted scouts who would deliver him a selection of international talents by the time football had truly opened its borders in the 1990s. From Bob McNab, the former Arsenal full-back, to Derby's own Archie Gemmill, it was these hidden connections which would serve Smith with the ability to use the international markets to build his squad. One of the names presented to Smith soon into his time in the Baseball Ground dugout was that of the Croatian.

'What was fortunate about Jim, which is very important, is that you have to look back to the war, when it ended in the Balkans,' admits Peter Gadsby. 'Štimac had earned no money because football had ceased there for a year or so. All those players didn't play for 18 months to two years. They were on no money and Jim had spotted that very quickly, because he suddenly started to talk about him.'

The story of how Štimac would arrive in Derbyshire is reflective of British football's inexperience with overseas talents at this time though. For all of the impact that the likes of Eric Cantona and co. had on the newly formed Premier League, there was still a lack of professionalism in the way players would be courted. Igor is exhibit A, and as he made very clear in advance of explaining how he came to Derby, 'Don't laugh.'

* * *

'Oh, it's a fantastic story,' chuckles the current manager of the Indian national team, before lighting another cigarette. 'When I received the call from my agent at that time, he told me about an offer from England and I immediately said yes – but I was not told where I was going. With the same agent, some others were trying to get involved in my transfer and they destroyed another transfer. It was like that a lot, but I was not told where I was going; for me it was just important to go to England and play there. But obviously I was not thinking that it wasn't going to be a Premier League side. So, I landed at Heathrow Airport with my agent and two guys were waiting for us. But going back to 1995, you need to know that in most of Europe people were following Man United, Arsenal, Liverpool, Tottenham, four or five clubs at the top. The rest were all going up, going down. We had not so many games on TV, but you could watch one game from England a week.

'So, I'm going there but I don't know which club. Not for a single second did I think the club would not be in the Premier League. So, we landed to Heathrow, we took a ride with their car, and I knew we were going somewhere in the Midlands, but I didn't know where. They stopped the car and I'm thinking, "What the fuck is this? We are somewhere in the middle of the night; it looks like a factory or a jail or whatever it is." These English bricks, I can't recognise anything, but I see "The Baseball Ground", the written sign saying "Home of Derby County". I said, "What the fuck are we doing at a baseball ground? I'm a football player!"

'We go in these tiny tunnels to Jim's office, and he is waiting there. We sit down and we speak, and I'm still not thinking about Premier League or Championship or that. But he is telling me about the team, the contract details, and then he started to mention that the club is trying for seven years to go back to Premier. I said, "For Christ's sake." But I could not tell him I didn't know. That's when I found out that Derby County was not in the Premier League. Of course, I had heard of Derby but I didn't follow them, I didn't know much about them.

'So after that little chat with Jim and agreeing contract terms and all that, I go to a room where the journalists are waiting. One of the first questions was, "Why did you choose Derby? Why did you choose a Division One club? You are an international player." OK, the answer was simple. "My dream was to come to play in England. So, at the moment, for me it was not important, it was just important I was here, the rest will follow." The second question, "We are trying to get back [to the Premier League] for seven years, but not having luck. This season we are 17th, what do you expect?" And that's when I said, "We are going up." I remember somebody took a photo of me doing this [places his thumb to the sky] and saying we were going up. They started selling shirts days later with my photo and my thumb up, "IGOR SAYS WE'RE GOING UP!"

'It's nice to remember these things and everything which followed. It looked impossible to get promoted but nothing is impossible in football or in life. If you wish so hard to do something to achieve something, if you work hard everything is possible. But no, I didn't know where I was going to.'

He would prove to be the greatest accidental signing in the history of Derby County, and he would officially be signed off by Gadsby, who said, 'I recall well that Lionel left me a message saying, "Are you coming? This Iro … this … this foreigner's here." So I went to Ednaston and they needed somebody to sign the documents. I was just moving house but he said, "Are you coming? You have to because they are going soon." So, I went down there, walked into this room and Štimac was there. Immaculate. That jaw. Bloody hell, that'll do for me. Christ, he looked a player. "I like this place, I like you people." We didn't pay a lot of money for him, did the deal with his agent and that was it. I remember I said, "I want to be there when he moves in and bring an electrician." I went down and Štimac is just on his sofa watching the television. His wife was seven months pregnant, carrying boxes upstairs. She was Miss Croatia, carrying boxes up. And he was going, "Up in the top room!" and it was incredible the way he was. It was just Igor!" Štimac would arrive for a fee of £1.57m, at the time the second highest the club had ever paid out.

* * *

But despite the fanfare, the excitement of the decision-makers and Jim's confidence himself, the debut of the Croatian was perhaps the most disastrous result of Smith's entire tenure; that 5-1 loss at Tranmere. 'The Tranmere game was a one step back, two steps forwards scenario. Igor came in as a centre-back and what it did was it showed us that Igor was not a centre-back,' said Robin Van Der Laan. The club captain could see there was *something* about Igor in his display, he just didn't quite know what it was. The seven-figure addition scored on his debut, but it was more the five goals which slipped by him that was of greater significance.

'Tranmere away was really the catalyst for it,' reflects winger Paul Simpson, 'because it was a really strange game. We'd just signed Igor and, on the Friday night in the hotel, when any players come into the club, particularly foreign players, Jim leant on me a little bit and sometimes my wife Jackie to help them settle in when they had families, and I was leant on to help Igor settle. We played Tranmere away and we were in the hotel up at Haydock Thistle. We were just having dinner on the Friday night where we all used to sit down at seven o'clock; Jim and the staff went separate from us. Igor said to me, "Simmo, I'd like a red wine." I said, "No you can't have red wine, Igor." "Why not?" "Well, it's Friday night, we've got a game tomorrow, we don't drink red wine." Now obviously in foreign countries it's normal to have a glass of red wine with your dinner, but I said, "You can't have it, you're not allowed it." "OK, no red wine then I won't play."

'I go through to speak to Jim and said, "Listen gaffer, Igor's asking for red wine with his dinner. I've told him he can't." And he said, "Ahh just let him have a glass of red wine, don't worry. Get a couple of bottles on the table." So, he allowed Igor and then a few other players had a glass with dinner, but we came into the game on the Saturday and got absolutely murdered. When the fifth goal went in they cut through us like nobody's business and I'm thinking, "Where's Igor? Where's our centre-back?" And he was further up the pitch than I was, not even doing his job defensively. Bloody hell, what have we signed here?'

It was the same process of thought that would hound McClaren too: 'You could tell from day one with his stature, the way he came in, he was going to be a leader. Igor played in a [defensive back] four and I remember he picked the ball up, and don't get me wrong he was probably at fault for all five goals, but he did pick the ball up, ran all the way through, had a shot and scored our only goal. And from that, we kind of put our heads together and went, "We need to get the strength of Igor into the team. He can't play in a four, he can't play in midfield."' What he could do though, was play in a five, or alternatively in a three. That much he made clear to Jim Smith the following day.

When looking at what caused Derby County's resurrection in the 1995/96 season, there are some discrepancies between three parties as to who exactly sparked it. Jim Smith and some of his squad maintain it was due to him. Peter Gadsby and some of the squad believe it was a Steve McClaren masterpiece. Igor believes that it was himself: '[After Tranmere] Jim invited me into his office, we spoke about the game, about the problems and I suggested to him to change to three at the back because we had a really strong team with Dean Yates and Gary Rowett, who was a young boy there performing well. The three of us could handle any front players in the league and all we needed was to put more bodies up front, more offensive full-backs and more people in the middle. We had [Marco] Gabbiadini, Paul Simpson, [Dean] Sturridge up front – we could beat anyone. Everything went well from that day.'

It was on the Monday that not only did the great side of the 1990s first take shape, but it was perhaps the first inkling at Raynesway that McClaren was destined for greatness beyond his current employment. Aware that his new foreign import would be unable to fit into Smith's conventional 4-4-2 shape, from Sunday morning he would begin to jot ideas for how he could turn an underperforming side who looked destined for a relegation dogfight into one that could, at this stage at least, compete in the upper echelon of the division.

McClaren said, 'I remember we'd talked about it and, to this day, I remember it. I did one session on the field, put us in that formation and we just played a little practice match, worked on a few things and I went, "Oh my God, we've got it." It was just … it was just perfect. Round pegs, round holes. A lot of teams I say, and I've done it myself, you're putting square pegs in round holes and round pegs in square holes, so you are getting everything wrong. You've got the personnel, you've got the right players, you're just putting them in the wrong positions. Everyone was in the right position, it was perfect for Igor, our full-backs were attacking so it was great for them. Defenders were man-markers so Igor could sweep, they could mark. Darryl Powell and Van Der Laan so you had someone who could sit, someone who could run around. Ronny Willems was a massive, massive player for us in that ten position and it allowed us to keep two up front with Sturridge and Gabbiadini. And that training session, it needed no coaching, it just worked. And I came back in and saw Jim in the office and said, "We've got it. It's took us a long while, but we've found it."'

It was the session which would dictate not only one game, not only one season, but it would become the staple of Smith and McClaren's vision for taking Derby County to the Premier League and beyond. Conducted on the boggy grounds of Raynesway, the squad of players sensed it just as much as McClaren. One member of that squad was Dean Sturridge, who recalled, 'I was injured for that Tranmere game but the week afterwards they did the training and they had three defenders at the back, with Igor sweeping. Darryl was in the midfield, me at the top end of the pitch. We were playing against the reserves or the possibles vs the probables as it was back then. I was in those probables, Igor being at the back in the three-man defence. There was a scenario in that game and we won it 4 or 5-1. And Igor passed it to Darryl, Darryl passed it to somebody else in midfield, the midfielder passed it to me and I ran at the right time where I got in behind the defence, took one touch and side-foot curled it into the bottom corner, similar in a way to the goal that was scored against Crystal Palace in that penultimate game, something like that happened in the training session. Darryl said, "Wow, we've got a team now. We've got the pieces of the jigsaw." And that was the training session. I've never talked about this to any team-mates or anybody, but at the time, seeing what happened in training and hearing your team-mates going "oh my God" or making comments, you just know that the penny has dropped and the ingredients are all in place. But I personally knew from that training session. That training session was the wow moment for me. In that session I just knew there was something different and we had the ingredients in the team to make something special.'

* * *

Gone from a standard back four, Derby's build was now centred around a shape which would only become popular decades later. That four became a five when defending, seamlessly becoming a three when heading forward. Within that three routinely saw the Croatian supported by Dean Yates and Gary Rowett, who remembers the moment of change fondly: 'You could see the strengths of Igor as a player, and it just suited a back five. It was a quick decision by Jim and a brave decision, and I just think it clicked into place with everybody because it was just a formation that just suited the players so much. Igor was the heart of that and it gave him a little bit less responsibility for him to then do what he did the best, which was take the ball and go forward, organise people and the likes of myself and Dean did a lot of the donkey work. But I think it suited the forward players as well. Ronnie Willems just behind the front two, the likes of Gabbers and Sturridge were top, top strikers at that level. It was a move that came about a little bit by circumstance.'

It would prove to have instant success, the Rams' best performance in those early months immediately following the switch as they eased to a 3-0 victory at home to West Bromwich Albion. Then they would beat Charlton with another clean sheet, before an eye-opening 4-1 victory at Birmingham City, a victory that supporter Andrew Beckett described as 'a turning point for us'. With just one training session, mid-table obscurity to the most optimistic of supporters had become something much, much more.

It was important for more than just Smith and McClaren's jobs though. Having shipped five on debut, Derby's new international star was facing early questions. Igor explained, 'That was a really strange game to be honest, because I was not worried and coming very easy in front of our box into the final third, so we needed to sort only a few things and the change of the system, the change from 4-4-2 to 3-5-2, everything changed. That was the crucial point in that season.

'When Jim decided to change it, he made it much easier for me, although I know the next two games after Tranmere we were at home, and that impression in front of our own fans needed to have an impact on everybody. I decided to have the best games of my life in those two games and to make sure that Derby won these two games, and with six points we would start rising. And that was the crucial thing for us.'

In among the turnaround on the field and the adaptation to a system more suiting of Igor and his team-mates, he did have the notable issue of becoming used to a new world in England. Ron Willems aside, Štimac was the pioneer of international footballers descending on sleepy Derbyshire and, as such, he found himself in a city and with an employer not so attuned to the requirements of an international footballer.

'I adapted to a new way of life, but it was the biggest challenge for my family, definitely. Coming from sunny Split and the coastal part of Croatia, which is one of the most beautiful parts of the world, coming to Derby was not easy. I was lucky to have great support from my wife at that time who supported my decisions and not making it more difficult, but that's the path we chose and there was no way back. But I know the kids, even my younger daughter who was born in Derby, it was not easy for them because they were missing their cousins, their grandparents. But that was life. Job would dictate what you need to sacrifice, and we did well as a family to be honest. The challenges were bigger but our response was even bigger and greater than that.'

One of those challenges came in relation to language. There were no dedicated linguists helping overseas players such as Igor and his family become accustomed to English, although he does recall, 'I learnt to understand when Jim swore, that became easy to understand!'

But in those early weeks, the biggest – and most ultimately disastrous – oversight came in not offering Štimac a driving lesson or two. Presented with a Honda Civic from a partner of the club, he was entrusted to drive himself to his home for the first time alone, but neither driver nor club had banked on his confusion when it came to left-hand driving.

'I hadn't even played my first game. I was so impatient and annoyed with all the cabs and taxis, I was using them four or five times a day. I'm a good driver and I was just thinking, "I cannot keep calling cabs and being taken and waiting all the time," so I complained, I was invited to an agency and they prepared a car for me. It was a new Honda, green colour, and from the office, which was in the city centre, first there was a photo taken of me receiving the key with the car behind. Nice smile and all that. We shook hands, I left the building and then I missed one turn. So instead of going back to my apartment, I was on the way to the A52 towards Nottingham. I was looking to turn around and go home, but of course that was the motorway and just one-way traffic. I was not aware that once I turned and went on to the bridge, there was two-way traffic.

'So instead of keeping on the left, when I got up on the top of the bridge I was on the right side, and then there was a car in front of me. And instead of going left I went more right and that was a direct crash. My God, what was going through my head in that time … you stupid son of a bitch! You didn't even play one game; you are going to jail now. I felt my knees hurt and I saw two old people in the car just not feeling well. The cars were in the shit, but soon the emergency car and the police came, and thank God everything was OK with these guys in the other car, which was an old Citroën. I'm not sure even if that car had a seatbelt, but it was a very old car, and I was afraid people might get hurt. That was before my first game.

'When I got back home, I received a call from the club, we went to pay a visit the following day to the couple, and it was funny. They were season ticket holders and they said, because I was apologising and we brought some presents and flowers, I started apologising and they said, "Oh Igor do not apologise, only God sent you to Derby." And I was crying at that point. I just hope they are well and safe if they are still alive. I felt lots of pain. I shouldn't have played the Tranmere game, but I couldn't say that it hurt me a lot.'

But play he did, and without that crash, there is little telling just what could have become of not only that season but the overall reign of the managerial team. The new-look Derby County, masterminded on the training pitch by a concoction of McClaren, Smith and Štimac himself, would embark on the longest unbeaten run within a single season in the history of the football club; a spell which took the Rams to the very top of the First Division.

3

THE PROMISED LAND

HAVING TAKEN some time to find a formula to work around this new-look squad, Smith and McClaren could scarcely have believed what they would experience over the coming months. From sitting perilously above the bottom three in October, the nature of the division at that time meant a pair of home victories over West Brom and Charlton had taken them nine places higher and only two short of the top six. With those two wins offering signs of life in the management duo, it was away at Birmingham in late November that hinted at what would come next. The Blues, third in the league at the start of play, had been without defeat in 15 games, picking up 20 points from a possible 24. Add to this Derby's consistently poor form at St Andrew's over the decades and it looked a mammoth task. Derby won 4-1. Things were moving.

They wouldn't taste defeat in the league again until March, an eventual unbeaten run of 20 becoming a club record for a single season; Brian Clough's team racked up 22 at the end of the 1968/69 and the start of the 1969/70 seasons. From the turn of the year they would never drop out of the top two. It was a revival unexpected by anybody who had endured those first months of the season. Supporter Jamie Allen remembers: 'It was like you'd just opened your Christmas present, and got exactly what you wanted. It was something we had been starved of for so long. We tried all different ways when Lionel Pickering came in and he tried to buy his way up like Jack Walker did [at Blackburn Rovers], with all the best intentions. But this team, the momentum just built, and it kept going on.'

To understand how it all came about though, it's important to get to know the people who made it happen: the players. The last two Derby County promotions to the Premier League (and in fact the only two since its formation) were made of squads who on paper did not look like top-flight groups. While the side which got promoted in 2006/07 was made of journeymen and promising youngsters, the one built by Jim Smith was considerably different in nature. Money had been spent on Štimac, but for the large part this was a side created on a shoestring budget when compared to those previous seasons.

Take Robin Van Der Laan as an example. Before signing for Port Vale, he was banned from playing in his home nation. Known as a talent on the ball and a man to potentially build a side around, the Dutchman came to Derby in those uncertain circumstances, as explained a couple of chapters earlier. 'What clinched it for me was that Jim wanted to make me captain. He knew that already, which was not necessarily a deal-breaker but was a massively important part of the decision-making process because it would mean that I would be starting at the start of the season. I would never claim I was the most technically skilful player on the face of this earth, but I always wore my heart on my sleeve and I go in with my head where other people wouldn't even go with their boots. I'd always fight for the cause.'

That was what Smith was after. By giving the armband to the man who would become known as Captain Fantastic across the Baseball Ground, he provided a demonstration of how he wanted his side to look and to perform on the field. Taking a group of players who had arguably failed to build their identity in the previous couple of seasons and moulding them into one which would put bodies in where talent lacked was vital in the ethos the Bald Eagle was looking to develop.

The same can be said of Gary Rowett, a youngster who had failed to make the breakthrough into first-team football at Everton. He remembers his switch to Derby and those first moments with Smith: 'I came back on the first day of pre-season and I got called into Joe Royle's office, who had taken over from Mike Walker the season before. He pulled me in and just said, "Look, we're trying to sign Craig Short, but Derby want you as part of that deal." I was about Shorty's little toes' value's worth in that deal, but I ended up going to Derby as part of that swap. I suppose from my end and from Derby's end there wasn't a massive amount of expectation but, nevertheless, when I went in there it was clear to see that there was a very new group of free transfers predominantly, cobbled together by Jim and Steve.

'I turned up at Derby's ground to meet Jim with my agent and, a few stories later, I was playing for Derby. I remember you would get down to money and it was all done in front of you, so it was quite a unique experience. Halfway through, Jim called my agent a greedy so and so, and when I look back at it, quite what he thought was greedy about the wages I don't know because they were very, very modest at the time in footballers' terms. But that was Jim, he chucked my agent out of the office, chucked me out and said, "Sorry son but your agent's a greedy sod." And I had to walk out. We drove down the road and my agent was panicking, saying, "Don't worry, he'll call in a while!" It went half an hour and I sat there having a coffee, thinking, "What the hell's going on?" and then we finally got the call back to go back in, and it was all sorted. It was all part of Jim's experience and man-management, he'd done a million of those deals before, but for a young 21-year-old footballer looking to make his mark at a club like Derby, it was probably quite an awe-inspiring moment and worrying in truth.'

Smith always wanted to know the personality of those he was bringing to the club, and through both of his encounters with Van Der Laan and Rowett he was able to build a definitive picture. But throughout the course of the season, though his summer additions and Igor had propelled the side following the formational adjustment, it was a forward they already had on their books who would emerge as the difference between a solid but uninspiring side and one built for bigger things than the First Division.

* * *

The Dean Sturridge of today is a busy man. A football agent representing a series of clients across the top divisions of English football, the knowledge he built up from his 16 years a professional is now used to drive the likes of Tyler Roberts and his own nephew Daniel Sturridge on to the next stages of their career. Across 16 years Dean played almost all of them in the top two divisions, scoring goals across the Midlands for Derby, Leicester and Wolves. On paper it looked like an inevitable growth to stardom. For a man blessed with raw pace and brutal power, his attributes were always designed to terrify ageing defences. But his transition from life on the estates of Birmingham to first-team football had significant hurdles across the board.

Sturridge begins, 'When it came to me leaving school, I pretty much didn't have a football club who believed in me or wanted to offer me a YTS contract. A man called Jim Thomas, who was one of the biggest scouts in Birmingham and had scouted my brother Simon and brought him to Birmingham, was now a scout for Derby. Basically he presumed for years that I would be getting a YTS contract, but lo and behold when it came to my last year of school, I was scratching my head thinking where am I going? And in some ways my family were thinking I wouldn't be going down the football route because he hadn't got a guarantee. Jim spoke to Gerry Summers about me. I played for Derby against Aston Villa, Gerry was the manager of this under-16 game and, to be honest, I had an absolute shocker. I had one moment where I beat three or four players, and Gerry said, "I took you on based off that one moment. Just below me there were other players like Mark Stallard who was really the big name emerging as I got to about 18, 19, and at that stage there were me and Lee Carsley, Jason Kavanagh, Jason White, numerous players in the YTS.

'Lee Carsley and I and Michael Moore would travel in from Birmingham together; Kevin Francis who came from Mile Oak and was signed by Arthur Cox, he would pick us up. But at that stage I was playing as a winger on the wide right, and it was all about my pace and being direct. In my second year I started to play up front a little bit more, so I was competing with Mark about who the next striker was who would get into the first-team squad. Mark got into the squad before me under Roy McFarland, who was the reserve team manager at one stage and in the first-team environment it was the same situation. Rightly so because Mark was a ruthless finisher whereas I was playing pretty football between the halfway line and 18-yard box. Showing pace, doing good things but not really hungry to score goals; I didn't realise how important goalscoring was. I was happier doing flicks, bits of skill, playing the game in an aesthetically pleasing way but not being ruthless enough. If there was a 5-0 win in the reserves, it would be Mark scoring three, I may have got a couple of assists and no goals, and that was happening regularly at that stage.'

While finding goals difficult to come by prior to developing that selfish edge, it was off the field where Sturridge's development was most telling. Having become a dad aged 17, the youngster was travelling between Derby and Birmingham and with this came its own costs and heartache, resulting in a heart-to-heart with then manager Arthur Cox. 'I remember when I went to Arthur's house and negotiated my own contract. Nobody at the football club knew at that stage, but I said, "By the way boss, I'm a parent so I need a little bit more money in wages." And Arthur accepted what I said, he didn't shout or say, "I can't believe you've become a parent at this age," he just said, "OK, I understand. We'll top your contract up because I believe in you, and I think you've got a chance of being successful at this club."'

Though supported, the departure of Cox in October 1993 would leave Sturridge on his way out, with Roy McFarland not favouring him for a starting berth. 'He [McFarland] told me Torquay wanted me on loan and when I left the office I felt like I wanted to burst into tears. I felt that going to Torquay, which was the end of the earth at Christmas, it was a big sea change and a big culture shock for me in having to make that kind of decision. Roy probably sensed I wasn't focused enough, wasn't as determined as I should have been to have been scoring goals regularly or doing what a striker has to do.

'So at the time it was a bit of a rejection and it was hard to take, but in another way it was a great opportunity for me to play first-team football, toughen up and mature and go into men's football. 'Going to Torquay was very, very important for my development in realising that League Two [the Third Division as it was at the time] football, washing my own kit, getting on with the manager and getting on with the lads. There were people there I went to school with in Birmingham, people like Darren Moore who I represent now as well as an agent. But having Darren and Chris Curran as Birmingham boys in the changing room really settled me down and made me relaxed in my environment. I was a confident, cocky, brash young lad anyway when I was at Derby, nothing changed at Torquay and I went in, scored five goals in ten games and 'it was a good education for me.'

It wasn't until the summer of 1995 that Sturridge felt properly wanted though. Almost moved out to Torquay permanently, the Gulls couldn't find the necessary funds to bring him in and instead he would become part of the thinking of Smith and Steve McClaren. 'Jim and Steve coming in was the next defining moment for me. In that pre-season I was training with the younger lads and playing games where I hadn't even signed a contract at that stage. So I came back as part of it, was under no contract, so if I got injured or anything went wrong, that would have been my career up in flames. But I remember Jim saying in the lead-up to the first game of the season, "Sign the bloody contract because we rate you and we believe that you are going to be on the bench at the weekend." Second game I came off the bench against Luton and scored, and from there it just snowballed. My confidence got higher and higher, I was playing in the position I always wanted to play in as a striker, and now the player who was happy to play between the halfway line and 18-yard box in the Pontins League and looked pretty, I was now not caring what happened on the halfway line, it was about me getting into the box and being on the end of things.'

Across the season, Sturridge would find the net 20 times. No other Rams player would reach that number for another two decades. Through the decision to implement the forward in a central position and most likely partner him with the vastly more experienced Marco Gabbiadini, McClaren could see on the training pitch that they had a man as important to their new setup as their Croatian import. McClaren said, 'Once we'd found that system, we really coached it individually and collectively. And we played to players' strengths. Deano was an exciting talent, but you can tell with Deano why he would fall out with some people. I made sure that we built a relationship, and he had that love/hate relationship with Jim. Jim really did love him, but he also showed that he didn't like him as well! He wouldn't run around; he wouldn't hold the ball up. But we just found that him and Gabbiadini, Ronny Willems behind, we played some football. And he was fast, quick, strong. And we put the ball behind, and he could score, so we just gave him confidence and we believed in him and we gave him tough love. He was a fantastic player, we did love him, but Jim was tough with him as well.'

Even Peter Gadsby was aware of Jim's tough treatment of Sturridge, recalling Dean was very temperamental and had to be cajoled or patted on the back: 'I remember one occasion enquiring in the boardroom as to why our leading goalscorer was not playing on Tuesday night. "Jim, I see Sturridge is not playing tomorrow night?" "No, that bugger has got Barnsley hamstring," after a wet Tuesday night at Barnsley; but to Jim it was a bloody Barnsley hamstring.'

Though he would often find reason for irritation in the gruffness of his manager, Sturridge himself recognises a man who knew how to get the very best out of him and rejuvenated his career: 'Jim's attitude was always very easy-going. He was a very flamboyant character. I remember sometimes he'd have a go at me on a Saturday if I hadn't scored, have a go in the changing room, and I would be walking tentatively past his office on a Monday morning at Raynesway because you're thinking, "Oh I don't feel excited here, he's hammered me. He'll shout again," but no. You'd walk in on a Monday morning and just hear, "All right Deano, good morning!" and it's like a new character. He would move on very quickly and he wouldn't dwell on things, so our personalities got on very well and I reacted to that in a very good way, because he was very relaxed in his approach and he'd always just say, "Go ahead and do the business, score goals, be a threat."'

* * *

Over the course of the campaign, the general setup of the Derby side changed relatively little. Between the sticks would be the reliable Russell Hoult, who held the number one shirt after his half-time replacement of Steve Sutton in that game at Sheffield United, with Igor sat in front. Gary Rowett and Dean Yates would sit ahead, with Shane Nicholson on the left and Lee Carsley on the right, often sharing duties with Sean Flynn. In midfield would be Darryl Powell and Robin Van Der Laan, with occasional cover from Flynn or Paul Trollope. The front three was routinely Sturridge, Gabbiadini and Willems. With that rigid structure in place – at least in terms of personnel – Smith would reap the rewards of the side he had built and when it came to the training pitch he could at least take a step back. Preferring to allow McClaren to manage things, the duo grew ever closer over the course of the campaign as the tactical insight of the assistant paved the way for the unbeaten run. Smith's willingness to hand over responsibility to his young apprentice was testament to the relationship the two had built considering their first weeks together when McClaren would be at the mercy of his new boss. We'll go into that more later.

In those first weeks, it wasn't only McClaren in the firing line of Smith though. Paul Simpson, who found himself in and out of Smith's plans throughout his time under him, thinks back to those first meetings, saying, 'For the first month or two months, he was horrible to everybody. He was so strict and strong in everything he'd say, and I don't really remember him giving any compliments out to anybody, he was just on everybody every single day, every minute we were together he was driving standards and having a go at people when we were training. Then off the grass he was really friendly and pleasant. But on it, I have this picture of him just being horrible to everybody. Then after that first couple of months when he'd set his standards and put a marker down, he livened up a little bit and he would be certainly calming down. But the first couple of months that he was in the club, he certainly made his mark, and everybody knew where they stood with him.'

Smith's ferociousness would be with the best of intentions, however. Designed to reach the core of his players and done with the knowledge of who could take what, often his focus would be on those he had built up the best relationships with, such as Darryl Powell. 'There would be times he would have a go at Darryl,' says Sturridge, 'but maybe because he knew Darryl so well from his Portsmouth days, he knew he could hammer Darryl who would take it on the chin. Sometimes I'd feel sorry because I'd think, "How is he taking all of this verbal assassination?" But he would take it on the chin, keep on coming back and still be playing on matchday. Jim had an unbelievable knack of man management and knowing what the mood was, what somebody needed.'

Another man – and even another Powell – would experience Jim close up. Coming into the side mid-way through the campaign, Smith looked to build his options even amid the great run when acquiring left-back Chris Powell from Southend United. In his first session, he would be quick to understand just the type of character Jim could be at Raynesway, laughing as he explains, 'I had to get used to Jim's ways, which were quite tough, because he demanded a lot from us every day. We knew the team on a

Thursday, which was new to me, but he needed everyone to be working so, so hard. We used to train at the Baseball Ground on a Thursday because that was the team preparation for the game on a Saturday. And I think I maybe got a pass or a cross wrong, and Jim just went ballistic. I remember Darryl just running past me saying, "Just get used to it, it's what he does. He wants you to be your best at all times and that's what he's like. You've just got to get through it," and that's exactly what I did. It was either sink or swim. I saw plenty of players who couldn't handle the combustible Jim, and that was just the way it was. Maybe it wouldn't be like that these days – it would be demanding but maybe in a different way because times have changed. But we just got on with it – we got on with it as a group, as an individual and you just realised that's your manager, that's how he was and he's been successful previously, so why wouldn't he be now?'

The signing of Powell signalled another masterstroke as he went on to become a never-to-be-replaced asset in a Derby shirt. Even now, 26 years after his signing, a left-back has not bettered him. Powell said, 'I was at Southend for five years and over that time we were seen as a side that had good young players. I replaced Justin Edinburgh who went to Tottenham, Dean Austin went to Tottenham, Stan Collymore came through and I was the next one being talked about going to a Premier League side. I was very close to going to Manchester City when Alan Ball was the manager and Southend turned the deal down three times. And that was disappointing, but I think it alerted one or two other clubs that I could be available, and Derby were top of the Championship then, obviously the same league as I was in with Southend.

'Southend agreed a fee of three quarters of a million and I had to meet Jim at South Mimms service station to have a chat with him – that was my first time meeting him, but I obviously knew all about him from his exploits with QPR and Newcastle and Portsmouth. But he had a one on one with me, and typical Jim, he was just finding out about me. He'd seen the football and his scouts had seen me, but it was more about: "Are you single?

Are you getting married?" And I was getting married six months from then, and he just wanted to know about me, which I thought was, when you think about it, great management early on. I hadn't even signed for him, but he wanted to know about me. After that meeting the deal was tied up.'

Not only was Powell joining a side at the top of the division, but he was also entering a defence that had tightened up considerably after some early season wobbles. Before Powell's signing and as they reached 11 games without a loss, Russell Hoult had only been beaten six times in that time. For Powell to enter that defence was a daunting task, even for a man who was being headhunted by Premier League sides. 'I was at Southend for a number of years, won player of the year and was known as a player that might move on. And there was no pressure on us. We went under the radar because we were seen as a small club in a very competitive league, and we were holding our own. But then I went from there to pressure. To a one-club city where everyone walks around in black and white, and the pressure was on because they saw themselves as a Premier League club. I went from a seaside town to a real hotbed of football, and that was pressure.

'And I was playing in a new position at left wing-back. When I met Jim he said, "I think you've got all the attributes to play there," but I'd only ever played in a back four, so I had some playing adjustments to make, which took me a while to be honest. But Jim and Steve were very supportive and the players. Igor, Dean Yates, Matt Carbon, we had some really good players defensively. Lee Carsley was at right-back, Gary Rowett as well. And then we had some real talents ahead of us. There was a real eclectic bunch'

But prior to Powell, by Christmas Derby had sailed to the top of the division with a 3-1 victory over Sunderland and wouldn't drop out of the top two again. That win, two days prior to the festivities, was the moment many supporters knew the side had what it took to go the distance. Jim sensed it too, writing in *It's Only a Game*, 'Even I had to catch my breath at the way we had rocketed up the table. I remember in early November, when we were in the bottom half, Yvonne [Smith's wife] and I had dinner with Trevor Francis and his wife at Howard Wilkinson's house. I told them then that we would go up. I felt so confident that everything was coming together. We jumped from 17th to number one in 43 days on the back of a golden December. The turkey had never tasted better.'

Not only were supporters excited by the buzz of the unbeaten run, so too was Brian Clough. 'I heard a familiar voice when I caught up with my messages,' wrote Smith. '"Eh, Mr Smith, this is old big 'ead Brian Clough here. I just thought I'd ring to say thanks for putting the smile back on the faces of Derby supporters." That meant everything.'

Having consolidated their spot in the automatic spots, the battle was on with Sunderland for who would move ahead at the peak of the division. Naturally, it was on a visit to Roker Park that things would take their biggest turn yet, with the task of extending the unbeaten run proving one ask too far. A convincing 3-0 defeat, coming after 20 games without one, threatened the character of the squad. Heading into the final months of the campaign, a loss of that nature could not only damage morale, it could feed into any hidden doubts individuals may have had about dealing with the weight of expectation. By this point, however, Derby County had a secret weapon in their ranks in the form of sports psychologist Bill Beswick.

'I can tell you the true story of that,' begins Beswick, who had joined the club on a freelance basis weeks earlier. 'We had the long run and Steve was anxious; he thought the team was running out of steam. He came to see me, and I said, "Well that's always the way in sport. You can't keep running all the time, keep winning. It's a question of how you handle the first defeat." You either fall off the horse or you get back on the horse. So, Steve said, "Would you go and talk to Jim about it?" So I went to talk to Jim and I told Jim a story. Now I didn't tell him what to do, you never told Jim what to do, I learnt that! But you worked your way around it, so he got the idea for himself. So I used to tell him stories about other coaches to get him to think, "Oh, I could do that."

'I told him the story about a coach who was beaten after a long run, walked in the dressing room and said, "Thank fuck for that. I was getting so tired with this bloody pressure of winning. I'll sleep tonight. OK boys, let's have a drink on the way home." And Derby got beat at Sunderland for my memory. And Jim walked in the dressing room and said, "Thank fuck for that! I'm so pleased, it was making me sleepless. We'll have a drink on the way home." He was a good learner was Jim. If you gave him an idea that was good, that's really what my job was, to set the mindset, and that first defeat after a long run could be a very damaging thing to the mindset unless you took it the right way. If Jim had gone in and blasted them after such a good run, it could have really caused damage. But he went in and let them off, and he laughed with them, they all laughed and relaxed.'

Beswick's impact was by no means the only reason form didn't deteriorate, but it was a vital inclusion that indicates how, although his temper was seen as fiery, Smith was able to vary his dressing-room behaviour to match the situation and utilised the skills of others to tailor how he could get the best out of his squad.

* * *

One man who found himself on the fringes of the squad more often than not was Paul Simpson. Despite a stellar goalscoring record for a wideman, he found opportunities limited under Smith despite having been an integral part of the squad for three years. So much so, he was offered an opportunity to move to Leicester on loan, with the manager looking to do a deal which would have brought Lee Philpott in as exchange. Positioned as a like-for-like swap with the intention of cutting the wage bill, the idea was nixed by Smith himself as Simpson remained at Raynesway. It would be a crucial decision in those closing weeks.

Because, as the side threatened to let the occasions get the better of them following the end of the run, Simpson was the man to step up, notching six goals in 11 games, including a hat-trick in the 6-2 demolition of Tranmere. To do the job on the side who had inflicted the heaviest defeat of the season to Derby, it provided scoreline evidence of how immense the turnaround had been. Crucial as that hat-trick was though, it was a goal on an afternoon in Oldham which had more significance. The Sunderland loss had quickly been followed by two more defeats, both in East Anglia against Norwich and Ipswich, and with Oldham's Boundary Park never the easiest of destinations to visit, anything less than a victory there would have opened the door for third-placed Crystal Palace – who were on a ten-game unbeaten run of their own – to add to the anxiety.

'We all knew how big a game it was away at Oldham,' Simpson says. 'We went up to Sunderland and actually got battered there, and it was our first defeat for a long time. We then started to shake a bit and we were under a little bit of pressure. So we go to Oldham and it's a really tight game, it's running towards 90 minutes and we get this penalty. As normal when there is a controversial late penalty, there was a long time between it getting given and me taking it. At one point I was stood holding on to the ball and my legs just started to go on me. They started to shake and I had never had that sort of feeling before. I started to realise how important it was, so I just had to walk away to the side and just started juggling with the ball a little bit, and my legs came back to me by the time I got to take the penalty.' Simpson would tuck it away, the only goal in a 1-0 victory, at the same time as Palace lost 1-0 at Leicester.

Simpson's contribution was massive, responsible for turning draws into wins and salvaging points with his goals. But though his time in a Derby shirt is remembered even more fondly today, at the time his team-mates knew exactly what he brought to the side, with Dean Sturridge saying, 'I remember when we used to play in the reserves years previously, and whenever Simmo had got demoted to the reserves, I would play with him and think, just what an intelligent footballer. A wand of a left foot and he would score week after week in the reserves. It was like an "up yours" to the management team at the time. He would always have time in the reserves for me, talking to me and giving me information, and he was exactly the same in the first team. Playing with him in those last 12 games where he got so many assists and goals, it went back to playing in the reserve team with him again in that I knew what he was gonna do, I knew his thought process, knew how he played the game.'

As is the nature of Derby County though, the Oldham and Tranmere victories didn't lead to a serene journey to guaranteed automatic promotion. Ever the tale, particularly in more recent times, just as destiny was in their own hands a Derby side threatened to relinquish it. It's the Derby Way, as someone once said. First came a goalless draw away at Charlton, then a 1-1 at home to Birmingham in which Simpson scored the Rams' only goal again. It left Sunderland with a clear run at the title with Derby made to rue their late-season wobble. On the same afternoons, a Palace side managed by Smith's long-time friend Dave Bassett had beaten Southend and Wolves without conceding a goal. The final home game of the campaign, on a Sunday afternoon in late April, in front of the ITV cameras, would be a do-or-die encounter. Three points for Derby and promotion was sealed. Three points for Palace would put fate in their own hands. A draw would leave Derby needing a win in a difficult-looking tie at West Brom on the final day.

* * *

Before social media and forums were used to raise fan awareness and begin campaigns, you had traditional methods. Flyers, interviews with the great Gerald Mortimer in the *Derby Evening Telegraph*, maybe even a television appearance if you were feeling especially needy. What Keith Loring offered up for the Crystal Palace match was all of the above and much, much more. The Rams' chief executive had become a key player in the off-field development of the club during his first season at the BBG. Less of a public persona than Jim and Lionel Pickering, it was the unseen work of advancing the business which would have the longest lasting impact.

To the backdrop of the 'Roar 'Til You're Raw' campaign, Loring and his staff set about transforming the Baseball Ground into a black-and-white paradise. Steel outside of the stadium would be turned black and white, matched inside by balloons and placards for supporters. And those same supporters did their bit, several sporting face paint and thousands more wearing Rams shirts from over the years. In fact, the city was so encapsulated by not only the event but the squad as a whole that, from struggling to reach five figures in attendances at the beginning of the campaign, there was clamour for tickets come the end of the season.

While the city of Derby prepared for the make-or-break afternoon, Smith utilised his contact book to take the focus away from his squad. Having spoken with Howard Wilkinson, he would take his charges to use the facilities at Leeds United's training base in Wetherby, as well as a trip to Champneys Health Spa, providing an opportunity to relax and be taken away from the heightened expectations. Come gameday though, there would be no getting away from the severity of the situation. When looking back today at grainy footage of the afternoon, players arriving at the BBG had grins across the board, which could be perceived as confidence or just an excellent poker face. Dean Sturridge remembers, 'The cameras being there as I was walking, and I looked back at the day after or when it was in the archives. I looked at myself and you could see me smile to the camera as I was walking in, and that was the inner confidence. I had a strong belief that we would win that game and that I would score. Jim knew what the squad needed, and he put us in a bubble away from the pressure.'

The decision to head north wasn't a one-off either. Smith would do it again numerous times over the years, taking his players to locations with few supporters to clear minds. Simpson recalled one similar occurrence where the squad ended up in Blackpool, and spoke of the Leeds trip taking in almost as much golf as football training, as well as a few nerve-busting beers.

Gary Rowett adds, 'I remember turning up at the ground, and Jim had relaxed the players. He didn't put too much pressure or too much stress on the situation, which again was part of his experience as he'd been there many times before. We used to park at the top end near the sports centre or the community centre, then walk back down past the fans into the ground.' Even upon arrival hours before kick-off, Rowett and team-mates were mobbed by legions of locals of all ages.

There was a reason to worry underneath the face paint. Player of the season Dean Yates had been as integral to the side as the more heralded Štimac but had failed to escape a knock he had picked up in Leeds and his run of 42 straight appearances would come to an end on the most important day of all. In his place came Matt Carbon, an inexperienced defender who had still not made his full debut. Luckily for Smith, that was where the selection panic would finish, with Štimac emerging fine from his midweek international appearance against England and Sturridge back in the side following suspension. There was also a recall for Gabbiadini at the top, replacing recent signing Ashley Ward.

'We didn't feel an ounce of pressure,' reiterates Sturridge. 'It was more an excitable kid kind of "I can't wait to get on the pitch and show you how good I am, and I'm gonna make the difference". In the lead-up that's what Robbie [Van Der Laan] said to me, and Darryl. "We just want one moment from you. One moment to win the game for us. You will help us get the three points." That was always ringing in my ears, in my mind and at the forefront. You've seen the culmination of that in me scoring very early in the game. Igor played the ball to Simpson. I was on the move as he was receiving the ball, and just knew he would put the ball into a certain area and managed to get on it. As I always looked to finish generally, I always looked to side-foot and curl the ball into the corner of the net, and I put it past Nigel Martyn. That settled the nerves of the team. Not that I had any.'

Sturridge's goal within the opening three minutes had lit the fuse of the afternoon, and an instantaneous equaliser from

West Ham loanee Kenny Brown only raised the temperature of a matchday with millions of pounds at stake for both clubs. The two sides struggled to test either Hoult or Martyn for the next hour though, a frantic opening descending into a cagey affair inside an increasingly nervous Baseball Ground. That was until the introduction of Ron Willems from the bench as one of his first touches saw the Rams win a corner.

Simpson took it from the right and found Captain Fantastic, Van Der Laan. 'You think for a minute, "Are we gonna have enough?"' Sturridge questions of himself when analysing that second half. 'Then Robin pops up with a header, his blond locks waving about everywhere, and he was the match-winner. It was a big thing because he was such a good captain, always having banter with the boys at the right time, always being serious when he needed to be serious as well, and just always thoughtful for the players in terms of off the pitch as well. Those little things like [getting family] tickets and being accommodating to make it as comfortable for families. All those little things people don't know about as such in terms of fans, but behind the scenes you appreciate it because it takes the stresses away and you can concentrate on the game.'

What followed was pandemonium and an iconic greeting between Van Der Laan and Carbon, as already disintegrating BBG stands threatened to disintegrate into chaos. The skipper blushes when bringing up the seconds after nodding home: 'The celebration just happened! There was no practising or thinking about it beforehand, and you know, that season I scored a few goals and my celebration was so stupid; I cringe sometimes when I see them. But that one was probably perfect for that moment. I don't know why it happened, but the photos were perfectly made from the right corner. It turned out to be a really nice image, so I'm glad I didn't do one of the previous ones where I looked a bit of a fool! When you score some but not too many, you don't have your set celebrations, not the Alan Shearer sort of hand up in the air, but that one was pretty good for the occasion.'

The 20 remaining minutes felt like quadruple that for supporters, and yet for the players – at least in Sturridge's case – they never felt the result was in doubt. 'It was just uproar and mayhem,' says Colin Gibson, who was broadcasting on the pitch for BBC Radio Derby before the game. 'For Lionel, who had backed Arthur Cox and spent that money and it didn't work, and then going to Wembley in '94 and losing to Leicester, you have this seminal moment of making all these changes, bringing Jim Smith in, and in one season it's all paid off. It was just a celebration.'

Already knowing they would be heading into one final season at the Baseball Ground (we'll get to that), anyone of a black-and-white persuasion defied the security presence to kiss, hug and in some cases, do even more than that to the players who had returned Derby to the top division. As supporter Andy Margett reminisces, 'I remember getting up to celebrate, and my dad was one of the very first ones on to the bloody pitch from the Normanton lower. I just lost him in the ground, didn't know where he ended up. Then I see him at the other side of the ground with Russell Hoult's gloves that he'd managed to nick off him. I've still got them in the house somewhere!'

Another fan, Jamie Allen, celebrated in a different way: 'I'm not afraid to admit that I almost broke down in tears, it was just unbelievable. I was in the Co-op Stand that day. We did the normal Derby thing where we have to do it the hard way as we always have done, but it was a proper carnival day, all just living in hope. But there's always that niggling doubt in your mind. When we scored that goal, rising up and I can see him [Van Der Laan] now, back across goal and into the top corner, the roof blew off. It was about 70 minutes in so there was still a way to go, but it seemed like forever. When that final whistle went, I felt myself well up, I really did, and I couldn't actually believe Derby County were back in the top league.'

Captain Fantastic himself adds, 'It was such a high-pressure game and suddenly everything is lifted and you end up being

Premier League players there and then. It was just such a feel-good time. I always have a laugh with Gary Rowett about it because we had a photograph in the paper and he was on my back, and the caption underneath said, "Robin Van Der Laan celebrating with a Derby fan", and it was Gary on my back. You've got the interview after with Jim Smith on the TV, then coming into the dressing room and it was a fantastic time for us. I have no idea where the cigars came from, but somebody must have raided Jim Smith's office drawer! It would never happen now because it would completely set the wrong image for young fans but, at the time, it was more acceptable.'

The players would accept the plaudits of supporters on the field before returning to the sanctuary of the home dressing room, where cigars and bottles of beer would be handed out across the board. When emphasising the togetherness of any squad that achieves promotion, it tends to go beyond simply the footballers and their coaches. Darren Moore recalled for *Pride* how everyone from the players to the tea ladies were part of the inner circle during the 2006/07 season. With the 1995/96 squad, that included the assistant groundsman at the time, Andy Croft, who would find himself invited to celebrate with the players. He said, 'We were sat behind the dugout, and all of the lads went into the dressing room. One of the lads came out and said, "Gaffer wants you to come in and join in the celebrations." For the three ground staff that were there, we were in the home team changing room where we'd just beat Palace to go up, now drinking cans of Carling with all the players and having a laugh. That's what it was like. He would make sure, because they had two open-top buses, even we went on one. It was mad and it wouldn't happen now, but things like that at the time. Ground staff going into the changing room with Igor and Van Der Laan and all the lads and having a drink? That doesn't happen. You couldn't make that sort of stuff up. Everyone is out there destroying the pitch and the ground staff are getting drunk with the players in the changing room!'

The release of emotion was also vital for Igor too. Having been convinced he was joining a Premier League side in the first place, the realisation that his journey to England had not been in vain was a welcome relief when celebrating: 'I remember it was crazy at the ground after the game and in the dressing room, there were a lot of Cuban cigars. I love after the games and successes to just go home to spend time with my family to be honest. Not enjoying big celebrations, because the body is exhausted and all you need at that point is to go to a peaceful place where you can feel alive and stay in peace.'

Saying that, there would be time for one celebration. As we'll see later, Jim Smith was not a man to pass up on an opportunity to raise a glass of wine when the situation called for it. Having suddenly realised no plans had been put in place on what to do following the final whistle, he tasked Simpson with the responsibility for managing to get a group of around 50 people into a restaurant within the next couple of hours.

As he had done in those dying weeks of the season, Simpson delivered again: 'At the time I was one of the longest-serving players at the club, so it was me and Jackie [Paul's partner] who used to sort of organise the get-togethers and things like that. I think we ended up all going to La Villa up in Mickleover or Littleover, wherever it is, just off the A38. The owner of La Villa was a guy called Salvatore and he was a real top bloke. We had nothing organised so it was a case of ringing him at the end of the game and saying, "Listen Sal, are you open and can you accommodate 50 people for a bit of a do?" He was always brilliant, and he told us to bring everybody up. So I think we ended up going to La Villa that night.

'I know we did on the way back from Wembley when we lost against Leicester. I rung him on the coach on the way back and said, "Look, everybody is really gutted but it's still been a decent season. Can you put some food on for us?" I'm quite sure we did the exact same thing when we got promotion, and we ended up going up there with a big group of us with the players and partners, ended up celebrating into the early hours of the next day with what we'd achieved. It was better than Wembley.'

And for Dean Sturridge, who had seen his career go full circle from 12 months previously, it was an opportunity to take in the celebrations of what had been achieved – even if McClaren had tasked him with getting his 20th goal of the campaign in the final match. 'We booked that restaurant out, and it had a magnificent bar that we drank copiously from. Jim was on the dance floor dancing with my girlfriend as she was then, quite a few of the players' girlfriends, just living the dream, smoking! He talked to me and told me he believed in me, and that's one that will always stick in the memory because it's a relief that all your hard work for those nine or ten months is rewarded with promotion, and you can really let your hair down and enjoy yourself, and just have a great night. And it certainly was that.'

4

BODY AND MIND

'WHEN MIND, body and spirit are in harmony, happiness is the natural result.' So said Deepak Chopra, the wealthy spiritualist who I feel I've heard mentioned far more than I ever cared to, without knowing anything about him. It's the first quote I could find when searching 'Body and Mind quotes' on Google, but it seems to do the trick. What goes on at the top of the being has repercussions all the way down. It's a basic fact of biology and yet, for centuries, it was almost ignored. Perhaps only in the past 100 or so years has it become a more accepted fact of life.

Take mental health issues. For those who have struggled with anxiety, you will know it's not just a panic in the mind. What goes on in the brain transgresses to the rest of the body, resulting in a racing heartbeat, sweating and perhaps even jitters. The same can be said of depression, which displays similar symptoms in the body and often leads to issues in the gut. Everything, from top to bottom, is intertwined. Therefore, if you look after the brain, your body will follow suit.

The same is true for elite-level athletes. Sports psychology has, become a necessary backroom team for sports clubs. Now, in 2022, they are accepted and demanded and squads would struggle to function without them. In the mid-1990s though, much like statistical analysis, they were almost nowhere to be seen. Step forward Derby County. Step forward Bill Beswick.

His is a name you may be familiar with, the godfather of the science in British football. Over a now 30-year involvement in the game, he has not just represented the biggest clubs (as well as the national team) but he has become the guru and example for all others to follow. Recent months saw an element of surprise at Manchester United when their latest universally acclaimed and inevitably unsuccessful manager Ralf Rangnick opted to bring Sascha Lense, his close confidant and psychological assistant, to Old Trafford. Lense would be the first man in the role in 20 years; the last was under Sir Alex Ferguson, and it was Bill Beswick. It's a sad indictment on the British game that it is one area yet to be fully welcomed in, when compared to clubs across Europe and beyond. But although there is still considerable room for growth, the reason it all came to pass in the first place was due to Beswick.

He explained, 'I had five years as coach of the England basketball team [where he won gold in the 1992 Commonwealth Games] at the same time as lecturing at university. It was through coaching all over the world that I became aware that performance was more than just talent. This was quite new at the time, because all the coaching I had ever watched or received was talent-based, physical or technical. But I was seeing psychology, I was seeing character in action under pressure of the team. I was seeing the mental strength of the player being more important than the talent-based. I had done a master's degree in my youth and I went to America where they had sports psychologists, I checked in with them and found some reference points, and then came back and made a decision that I was going to do a change of career.'

Though sport-focused, Beswick had switched his day-to-day work to become a principal at a college, before opting for an early retirement from what one would expect is an almost torture of dealing with adolescents daily. It was at this point, at the age of 50, that Beswick would be able to see whether his learnings in the USA would be of interest across England. His first port of call would be Carlisle, where Beswick would work alongside Mick Wadsworth and slowly be able to evaluate how psychology would have a positive effect on lower-league footballers as the club bounced between the bottom two divisions of the Football League pyramid. Alongside this, he would begin a series of talks at Lilleshall, the FA's then School of Excellence location, as he looked to at least plant the seed of psychology in the minds of coaches and budding young footballers. It was one of these talks which would transform the mind of a young man who would go on to change the face of English football.

'There was a red-haired guy in the audience. There were around 200 youth coaches there and quite a few of them came to see me afterwards because they had never heard anything before about sports psychology, it was brand new to them. But some of them were fascinated and they came to see me. And I watched the queue, and this red-haired guy kept going to the back of the queue. If somebody came to join the queue, he would go to the back, so I thought that he wanted a serious talk. And he came forward eventually at his turn and said, "I'm Steve McClaren."'

The then under-17 coach at Oxford United, McClaren had taken early retirement from the playing side but always had intentions of staying within the game, with his former Manor Ground team-mate Paul Simpson recalling, 'He took the youth team and got involved on that side of it, so I knew that, even though we were in the dressing room as players together, he wanted to go down the line of coaching. And I'd heard he was doing well on the coaching side, building up a good reputation as well before he joined the club.'

Just past the age of 30 at the time of meeting Beswick, from the moment McClaren found the courage to approach on that afternoon in Lilleshall he would change both his own career and also that of the man he was there to listen to. Beswick explained, '[McClaren told me] "If I'd have known you, I would have been a different player completely. Can I work with you?" We began some correspondence and about a week in I said to him, "I could talk to you about this but there is a great book you should read." Three days later he said, "I've read that, can you give me another book?" and I knew he was a student then. I knew it. Six months later he had gone to Derby.'

* * *

The 1990s was still a rugged time in football, so it's little wonder that the mind was ignored when it came to the sport. Though hooliganism was calming considerably when compared to the previous decade, and the sport as a whole was evolving, it was still a decade largely epitomised by alpha masculinity in and out of sport. Homophobia was still accepted as part and parcel of media and everyday life, with laws eventually catching up (the legal age of consent for homosexual acts was 21 until 1994). Sexism was prevalent, and the lads' mag culture was booming as *FHM* and *Loaded* launched to national acclaim. It was a time when men were supposed to be men and if you had something which others perceived to be wrong about you, you were ostracised. That fully applied to the topic of mental health too. When Andy Goram revealed he had schizophrenia, the chant 'Two Andy Gorams, there's only two Andy Gorams' was heard regularly. It even had a book about supposedly funny football songs named after it.

'Back when I played it was seen as a weakness to get help,' admits Dean Sturridge. 'I was brought up in a council estate as one of six brothers and a sister, where you are all battling for your own 15 minutes of fame as such. I built up a resilience and an independence and had a self-confidence from a very young age, just from coming from the family I came from. So when Bill came along, I thought, "I don't need him. I've got to this stage in my career and haven't needed anybody. I'm not showing any softness or vulnerability, I'll work it out for myself."'

That would have been a replication of the thoughts of not only most footballers at the time, but also most males, at least in the UK. You don't talk about your problems. Even though a softer and more compassionate world was emerging, mental health remained firmly on the taboo side of conversation topics, not helped by media which painted it in a humorous light. A

2011 Public Health report by Goulden et al. analysed newspaper coverage of the topic across various years. In 1992, 59 per cent of all coverage of the topic positioned it as bad news, meaning coverage centred around the dangers and stigmas. By 2000 that had fallen to 44 per cent. In film, an unsuitably overexaggerated number of 'bad guys' were justified to commit atrocities due to having mental illnesses written into their character. *Halloween*, *American Psycho* and many more would associate murderers with diagnoses such as personality disorders. Even real-life events like the Columbine school shooting saw the media try to attribute the two perpetrators with mental illness as a reasoning for hideous acts, regardless of whether they had been diagnosed or not.

So with a media response to occurrences in the brain so negative, it was little wonder that any sort of assistance hadn't been brought into sport in Britain. But as Beswick started to break the mould in certain circles, in McClaren he found a man who was intrigued by the possibilities of something new. Brought in on a three-day per week freelance contract during the promotion season of 1995/96, it was the role of McClaren to work out how this man and his way of thinking could benefit Derby County. To do that, he'd have to get the backing of Jim Smith.

Beswick said, 'Steve introduced me to Jim and persuaded him to take me, which wasn't easy apparently. But I came with a clear conviction that to compete in the Premier League consistently under pressure and fatigue we needed to build a squad with mental strength, not just physical strength. Initially he had great doubts and great fears, so the first time he saw me talking to a player in the canteen, when the player left Jim appeared and said, "What did he say? What did he say?" "I can't tell you that Jim, it's confidential. I don't tell them what you say to me, I don't tell you what they say to me." And he couldn't understand that. When I first went there, on the first day Jim told me he didn't believe in any of the psychobabble. He'd appointed me because Steve had insisted, but he didn't believe in it.'

It was little wonder, as British managers had long been built around running everything at a club. At his age why would Smith need to move with a new idea that hadn't been trialled elsewhere? Smith had long been the sole voice to players across multiple clubs, and everything would need to pass through him for much of his career. To then have a man on his team where secrets were part and parcel must have been a significant challenge. Beswick continues, 'Players used to run the other way down the corridor when they saw me coming and they would call me "Psycho Bill". There was an awful lot of resistance because it ran against the macho culture. British football has been brought up historically and traditionally on a certain sort of working-class ethic. Macho man. They all had to be stronger than ordinary men. Admitting you had a problem mentally and emotionally was like anathema to these boys. But I had some advantages.'

One of which was his age. Joining Derby in his 50s, Beswick would be on a par with Smith, two old warhorses in their differing professions. Had McClaren approached Smith with, say, a 25-year-old psychologist, he likely would have been instantly turned away. But age played a significant factor in encouraging Smith to at least embrace the possibility that this could improve his entire setup.

For McClaren himself, the decision to bring psychology to Smith could have gone one of two ways for his own career: 'Jim could see the advantage of that in terms of the team and a lot of individuals. And Bill was the kind who could build trust in the players and they would go and see him. Not everybody believed in what Bill did, and that was no problem to us. But those that did really benefitted. There is always a stigma behind it. If you're seeing a psychologist, you've got a mental problem or a mind problem. I call them performance coaches now. Do they improve your performance? If they can, use them. So you're not mental or anything, it's a strength. I remember the first time Bill was in the dressing room, he [Smith] said, "Steve, I don't want him in the dressing room. He keeps looking at me, I think he's reading my mind. He's putting me off!" [I replied] "Jim just put him behind you, don't look at him!"'

Beswick's work would largely be done at Raynesway, and he too would find the Prozone room crucial to getting his messages across to the wider team. But while it was wider messages which would help prepare mentalities for matchday, it was in the individual conversations where players would get the most out of a mental asset that no other club in the country had access to. As he alluded to earlier, the idea of speaking out as a player was alien to all, and so many of those like Sturridge in those early weeks and months would action wariness when in Beswick's presence. All were intrigued though, not least Sturridge himself: 'Some players didn't want to show in, inverted commas, "a weakness" at the time. I see it as a strength, but at the time I was one of them that felt a little bit uncomfortable. I'd been brought up in that mentality of you deal with things yourself, you're strong, resilient, confident. But as time grew, I realised it could be beneficial with Bill, it may help me one or two per cent.

There were some players who I'm sure would tell him, "Meet me down the motorway, not at the training ground." I was one who was initially not feeling I needed him, but when I did my cartilage and was out for a certain amount of months, it gave me the confidence, him saying, "Your knee is going to be OK, you can play. You've got a strength there because you've done all your rehab work and all the things that are needed."'

Sturridge's mention of meeting on the motorway was echoed by several others, and Beswick himself remembers a series of players looking to meet at a service station cafe to avoid the whispers of other players: 'I bedded down in the canteen with a cup of tea and mostly saw the players on the training field. Occasionally I would see them in the canteen, but it was very busy. I can remember Chris Powell and I walking round the training pitch, and we must have done miles walking around the edge and chatting and discussing his issues. Another player who I won't mention would only see me at the McDonald's on the A50 because he dreaded the thought of other players seeing him talking to "Psycho Bill". My office was wherever it could be. Car park, wherever, but it seemed to work. Football people are good people and, if you are there long enough, you win their respect and you build up a rapport. And if you share with them the pain and the joy of football, if you're there in the dressing room and you've been beaten and share the pain, or you're there and sharing their joy, eventually you become one of the family, and I did become one, slowly and reluctantly on many parts.'

What also aided Beswick's position was overseas players, who were more likely to meet him in public than to request separate discussions away from prying eyes. It not only had benefits for themselves, but they would become mouthpieces to the homegrown players. 'Mart Poom was always in my room, and the foreign players were comfortable about coming to see me. And they would go back to the dressing room and the English boys would say, "What's he like?" "Yeah, great!" So slowly I began to make progress and then I cracked a couple like Lee Carsley, and generally I integrated well. Initially I concentrated on the coaches and the environment because the players would need more time to come into my aura, but the environment and coaching was something I could work straight away. How do you coach players to be mentally stronger and build character? I had McClaren and Steve Round, Billy McEwan, so that was my initial starting point.'

Even Smith himself would visit Bill for psychological chats, whether results were good or bad. Beswick said, 'He was basically a lovely, lovely man. When you stick with a team through the difficult early phases and you share their life and share their experiences, you gradually become integrated. And Jim and I were a similar age, so we had things in common. And I have noticed with managers that they get very isolated, very lonely. The job of managing a team can be a very lonely job, but he found that with me he had a neutral friend. He knew I wouldn't tell anything to anybody else because he had tested me, but he knew he could talk to me about age and lack of energy, family issues, and I was on board with that because I had the same. Our conversations became more and more personal, and we became a lot closer.

'When the players went out to practice at 10am, I'd have a cup of tea with Jim, he'd get changed in his office and we used to chat. On my last day before I went to join Man United, Jim walked me out to the car. And when we got to the car, he gave me a kiss on the forehead, typical Jim. I said, "What's that for Jimmy?" "That's because you are the only one in football who ever asked me every day how I was. And you took care of me."'

* * *

Why it was that Jim Smith himself accepted many of the ideas presented to him will be explored later, but there is a secret reason why he particularly welcomed Beswick on board: Jim himself was a psychologist. To perceive him from the outside, it wouldn't be the first title you would throw at him, and even many of those who played under him would still not use it as a suitable descriptive. But in his role in management over almost four decades, he was the sounding board for many a footballer and coach at various stages of their careers.

'He was always very good at keeping your energy up,' says first-team coach Steve Round. 'He knew when you were a little bit low, he knew when you needed some rest and recovery, he knew when he needed to take you out for a beer. He just knew emotional intelligence. He also knew when you needed pulling down a peg or two or a firm word. He knew when the players needed a slap as well. Even though he did rattle a few cages, after that, players would still respect and admire him. You knew what he said was right. And it's not how much you know, it's how much you care. That's what he was about. He did have that ability and that humility about him that he could do that and he could get away with that. It's managing people. In this modern age today, it's very much about tactical application, physical capabilities, but there is still a massive part of management which is about just how you manage people. And he was exceptionally good at that.'

'He treated some of them with kid gloves. Honestly, he was a sports psychologist,' recalls physio and long-time friend Neil Sillett. 'He brought Bill in but Jim was still the psychologist. He'd say, "Nah, if Igor wants a day off, just give him a day off." All the players were upset that Igor wouldn't train, but he'd turn up on a Saturday and be unbelievable. And you don't see that very often these days.' Sturridge adds, 'He would hammer certain players and know he would get a reaction out of them on matchday. They would have to prove him wrong, and he'd just say, "OK, put two fingers up to me on matchday and show me how good you are, because I'm giving you stick."' Jim's perhaps less obvious strengths were built in both his humility and his general emotional intelligence, which will also be delved into in later chapters.

It was something even Beswick would become aware of the longer he would spend with Jim, as he saw the mind beginning to tick: 'His instincts were good, but if you intrigued him with something, he would take it and convert it to his. That's what I learnt with Jim. You had to drop something in the conversation and he was cute because he'd pick it up, and it would come back out in a team meeting. So I'd give him some ideas and then I'd hear them in a team meeting coming back out, but he would have adopted them.'

Ultimately, as with Prozone, psychology in football was an innovation simply too big for Derby County to contain, not that they wanted to. Smith could see what benefit it may have to the game, and McClaren would also eventually bring Beswick with him to Old Trafford to join Alex Ferguson. Beswick said, 'Derby was a very good classroom for me to learn how to be a sports psychologist, and without Derby I would never have been ready for Man United and then assistant at Middlesbrough and then England. So Derby was vital for me and it was a place where I could make mistakes and I did, and Steve and Jim would forgive me. That was important as well that they were good to me, because I couldn't get everything right and I would try things that didn't work. So I think looking back at my career Derby was a highly significant moment. When I started at Derby I was still experimenting, and when I finished at Derby I was more or less 80 per cent of the way to understanding what sports psychology in performance was.'

Bill would spend two years at Old Trafford alongside McClaren, before working with him across his managerial career. Even when he joined McClaren in the England national team setup in 2006, there was still reluctance to his position. Had it not been for McClaren's futuristic outlook and Smith's willingness to adapt to change, it could still be the same today.

* * *

That was the mind though. And for the importance it has on a professional athlete, a world-class footballer has never existed just on mind alone. It's irritatingly obvious to say, but football is about what you can do with your legs. And for a long time, the work which would go on in those legs across Britain's top footballing training pitches was focused around putting a spherical object into a net. And why not? It's the most important part. But in doing just this, you ignore much of what allows you to get into a decent position in the first place.

Within these early chapters, we have seen the science and the tactical nous behind the sport. But to be able to even get to the position where these are brought into your performances, you generally need to be good at the game itself. Yet what it takes to be good at football is as detailed as any other sport, regardless of the lack of complexity. For all the talk of a universal game and the relative simplicity that goes into football, it's not something which comes just from talent alone. Yes, there is heart; that goes a long way. But ultimately, what can distinguish an average non-league performer from a Premier League star is their fitness.

Take some of Derby's favourite sons in recent years. Craig Bryson is roundly regarded as a modern legend of the club for his long service under often chaotic circumstances. And let's not do Bryson a disservice, he was first and foremost a great footballer.

But what kept him in the plans of so many managers was his fitness levels. That was the same for the Derby side of the 1990s. Every Saturday afternoon, first the Baseball Ground and then Pride Park would watch teams boasting the likes of Stefano Eranio, Aljoša Asanović, Georgi Kinkladze – and Darryl Powell. Powell's ability was in his legs, but it was more in the amount of ground they could cover than what they could do with a ball in front of them. It's not something which just occurs though. Like any other aspect of the game, it comes from repetition and consistent training. And yet, like the psychology and the statistics, fitness training in the 1990s wasn't a thing. That was until Derby County and Jim Smith.

There were fitness elements to day-to-day training, that is a given; a professional athlete wouldn't be a professional athlete if they couldn't maintain 90 minutes of exercise. But generally, it was exercise in the loosest sense of the word. Player sessions would begin with a certain amount of laps of a given training ground, before ball work. Regardless of the club, it would be the same routine. It's little surprise considering where English football was in the 1990s. Despite a home tournament, the defining memory of Euro '96 is Paul Gascoigne's 'dentist's chair' celebration against Scotland to mock a heavy, heavy pre-tournament night of drinking between the squad. The nation that invented the game hadn't mastered it, instead opting for a few beers to keep it as a laugh rather than maintaining the lifestyle of an ultra-professional athlete. It's by no means a criticism of football or England as a whole; this was simply the culture of the time.

That's why, when Jim came to Raynesway, fitness was treated as a needs-must addition. 'I remember when we first started, Jim brought in a fitness guy who came in and he said, "Oh he's great,"' laughs McClaren. 'Jim said, "I had him at Halifax Town when I played," and he was older than Jim. We had a few disagreements around the fitness side because I'd done all the fitness work at Oxford myself and built up knowledge, had a good background in it and had planned pre-seasons from day one myself. But everything was about individuals, so I couldn't go around everybody. I just said we needed an individual fitness guy that everybody can go to for individual work. We were going into a more physical league and physicality was important.'

For the promotion season, fitness work would be taken on by mostly McClaren himself. But aware that they were entering a Premier League with a wider foreign influence that would be more physically able than his squad, it was left to the assistant to do exactly as he had done with Prozone and Bill Beswick and look for what his next game-changing development could be. His search would lead him to local fitness guru Dane Farrell.

'I played for some local teams,' begins Farrell, 'and was always interested in the fitness aspect. I did all my qualifications and was working with the police before I joined Derby, as well as fitness training with small local clubs in the city. Watching football, I thought, "What are these fitness tests all about? What does it consist of?" I just wanted to know, and I put together a letter, in those days it was the mid-90s, and sent them off to various clubs asking if I could come and observe. Together I gathered a pre-season programme which I thought would be of interest to them. I got some replies, and the best I got at the time was in the early days of Sir Alex Ferguson, which I didn't value a great deal at the time, but he took the time to reply. Steve McClaren replied and asked me to go up there [to Derby] and just have a look. And if I could put something together, he'd get a small squad of players, a mixture of reserves and first-team players, and put something on, because he was interested in what I had put forward.

'Meeting Steve and Jimmy, I just realised these guys are forward-thinking and it wasn't like the old archaic football which I thought I was venturing towards, which you would see on TV. There was some science and logic and progression using whatever was available in the football industry. So, I arrived at the ground, met the coaching staff and met a few players and just put them through their paces and had a little talk with Steve and Billy McEwan. They were pleased with what they saw, and where they thought this would really enhance the performances of the guys.

It all goes by the feedback and the players gave some very positive feedback. You could see they were enjoying the session and they could see the value of the session and it just moved on from there.'

That introductory session would act as a precursor to all that would follow, but it was primarily about giving the coaching team the views of their squad on whether it would be of use to them in their battle for Premier League survival in 1996/97. It also gave Farrell an opportunity to get to know exactly what he could do on a day-to-day basis. The session would involve a mixture of the key elements of Farrell's standard sessions: power, speed, agility. Elements of teamwork would be incorporated as well, but there was one key focus on at least his first practice session: there would be no football in sight. Those four key necessities were enough to convince an initially sceptic Smith that McClaren had offered him his third major visualisation.

Farrell said, 'Derby got promoted into the Premier League and we did not have the talented players that the top four would have. Derby's function was to retain Premier League status, so we had to work hard. Jim and Steve had the foresight to see that they needed something extra, and my letter came through just at that point where they were looking for that little edge, that little bit extra. So we were very physical, very fit and it was something very new to the players in terms of the demand I put on them through the training sessions. I explained it all, explained the science, the components where each individual player needs to attain that sort of quality of their physical enhancement to fulfil their role more effectively. So rather than a one size fits all, we would separate the players according to their positions. Goalkeepers would have more agility and power work along with some of the more explosive forward strikers. Players like Dean Sturridge who had thick, powerful thighs, we didn't want to distract him by sending him on long runs and hard, long aerobic work, because it would just distract from his main asset, which was just speed and power.'

Sturridge, a man who had all the credentials and speed a non-ball-playing athlete would boast, was one of the key men in the dressing room and his willingness to adapt his game to Farrell's demands would influence those around him. More than that, he was one of those who were willing to accept another outsider into the inner sanctuary of the changing room. Sturridge said, 'Apart from him being very good at his job, he also brought his personality. Every morning he would come in with a smiling face, cleanly shaven, head shaved bald, a body to die for, muscles on top of his muscles. You thought this guy is *fit*, he projects the right image, he's got the personality to back that up, he makes people feel good around him and he gives the information of what to do to improve, to get fitter, faster, stronger. All the players bought into it.

'Jim and Steve were good in terms of knowing you want a person to come in and to fit with the players, because players are very fickle. When a fitness instructor comes in – and it was new at that time – if they don't buy into the person and what the information is, Dane would have got chewed up and spat out within days or weeks. But Dane integrated himself into the group like another player, that's the biggest compliment I can give. Everybody, whoever it was, was relaxed around him. They enjoyed his company, and he was a fun character, but he never, ever overstepped the mark or got away from his role or got into people's faces away from what his job entailed. He was just a fantastic person to work around.' Farrell would later go on to work on one-to-one sessions with then England forward Daniel Sturridge, a situation Dean himself recommended.

As Farrell slowly integrated his way into a side then playing at the Baseball Ground and training on the choppy terrains of Raynesway, his work had to balance the uneven pitches his superstar performers would be playing on, adding an extra element of carefulness when it came to potential injuries and overworking of the muscles. He explained, 'It was an education for players to believe in the product we were giving them and they obviously saw the value from it, and worked well with it. You do get some resistance but the main thing with players is that they want to be match fit for every game moving forwards. One was around prevention of injury, making them more robust and hard-wearing to cope with the rigours of the Premier League, which was something new to most of those players. We knew it would be fast and furious and they'd get pushed about if they weren't up to it, but I think we did well in terms of getting those guys up to the mark and trying to bring down the injuries as best as we possibly could. Players would always play with knocks, but we had to develop the different muscles to make sure that they were able to cope with that.'

With fitness being a new focus, and as the Premier League began to morph into something bigger than its formative years, Farrell also had the additional risk to balance of footballer egos. '[I remember] Steve said, "It's difficult to motivate millionaires," and it was. They're the hardest group of people I've ever worked with because the people I worked with before, they came to me, they want to train and pay money direct to me. When I joined, players were regularly down the pubs getting pissed the night before and it seemed to be an acceptable thing. We had to help them believe in what we were doing, and they quickly found that they had more stamina, they found through the fitness testing that at one point, when we tested them again six weeks later, how quicker they were. And that made them feel good. That made them believe in the package that I was offering. There were times where I would work with a coach as well and we'd do ball work with fitness as well, because the ball is always a carrot for a player. They love to work with the ball, but sometimes you had to take them away from it and just work on the fitness side.'

Perhaps the biggest hurdle facing Dane was the squad Jim was building. While that initial Premier League campaign could boast the beginnings of international stardom, there was also that complicated task of teaching English footballers how to not train with a ball in their possession. 'We got it a lot with the foreign players, whereas the British players were a little bit reluctant. They just wanted to get on the field and play football and didn't see the value as much, but when we did the fitness test and the body fat testing to make sure they would be down at about 10, 12 per cent, they knew they had a target to attain, where the opposition are a little bit quicker and a little bit fitter than them. To get that you've got to put the yards in. Then there was Igor, who brought his own physio.'

To maximise this, over time Farrell would use the international players as his unofficial spokesmen, just as they had been for Beswick's methods. As the years progressed, Stefano Eranio would arrive and spread the word on what a footballer should live by. His team-mates, seeing what he had achieved with AC Milan and how he consistently performed in a Derby shirt, were left in no doubt that when they grew up they wanted to be like Stefano.

Another man who would focus on fitness and particularly strength was Mart Poom: 'I knew English football was physical. You had to be strong to play in England. I had to do extra in the gym to be able to handle it, but that gave me confidence on the pitch because I felt stronger prepared for these challenges in the game. We had this gym which had a little indoor hall so you could play a bit of basketball, which [Paulo] Wanchope was good at. Next it was a small weights room downstairs and then a little fitness room with boxing bags. I used to go there before training and do my exercises and a bit of boxing to try and get more aggressive. Jim was very demanding of his goalkeeper dominating the box, getting every ball and it was my strength. I remember I would run against the boxing bags and then jump against the wall, you used all sort of tricks. But I was a fitness-holic so I was sometimes told off that I was doing too much. But I liked doing that physical work. I wasn't ready at Pompey [where Poom had played before returning to Estonia and signing for Flora Tallinn ahead of joining Derby] for this physicality, so I adjusted my game at Derby.'

Though Sturridge, Poom and others spoke freely and at length on the benefits of Farrell, some others only gave quick mentions to the fitness side of Raynesway training sessions. If the subject were to be posed to Farrell today, it's something which wouldn't come as too much of a surprise, purely due to cultural differences of the time. He said, 'The British players thought a Friday night piss-up was the in thing. The sort of backlash I'd get from the British players was "Bryan Robson would get pissed on a Friday night, play a blinder on Saturday and play man of the match". That is what I was up against. He could do but the likes of Seth [Johnson] and Danny Higginbotham, they could not. Danny, another wonderful player and person who buckled in and did very well with the training – he appreciated it. The science behind it, the nutrition behind it. He was constantly phoning me up asking if he could do this or that, what is best? So he was willing to learn and be the best he possibly could be.'

Higginbotham was another one of those English players who were vocal on what fitness did for their career. 'Dane was a real larger-than-life character. One of the things, if you speak to any fitness coach or players, they get so much abuse because they are the ones that are making you run, they're making you do these sessions for you where you don't see a football. And the amount of stick you give them, because you can guarantee you just want to fall over because you're exhausted, and the only person you are gonna take it out on is the fitness coach because, as far as you're concerned, he's the one making you do all of this. But later on, you realise there is a reason behind this, because you're then gonna go and play on a Saturday and you have to go and take your body to the limit. Dane was great in that aspect and he'd have a little bit of a go back but, at the end of it, there was always an understanding that it was a necessity.'

But much like Prozone and psychology, though the idea would come from McClaren and Round, it would not have been apparent at Derby without Jim Smith. It's a chance that Farrell is all too glad he was willing to take: 'To work with Jim was an absolute pleasure. Just a pleasure to be working alongside the guy and for him to acknowledge my work. I'm going to say, but for an elderly person to acknowledge and embrace fitness as Jim did … well, I knew I must be doing something right for him to believe in my product.'

* * *

Farrell knew that all of his work could easily be in vain though. As the squad progressed into the Premier League in those early months and were met by a training regime focused at building their bodies physically for a bout of top-flight football, there threatened to be almost an element of counter-productiveness in their approach. By taking this revolutionary step into fitness-focused work, the Rams had positioned themselves as a club intent on taking care of the physical setup of their players. But it would all be in vain if the players continued to eat and drink like darts players. Innovation number four was on the cards.

It was one of Farrell's worries upon arrival. He could spend all the hours in the world on Raynesway with his new charges, but if they would leave the pitch and delve into a couple of bacon sandwiches, before having a smoke and a few beers in the evening, what would be the point? It was an understanding the coaching staff were already aware of, but for all of the introductions made to the squad, adjusting the lifestyle would prove to be the most difficult. A squad menu from early in the promotion season showed a pre-match meal menu including lasagne, beans and an alarming number of eggs. Go through any 1990s footballer's autobiography too and you'll get a flavour for what being a professional athlete entailed: not anything to do with the word athlete, mostly. It would be about more than changing a menu; it would be about changing a mindset. And for that mentality to adjust, the staff would lean on international imports to again bring English minds around to the idea of what it took to be a professional.

Farrell remembers, 'I would get them in a room with the players and say, "Stefano, what do you think to this diet? And this diet?" and I would let them pass their knowledge of what they did. Rather than it coming from myself – not a footballer – those great players who had done it and lived it, they would teach our young British lads to learn from them.'

By bringing established overseas players directly into the leadership group, the coaching staff found they were presented with ideas that hadn't crossed their mind either. There were other witnesses within the training ground too, one of whom was Ramm Mylvaganam. The consultant who integrated a key component of Derby's success found himself engaging with Stefano Eranio daily, and got a flavour for how the internationals perceived the setup: 'I remember talking to Stefano and Ciccio [Francesco] Baiano and I said, "I see you guys training, having a shower, jumping into your Ferraris and going home. Why don't you stay here?" And without any hesitation or exaggeration, "Ramm, you don't really expect us to eat that shit do you? I can cook better than that at my home. I'm an elite athlete, I want proper food." It was really eliminating people like Igor, who was built like a man mountain, he would go and eat his food. There was this lady just piling up stuff in there, which was quite interesting. But that was the reality. The first players I saw have a proper restaurant was when David Dein and Arsène Wenger created London Colney. They had a proper French chef and, wow, the food was amazing, I loved going there.'

It was an issue which would irk Farrell early on as well, as the professional setup he had in place needed dietary changes to have a full impact on the body. It was at this point that a change was made, the idea stemming from the coaching staff and leading all the way to chief executive Keith Loring, who brought a new chef into Raynesway.

'Briefly before it I was working at Pride Park as a chef,' recalls long-time Rams fan and the man tasked with feeding the squad, Mark Smith. 'One day I came into work and met the head chef at the top of the stairs, and they said, "Don't put your bag down. Make your way down to Raynesway." I was gobsmacked because I was a lifelong Derby fan, going to work at Raynesway. You could have knocked me down the stairs. It was unbelievable. I get down there and it was just a dream. These heroes of mine were in front of me. I was actually working for a catering company, and I worked there for six weeks and was doing a night function down at Pride Park. I came out the kitchen and walked along and Keith stopped me for a word. "Right, I want an answer now. I'm offering you the job down the training ground, full-time." My role was then head team chef. But that was just not at Raynesway, I also had to man and crew the Baseball Ground for the academy as well.'

Smith would work alongside the coaching team to develop a strict menu designed to maximise on the work of Farrell and the squad, and a menu which would be tailored to individuals with different culinary tastes: 'You had Italians, South Americans, Europeans, native English, Scots, Irish. It was a challenge. My ideas from day one when I went in there until my leaving, it was a complete menu I was giving. When I was there it was a straightforward athlete menu. At first it was hard to keep the lads at Raynesway because our aim was to get them in after training, get them fed 30 minutes after and try to build a bond there with them together. And then I had to report to Eric Steele and with his catering background [Steele owned bars after his playing career] we hit it off straight away. So, I started to put my own twist and ideas together and just grew and made the food better.

'In the end we seemed to get to know what they liked and didn't like, things like making a lasagne out of minced chicken prior to a matchday. It was complicated stuff but you'd try and look for something. European pasta bases and just different things like a veal, or herbed rice going through the centre with breadcrumbs. The week was split into two you see. Before a game in that first half, it would be what I just said. Prior to that, two days before a matchday you would have your chicken, pasta, beans, tomato sauce, then I'd chuck in a poached fish or any white meat, because that would break down quicker than red. We were looking for high carb intakes.'

It wasn't always possible though, and for Stefano Eranio, he would still find reason to bring some of Italy directly to his new home in Derby when he fancied some authentic pasta. He explained, 'When you live in a different country and you leave home, you try and keep the same things. You cook pasta, but the sauces you couldn't get [and] those Italian items. Sometimes we would call our parents to send parmesan, olive oil and things. But in our home, nothing changed. When we would go to play away before the game, we would try to eat just what was possible to eat. We used to get the pasta before the game and some Parma ham, nothing else. Instead the English style was beans and eggs, but I would try to eat what I used to eat.'

Food would ultimately become another crucial part of the setup and not only would it aid the players, it would also provide them with a reason to stay at Raynesway after sessions had finalised. For Smith, that would give him some of his favourite memories from his years within: 'There was a time when I had two girls working for me; Sandra and Hannah. All three of us were out the kitchen for a matter of minutes and one of the players snuck through the backdoor to the kitchen, next to the physio room. They came and turned the oven up.' Smith suspects it was one of the core group of jokers in those later years, consisting of Danny Higginbotham, Rory Delap and Seth Johnson: 'They didn't know what they were doing. Five minutes later I could tell something wasn't right. Five minutes later than that it would have been buggered. But you couldn't trust them. There was a great story with Danny. He was being interviewed by Sky Sports inside Raynesway, and Rory and Seth coming running into the kitchen. "Chef, chef, chef. Have you got any potatoes?" They pick the bowl up, run outside and throw them over the roof to try and hit Danny. Those three were the basis of the piss-taking club, to put it politely. They were at it 24/7.

'Stevie Elliot as well. One day I decided to do some horseradish sauce with beef, and it was fresh. So I get the blender going, open it up and it nearly knocks my head off. Like an idiot I said, "Steve, come in here a minute. I just want you to smell this sauce to make sure it's there. I want some body and depth." So being an Alvo [Alvaston] lad – and I'm a Chad [Chaddesden] lad – we were always having banter. He's on the floor, eyes running, I've got a pro footballer rolling on the floor, unable to get his breath. He gets up laughing his head off and going, "Chef that is a wicked trick, I've got to use it for a party at home! I know, let's do it again shall we. We'll get [Fabrizio] Ravanelli!" So, he calls Rav in and says, "Chef has just done this wicked sauce, you've got to smell it, it's brilliant." Rav goes, deep breath, and I have a million-pound footballer rolling on the kitchen floor, screaming. I'm thinking, "Oh my God, all this from a prank." About five minutes later he found it funny. "Chef, you're a bad chef you are!" and starts laughing. If you don't have that bond, you won't be doing anything.'

* * *

There's one bonus innovation as well, which has also stood the test of time. Synonymous with the moments before kick-off is the huddle, where the players embrace and listen to one of their colleagues shout at them before 30,000 other people then shout at them for the next hour and a half. But lo and behold, according to Farrell, the huddle itself was a Derby County invention within football.

'That was a product from Derby County. I'll always remember how it happened. We got beat 4-0 at Chelsea, heads were down and we went out by the river at Raynesway, and we were getting just nothing from the players. Nothing. They were battered and broken. And Steve [McClaren] said, "Come on in, lads." They stood there and I was just talking to them, and Chris Powell went, "Come on, lock in," just as they would in basketball. And that was it. Steve saw it and said, "Do that on Saturday." And that's what we did. On the TV, it said Derby County are doing this thing and it caught on and other teams started to do it. Brought on by Chrissy Powell, taken forward by Steve. It was witnessing the birth of how that happened in football. Regular in basketball and other team sports, but not in football and commentators were saying, "What are they doing in there?" But it was valuable because it was just a small unit where we could huddle together and push each other forwards.'

Derby County. Football wouldn't be the same without us.

5

CONSOLIDATION

THINGS HAD changed since Derby were last in the top division of English football, and not all for the better. In the time since they were relegated under Arthur Cox, a British sporting landscape had changed in name and look, with the 'old' First Division replaced by the new money-spinning plan to transform the game.

As we now know, that's exactly what the introduction of the Premier League did. But all wasn't quite so apparent as to the direction it would go by the time Jim Smith had taken his men on their first foray there. Of the side at his disposal, very few had played at the highest level in England, even fewer having done so within the new brand. Smith himself hadn't been there in some time, and the coaching staff had no experience of the highest heights. Paired with that you had uncertainty around the club and its immediate future (that's for the next chapter). Any nervousness heading into the campaign would not have been without merit.

But what the summer of 1996 did have supporters across the isles purring over was the home Euros. Euro '96 needs little introduction to anyone interested enough in Derby to go back almost 30 years, because it was the sporting pinnacle of this nation until the London 2012 Olympic and Paralympic Games. It probably even surpassed it for pure, scintillating, community-clutching fever. Three Lions were roaring, Gazza was slowly being dragged to his Scotland-bashing best from the dentist's chair and hope, genuine hope on a scale not seen since, was filling each and every Englishman in the country.

Hope ultimately became sadness as 30 years of hurt extended to the present day. But for the people of Derbyshire, hope sprung eternal during the summer. Not only did they have the opportunity to be overcome by the tournament and by an English side which dared to push boundaries, they also had the chance to cast an eye on what their future looked like for ten months of the year. And you know what? It looked pretty good.

Igor had changed the performances of the team with his switch from Croatia and, in conjunction, he'd cast a thought or two in the mind of Jim Smith. If one man from overseas could take him into the Premier League, what could a few others do? That level of thinking made the European Championship so downright intriguing for Rams supporters, because they had the opportunity to see their two new recruits in action. And they looked good.

'I remember watching Asanović and thinking, "Wow, I cannot believe we've got him."' Supporter Andrew Beckett puts the thoughts of a fanbase into one succinct sentence. Aljosa Asanović was one of the most impressive performers of the summer. Starring at the heart of the Croatian midfield and playing ahead of his compatriot at the back, it was a masterstroke from Smith who jumped the gun on his signature to get ahead of any other interested parties.

It was no guessing game on just where the thought had first come from, however: Igor Štimac. 'He was one of the best midfielders I played with in my life,' he states without prompt. 'He could produce magic and, at that time, we got promoted and I was with the Croatian national team preparing for Euro '96, and he was looking to go somewhere abroad. That was the time that I started engaging him to think about England, to think about Premiership, I told him about the club's plans for the new stadium, about what the supporters were like, the players, the manager. And when I felt him become interested, I called Jim and told him immediately to send someone to sign him before the Euros. That was the time when we could afford him. If we waited two weeks more, we couldn't afford him because the price before Euros was less than £1m. After, it was five or six.'

The timing of the signing may well have taken advantage of the skilful midfielder, who had he waited a month would have found himself with the established sides of Europe sniffing for his signature. And whether that would eventually lead to his frustrations at the club is without substance. With Croatia only eliminated thanks to a ten-man loss against Germany (with Štimac dismissed), Rams supporters got four games to look at their new maestro. And he looked good.

But while the man who would soon be known as Ace would become a glue that would ease the transition into the division, he wasn't alone when it came to new European recruits. 'It all started in October '95 and I came in the summer of '96,' Jacob Laursen remembers. 'I had a meeting with Jim Smith in Denmark at my club, Silkeborg. The club had agreed everything but, at that time, Derby was actually losing a lot of games and he ended up saying he needed someone with a bit more experience than me. I was 23 years old and he was looking for someone with a bit more experience than I had, so he ended up taking Igor. But he said to me, "I really like you, I like what I've seen and if we survive this and we go up to the Premier League, I'll definitely buy you because I'll have the funds to do that."

'So we had things agreed for a long time, more or less from February 1996. And then it was just waiting and waiting for Derby to finish the season and at one point they were ten or 15 points ahead. And then right at the end of the season they started losing points and every Saturday I was checking their scores. And so it was the game against Crystal Palace where I knew that I was coming over. And then I flew over because we were with the national team preparing for Euro 96. I got two days off, flew over and signed, did the medical. I think I actually bought a house then as well. It was done very, very quickly. I went to the Euros, went back and started packing everything to bring the family. And that's how I ended up at Raynesway!'

The switch was quickly secured and having learnt the best processes to go down after bringing in both Štimac and Ron Willems the previous campaign, chief executive Keith Loring knew the path to take in welcoming their internationals: 'I worked out how players were coming into a foreign country and how to live their life. So, for example, Igor. He's staying at a posh hotel down the road and he's sitting there with his wife and two young children, none of them can speak English. It's OK when he's playing football, but how is he looking at his life, is he happy, are is his wife and children happy? And we were so good at that. I used to go and see them myself and make sure they were OK, and so did my daughter. Because if you had the wife settled, it was good news. It wasn't rehearsed, it was all natural for us to do. That continued and then in the end we had members of staff doing the job for us.'

With the internationals content with their new lives (even if they had never heard of Derby before), all that was left to become familiar with was Jim Smith. Not the easiest of tasks, admittedly. And for Laursen, his realisation about the man he would spend the next four years with came after 45 minutes of a pre-season friendly in Bournemouth: 'At half-time, I have to tell you, my dad is a big guy and a blacksmith, and when I'd done something wrong he could tell me off and tell me, "This is not OK." But the way Jim Smith told me I wasn't performing at half-time, I was shocked! I had never, ever experienced anything like it. That experience was really good. It established a relationship between the manager and me because it meant a good understanding of how we do things. He found out he didn't have to tell me off all the time, he could just look at me and I would accept it. It was a very, very good experience. You couldn't do it today but in those days it was a good way of telling your new players, "We know you have a big ego but here we work as a team."'

There was one other significant change in the outlook of the Derby side. While Van Der Laan and Igor were to find themselves balancing captaincy duties, the big change came in the Dutchman's look. Iconic as his celebration is today, the Captain Fantastic who would begin 1996/97 was a different, shaven-headed beast. When pressed why, the answer was simple: he just fancied a change.

If Igor marked the baby steps into an international dabble, then bringing in Laursen and Asanović was a clear indication that when it came to Jim Smith's thinking he was ready to embrace a changing game. Not only had he brought through psychology late into his first season and a fitness coach after promotion, he now expressed serious desires to turn Derby County continental. His thinking wasn't solely overseas though, with another pair of signings arguably having the bigger impact over the course of that 1996/97 campaign. The first of which was Christian Dailly, secured from Dundee United, who was signed as a midfielder but would develop into another pivotal figurehead in the defence. But Dailly was only 23 and, having come in for an initial £500,000, it provided another individual who, like Gary Rowett and Chris Powell, would grow in the defence.

If there was one complaint about Smith's evolving side, it came in their lack of Premier League experience and to counteract this he turned to a man widely regarded as in the very, very twilight years of his career.

* * *

Paul McGrath couldn't run by the time he left Aston Villa in the early months of the campaign. He couldn't train, couldn't jump, and had few offers to prolong his career. He hadn't played Premier League football in six months and an X-ray of his knees would leave an unsuspecting surgeon questioning why he had been given the results of a man 30 years his senior. Having been omitted from a Villa defence which now boasted Gareth Southgate, Ugo Ehiogu and Steve Staunton, the man known simply as 'God' within the Holte End faced questions over his playing future, especially when

Brian Little decided to value the soon-to-be 37-year-old at an eyebrow-raising £200,000.

But having stuttered in the early weeks of the season with the defence slowly adjusting to the demands of top-level football, Smith recognised the need for experience and didn't baulk at what was an initial £100,000, to double should Derby avoid relegation. Rowett contemplates for a second before working out how to describe his defensive partner: 'He was ... close to being world-class.'

It's no exaggeration. You don't earn the nickname of God without being something significantly special, and that was what McGrath was. Surrounded by youngsters, his lifespan over the season only grew in importance, so far as to the fact he is still today revered by fans of Derby, Villa, Manchester United and perhaps most notably the Republic of Ireland. A wonderfully nostalgic 2021 article about McGrath in *The42* by Paul Dollery incorporates a comment section at the end. The top comment simply says, 'The greatest player to pull on a green jersey. My footballing hero.'

And while that is a gushing and appropriate description of a man who starred at Euro '88, Italia '90 and USA '94, it wasn't what Rams fans first thought they would be able to echo. Initial questions over the desire to bring in a player deemed long past his best were a suitable response, including by Rams assistant Steve McClaren during McGrath's first session on Raynesway. 'The first Friday,' McClaren begins, 'we had him in and did some set plays. They put the ball in, Paul was marking somebody and this person scored. And Paul didn't make an effort to jump; he looked as if he couldn't jump. Jim was going, "Oh no, I can't believe it. We've signed a cripple. He can't run, he can't move, he can't jump." We got a knock on the door, Paul McGrath walks in. "Err, gaffer, gaffer. I must apologise for this morning. I don't jump on a Friday. And normally I don't train on a Friday. I just play Saturday. But tomorrow Jim, I will be OK." The next day he was man of the match. He won everything.'

And over the course of a season McGrath would prove more than OK. So OK was McGrath that, despite playing fewer than 30 games in black and white, he was voted into a poll of the top 100 players in the club's history. Though joining in what it would be extremely kind to describe as the 'twilight' of his career, it's no exaggeration to say that his impact was a significant difference between comfortable safety and a possible relegation battle. Such was his calmness, not only individually but on the players around him, McGrath would turn losses into draws and draws into wins, simply from his air of assuredness.

'He was a player I watched as a younger player in the World Cup for Ireland in the middle of midfield and he was just unbelievable,' continues a starstruck Rowett. 'He'd come in intermittently and didn't train, he was very, very quiet and would often go on an exercise bike at the side of the pitch to watch us doing some of the shape and work. Then he'd come out on the Friday and then he'd play the game. But when he played, boy he could still perform at a very, very high level.'

That was the concern for supporters and coaching staff in the early days post signing. While all knew what McGrath had done in his career, fears continued about whether Smith had dropped a clanger in a man living off days gone by. How wrong those fears were, with Rowett continuing, 'I remember away at Wimbledon he gave the ball away. I think it was Efan Ekoku, who was very quick; he knocked the ball and Macca was about ten yards behind, but because he had given it away I had never seen someone move so quick, and he was an absolute Rolls-Royce, went and took it back off him, atoned for his error and you just thought, "Wow, imagine what he was like with two good knees."' Rams fan Jimmy McLoughlin remembers the same incident, adding, 'He had the most amazing reactions. Watching him was pretty incredible.' But among this, Smith's desire to bring in 'God' was another vital example of how he had the soft touch when identifying a character to fit into his squad. Rowett adds, 'He was a really nice, quiet, unassuming guy. Even in games he wasn't particularly loud but he just led by example, and he was an incredible example to the younger defenders at the club.'

And while McGrath would become the puzzle piece that allowed Smith and McClaren to build on what they had, the duo were left checking the box for another possible solution in the early weeks of their Premier League voyage. While an opening-day thriller against Leeds saw the spoils shared, the Rams struggled for consistency. Three points from the first four (including a spectacular Laursen free kick at home to Manchester United) were followed with back-to-back victories against Blackburn and Sunderland. But next would come a five-game winless streak, then five without defeat. Derby weren't in danger of being dragged into a bottom-of-the-table battle, but the topsy-turvy nature of their performances would give the coaching team a significant headache.

Sleepless nights would follow as the side failed to pick up a single win in two months between December and mid-February. And while the defeats weren't heavy when they did come, the issue came in finding the net, with only five goals in nine games. It was a time which would frustrate Paul Simpson who, despite appearing almost 20 times that season, never started a single game and felt he had more to give: 'Jim kept me involved as much as he possibly could and he was very honest in that he didn't think I was going to be good enough to play in the Premier League. In that first season I would have really liked to have had a chance, but the only chance I got was the first game of the following season where we got absolutely decimated with injuries and all of our strikers got injured. I played away at Blackburn Rovers, Jim picked me and Matt Carbon to be the two centre-forwards. Matt isn't a centre-forward, it's not my strongest position and I ended up getting dragged off at half-time and that was the only chance I got. So I still to this day, and I would because I'm biased, but I believe that first year in the Premier League I would have been able to do something for the team.'

But while Simpson wouldn't get given the gig, Smith was again looking into who could support. While Sturridge was clearly his key man and didn't look out of place in the Premier League, Ashley Ward struggled for goals in support and by March. Christian Dailly was the third-top scorer with three. Something additional was needed at the top end to capitalise on the ingenuity of Asanović, and there was an equal need for new cover between the posts as well.

* * *

Asanović had turned out to be a tremendous signing, albeit one who could prove difficult to manage on his day. Clearly a level above the lower mid-table side he had been poached for, frustration would seep into his game on occasion, and his ultimate decision to stay in Derby for just 18 months was little surprise by the end of the campaign. In contrast, Laursen would become a core part of Jim Smith's side for the foreseeable future. In a Rams career which spanned 140 games in four seasons, Laursen would be every bit as important as Igor was, lasting longer and providing Smith a loyalty even beyond the loss of his coaching staff. In his third season he'd claim the player of the season trophy too, becoming only the second player (after summer 1997 recruit Francesco Baiano) from overseas to collect it. Even the great Igor wouldn't pick up the accolade.

But the longer the campaign went on, and the more likely it looked that Derby would survive in 1996/97 with relative comfort, the more attentions would turn to what else the land beyond Britain could bring. Thus far, everything Smith had conjured up had come in the form of established overseas talent. Laursen was no unknown on the international stage, having appeared at the 1992 Olympics and Euro '96. The Croatian duo had a wealth of suitors behind them, while Robin Van Der Laan was a known name in the English game from his time at Port Vale. Only Ron Willems was the unproven one, but he had come in the early weeks of Smith's tenure. From then on, all followers came with pedigree. But even in the 1990s pedigree came at a price, with more attractive names aware of established talents. This moment right here was where Jim Smith's Derby properly begun.

That last sentence is unfair to the work that had gone on before and to the phenomenal efforts of the squad in both getting to and then staying in the Premier League. But when it comes to why Jim Smith and Steve McClaren were able to create an era of football in Derby that still tingles the spine today, the key moment happened during March 1997. Because Smith didn't decide to sign established stars at this point. What he did came with the help of a specially selected group of confidants and agents, as they identified three players from two unthought-of, bordering on unheard-of, countries: Costa Rica and Estonia. Welcome Messrs Wanchope (plus Solís) and Poom.

* * *

We'll begin with the latter, because he is just about easier to track down. Derby were in relatively safe hands with Russell Hoult, who had been steady during the promotion campaign, yet unspectacular and occasionally coming up short in the Premier League. And with defence strengthened with McGrath and Laursen, midfield bolstered by Asanović and the forward line continuing to fire through Sturridge, the goalkeeping position was the pressing one to be addressed, with backup Martin Taylor never fully recovering from the broken leg suffered in seasons previous.

'In the summer of '94,' begins Poom, 'I travelled to Pompey [Portsmouth] for a medical, but Estonia wasn't part of the EU so after that I had to then leave the country to wait for the work permit. But with Jim, I must have met him first at Fratton Park and I even managed to do some training in the pre-season, and he was surprised that I ran so well because he was just used to goalkeepers not running. I can't remember exactly but it was the summer of '94. Darryl Powell was there also, Deon Burton as well.'

Poom had been identified by Smith years previously, pointed out to him by Alan Hutchinson, the goalkeeping coach for the Scottish national team. And though he had lost the goalkeeper after a minimal amount of games on the south coast, Smith saw enough in his non-EU protege to keep tabs on him. It was no easy feat to formally bring him to Derby. First there were the work permit complications, then there was the match Poom was due to be scouted in descending into farce. Poom said, 'We had this famous replay against Scotland, that game which never went ahead. It was postponed because we didn't turn up, then it was rescheduled by UEFA for February in Monaco, and Derby and Jim were looking for a new goalkeeper or someone to push Russell Hoult. They had a bit of a difficult time then and were looking for a new one, because Martin Taylor was injured also so they needed reinforcements. He asked Alan to have a look at me and I had a very good game, think it was 0-0. We kept a clean sheet and soon after I heard of Derby's interest.'

The clean sheet would be the clincher for Smith, who saw enough of the younger Poom at Portsmouth – and within that 90 minutes – to be convinced he had what it took to push and subsequently overtake Hoult. Timing-wise it worked perfectly too, and by the time the deal was done the international break in late March allowed Poom another showcase against Scotland, and another admirable showing in Kilmarnock. Though Estonia's number one, competition at that time was scarce, meaning Poom's move to Derby drew little in the way of excitement.

The same can't be said of Paulo Wanchope and Mauricio Solís. By no means known names in the English game, the duo were anomalies to a Derby fanbase whose outside-Europe experience didn't go too much further than John Harkes.

'Over in Costa Rica we only had a chance to see Spanish football and Italian. And Germany as well, but not much of English football. But of course we knew about teams like Arsenal, Liverpool, Man United and all those big clubs. But we usually followed the Italian and Spanish football.' That was the childhood experience of Paulo César Wanchope Watson, perhaps the most '90s of all Premier League players. With his unique running style, semi-frequent fits of rage and double-jointed limbs perplexing central defenders across England, British football had a new maverick import.

'The first time I came over to QPR,' recalls the Costa Rican. 'That was because of Bob McNab [the former Arsenal player]. It turned out that he turned on the TV and there was a game, I think it was Costa Rica against United States for the qualifying games for France '98. He was watching the game and he saw me play, he thought I had all the qualities to play in England and so he made all the enquiries, rang up my club in Costa Rica, then he got in contact with me and my parents. So at first he wanted me to go to QPR, and I went over and made a trial. I played three games and scored six goals and nothing happened.

'So then when I came back to Costa Rica, he insisted I had the quality to play in England, and so he rang up Jim Smith. QPR were in the Championship, Derby were in the Premier League. So I went over and played two [trial] games, didn't score and was a little bit down and a little bit worried. But everything went great and they gave me a contract, and the rest is history. They were very experienced coaches and they see all around the player, they know that we as strikers have bad moments. And maybe they realised I was a little bit nervous. But all around the game they saw something, that's why they made the decision. I went to QPR and scored six goals, I went to Derby County and got no goals. But thank God that they saw something in me.'

What that something was is up for debate. For Smith, a forward in his own right, he had the capability to see a predator in front of goal. McClaren, though, remembers the minute detail that made up their minds: 'We played some non-league team, organised a game and the agent said, "He can play in a trial but it has to be under a different name.' Where's he from I asked. "Costa Rica." So we went to this game and the ball came across, six yards out and he missed a sitter. And another chance. I went, "Bloody hell, Jim." All of a sudden the keeper kicks it and he leapt, I remember it to this day, he got unbelievable height, chested it down and volleyed it out wide and then got in the box. Me and Jim looked at each other and went "get him off at half-time, get him signed". The rest is history.'

And while a breathtaking piece of control was the deciding factor for Smith and McClaren, it could all have been so different for Wanchope had he gone professional in another sport. Prior to Derby, it's a little-known piece of knowledge that the great forward actually had serious ambitions to make it pro in basketball, so much so that he spent 18 months in California pursuing his boyhood goal. Conducting a scholarship and finishing his studies in the Golden State, part of his reasoning for the move was to embark on that new career, but football claimed Wanchope. So far removed from basketball did Wanchope become that in all his time in Derby he never even took to a court for practice.

Accompanying Wanchope would be another Costa Rican, Mauricio Solís. Older, perhaps wiser and very much a different style of player, it was thought that Solís came as the main prize, Wanchope being merely the secondary option, yet his time in England never worked out as expected. Making only 11 Rams appearances, a mixture of getting married, failing to adjust and struggling to squeeze into a squad that had to adhere to overseas player limits during the 1990s meant he couldn't call Derby home in the same way that Wanchope could. But that Wanchope could ever get to that stage is once again testament to a man he had a fractious relationship with: Jim Smith.

'Jim would always ask for opinions,' recalls former physio Neil Sillett. 'He would see something that other people couldn't. I've been in recruitment in football for a long time, and it's those people who make quicker decisions because they've got that picture in their mind, and Jim would have that. I think in the early days at Portsmouth, my dad [former manager John Sillett] always taught me – and Jim liked the line, "When you're watching them, imagine you're playing against them." And when he first saw Paulo, he said he remembered what my dad said, and he didn't want to play against Wanchope because his arms were all over you, his legs would go higher than your head. "You don't know what he's going to do and he doesn't fucking know either, but that's difficult to play against." And he stayed like that through his career. Now Wanchope did know what he was doing but some people thought he didn't just because he looked ungainly.

Throughout *Groundwork* has been (and will be) the theme of Jim Smith the sports psychologist; with few players has it been so clear as with his long-distance import. Much is made in sections of this book about the relationship the duo had, not least in the Smith-centric chapter which looks at their tendency to fight in the changing rooms. But when it came to Smith, he knew the right side of the line to walk with Wanchope more often than not, and it was in his very first days that he put the plans in place for their intriguing relationship.

* * *

Before getting to a no-doubt anticipated 90 minutes at Old Trafford which marked the first Rams appearance for Wanchope and Poom, there were a handful of days for Smith to acquaint them with his side. Coming in off the back of three defeats followed by a heavy win over Tottenham, the 5 April encounter presented an opportunity for the Bald Eagle to experiment with his side. Hoult had faltered, and while Sturridge and Ashley Ward had found the net with a little more regularity, an away day in Manchester was something of a free hit. Nobody was prepared to see either recruit in the 11, but such was the lack of expectation around the match, it was a relatively nothing decision for the coaching side. But for Wanchope, it was the biggest day of his young life and marked an afternoon which would change everything going forward.

Wanchope explained, 'He told me the day before that I was going to play and that night I couldn't sleep. I was a little bit anxious because I wanted to play well, and I would sleep for two hours and wake up.' Knowing this, and knowing the importance of integration, Smith used something few other managers could: empathy.

'When we were on the bus and we were going to Old Trafford, Jim just said to me, "What kind of music do you listen to? What do you like?" And I was with Mauricio and we just said we liked salsa music. "Well let's put it on." Just like that he put it on on the bus and everyone was trying to dance and I was dancing, so that was a nice thing from him that made me feel like I was in my country and just more relaxed. It's why I went to the game with no pressure. I can imagine he sensed I was anxious, and he helped me a lot with that. And you could see it in his eyes because he was really making eye contact with me.'

And while Wanchope would take to the field with salsa running through his mind, Poom would enter with something a little bit different, in the form of somebody else's shirt. As told in *Pride*, the player fast-tracked into the 11 didn't even have his own shirt, leaving Gordon Guthrie to take Hoult's number one jersey, black out his name and get a replacement printed on top at the official United shop. Never, ever say football in the 1990s wasn't the height of professionalism.

Supporter Jimmy McLoughlin recalls the afternoon as the greatest day of his childhood. Having massed out on the home meeting with the champions the previous September thanks to an ill-timed family holiday, it was down to his dad to take Jimmy to Old Trafford for a day he would never forget, nor expect: 'I remember the radio saying there was no point Derby fans going, you're going to get hammered 5-0. And I remember, I thought Wanchope was called One-Chop-Aye because you didn't know these things at the time. And I couldn't work out every time Poom caught the ball, it took us ages to work it out because we thought they were booing him.'

For Poom himself, that would pose an initial hurdle, so unsure was he over why his new audience were jeering his every touch. He wasn't alone either, constantly having to tell his friends and family he wasn't a victim of hatred: 'A few times people and away fans would say, "Why are they booing your name? What have you done? Why don't they like you?" No, they do! They're showing their appreciation because they knew I'd catch the ball, and it was always a good feeling knowing that they're not booing me!'

But back to the day. United had lost a solitary match at home all campaign, while Derby came into it off the back of three successive losses on the road. Not that it mattered. Ashley Ward's unconventional finish – off the back of a Wanchope header – had eyebrows raised, but it was what happened six minutes later that shook the table-toppers to their very core and launched a Premier League career for the first Costa Rican ever to appear in the top flight.

Wanchope will take it from here, just as he did that day: 'I just kept running and trying to see the gap. When you see that video and that goal, you can see a run from Dean [Sturridge], who makes a diagonal run, and that was a key moment for me to keep going because he opened up the space for me. I know it's difficult but when you are with the ball you need to be aware of what's happening on the pitch and when I saw that run from Dean I kept running and I was almost in the box and tried to shoot on the side of the goalkeeper, and that's it! At that moment you don't realise anything. I've always said that when I celebrated, when the ball went in, my face was like a big surprise because all of the memories back in my hometown when I was playing on the street.'

Almost on cue, Wanchope (who may I just add clocked on for our call at 7.30am his time) is interrupted by what one can only assume is a Costa Rican paradise. Birds chirp in the background as he pauses over where to go with the sentence next: 'I dreamed for that moment, that moment to be in a special league, to play around good players ... great players. Of course it was a big joy with Mauricio afterwards, and then I had a chance to speak to my parents and my brothers. And back in those days it was difficult to get the news, but my family were the first ones I managed to speak with. "Oh Paulo describe me the goal, we're still waiting for the goals to come on!" and so I was describing it. Of course they were really happy with that!'

The significance of this moment cannot be underplayed in what would follow over the next two seasons. Though he beat half a side, what Wanchope did wasn't Maradona-esque. Everyone knew what Maradona could do before he did it to England in 1986. But even Wanchope would hesitate before saying he knew what he could do before the goal happened, such was the distinctive style of play he brought to the English game. And as Graham Richards said on BBC Radio Derby's commentary, 'He treated Manchester United's defence with absolute contempt!'

United would strike twice either side of a Sturridge goal in the second half as Derby collected their most famous victory in many years. There were concerns on the day though, beyond the ones at the heart of the United defence. Coming during the same weekend that the Grand National was postponed due to a bomb scare, tension was so high that even those in the away end, such as Jimmy McLoughlin's dad, were approaching stewards to check if there was any chance of an abandonment, particularly as they were at the biggest attendance of that weekend. There would be no scare, and Jim Smith would be so content that his pre-match conference would be conducted over a cigar or two. If Igor and Ace had been his starting points, Wanchope and Poom would mark the beginning of the next era.

But the old guard, if you can call them that, more than had their part to play, as Chris Powell attests to: 'We played man for man and that preparation that week, we were all thinking, "Oh I don't think that's gonna work," but when you watch the highlights, I was with Beckham, Trollope was with Cantona, I think Darryl was with Roy Keane or Nicky Butt. He [Smith] just felt going to Old Trafford we all needed to take responsibility and it was just clever. We started off a bit shakily but after that you have the Wanchope goal and we were just brave. We played three up top away at Man U because he knew the seven behind would do the job they were asked. Or the eight with Mart Poom who made some good saves. I look back and just think Jim was really, really ahead of his time.'

* * *

Derby would consolidate over the course of the campaign, and despite a winter wobble, the late-season revival of four wins in eight put a newly promoted side in the extremely healthy position of 12th, six points clear of the bottom three and only behind Leeds and Tottenham on goal difference. Had anyone of a black-and-white persuasion been offered that when Van Der Laan struck against Palace in April of the previous year, it would have been warmly – and eagerly – received.

But there were elements of what could have been in the campaign, not least in the way of an FA Cup run which threatened so much. Tom Flight's *Yer Jokin' Aren't Ya* analyses Middlesbrough's scarcely believable 1996/97 season in which they had a player disappear, had points taken away from them, the White Feather of Fabrizio Ravanelli at the helm, two cup final appearances and a relegation. But when it comes to cup finals, it could have been Derby.

As is known and not remembered, the only cup triumph in the history of Derby came in 1946 and there has barely been a whiff of anything similar ever since, bar a couple of FA Cup semi-finals and two in the League Cup. That's why what happened in 1997 – at the hands of Boro – still stings. Derby had got past Gillingham, Aston Villa and Coventry to line up an intriguing home tie against the Teessiders. Yet a 2-0 home loss put paid to Wembley dreams and ruined what could have been a semi-final against Chesterfield. What might have been.

But as nice as a Wembley day out would have been, there was only one place on the mind and in the hearts of the people of Derbyshire in the final weeks of 1996/97 – the Baseball Ground. Largely ignored thus far in this book is the biggest movement in the history of the entire football club, which occurred right in the midst of this timespan. The full overview on the process which saw Derby leave for Pride Park will follow, but for the purposes of this chapter, the closing paragraphs focus on the emotion of the final afternoon at home to Arsenal.

There would be no fairytale ending, no sweet goodbye. The last day at the BBG ended in defeat against Arsène Wenger's ever-improving side, but it was an irrelevance in the grand scheme of things. Ashley Ward's opener would be counteracted by three Gunners goals in a comfortable away win, but it mattered little to most. On a day that saw legends of the club parade the pitch, fans embark on heavy nostalgia of years gone by and a full house say a tearful goodbye, football took a back seat to all but those on the pitch and the coaching staff. It's something Chris Powell, crowned player of the season on the day, can attest to after being on the end of perhaps Smith's last rollocking at the famous old ground.

'Arsenal at home is always a big game and we knew a lot of the old players like Charlie George and some of the heroes from the past there. I got out of my car and the fans were saying, "Oh you're the player of the year!" which I didn't know. It was on the front page and I was signing autographs and I was so made up. So I knew then, went in and everyone was excited because we wanted to be in the Premier League for the new stadium, we had this brilliant last game, packed out. And my sponsors at the time said … I can't remember his name who wore white boots. Alan Hinton? That sounds right! They said, "It'll be a good idea and a mark of respect for the old players that have gone before," and I thought, good idea! Then I thought no, Jim won't like it. And they were telling me to ask him, but if I asked him he was definitely going to say no.

'So I got presented with the trophy before the game, which was a great moment for me in front of my family and friends, as the last player of the year at the BBG. It was just working out so good. And then we played the game and at half-time I thought, "You know what, this is going well. There's a carnival atmosphere." I think we were 1-0 up and I just thought, put the boots on. He won't mind, it'll just be a nice finish to the day. So I put them on, never told him and ran out and of course we lose 3-1 and it's a little bit of a dampener on the day. And he absolutely nails us, but particularly me. "What the frigging hell are you doing wearing them? Who do you think you are?" And we'd just stayed in the Premier League, and he was still saying it wasn't right. And he taught me a lesson that day that actually, OK, the euphoria is right but leave that to the fans, be professional and do the right things. And you know what, fair enough. But to be fair to him, we all got on with it afterwards, but he didn't let that go for a while to be honest and it taught me a lesson.'

I never saw a Derby County game at the Baseball Ground, but I like to think I know what the place meant to thousands who did. And so rather than falsifying memories, I'd like to round off with a passage from David Moore in the final ever matchday programme from the BBG: 'Leaving the Baseball Ground is a terrible wrench for many of us and we all have our own special memories. The lucky route to the ground, the familiar streets and the hustle and bustle outside the stadium. The same old seat in our favourite stand. The muddy pitch and the friendly faces. The anticipation before the first home game of the season and the despair if we lost it. Playing on a snow-covered surface in midwinter. Offilers' Ales, the meat pies and toilets in that order. Being admonished by a goalkeeper's aunty in the Normanton Stand for shouting at "Our Terry" when he had a stinker.

'The laps of honour, the trophies, the promotions and the championships. The relegations, the High Court, Stuart Webb's heroics, Robert Maxwell and Plymouth Argyle. Lionel Pickering, owner, chair and supporter. And the managers, all 19 of them! But above all the players, the great ones, the good ones, the ordinary ones and the bad ones, they all had one thing in common. They were lucky. Lucky to have had the privilege to play at the Baseball Ground.'

Amen to that.

6

NO HAIR, DON'T CARE

WHEN JIM Smith first joined Derby, he was perceived by many as a relic. A manager from a bygone era who had effectively left the game when he decided to move behind a desk with the LMA. Some people I spoke to in the writing of this book labelled him 'elderly', one even as a 'dinosaur' when referring to the perceptions they had before linking up with him. But to thousands across the game, in cities from Newcastle down to Portsmouth, Jim Smith was everything football should be. He made the game fun, injecting his highly infectious personality into sides and fanbases across the country. And he delivered success, not least in Derbyshire.

To understand how he did that, this chapter is a diversion from the footballing side of life in the 1990s. Instead, the next few pages will assess the man that Jim Smith was for colleagues, supporters, players and, ultimately, friends. Because, as Keith Loring assessed, nobody else could have done what Jim did at Derby.

* * *

This chapter isn't a comprehensive history of Jim Smith. For that, you can still get copies of his *It's Only a Game* autobiography across the internet. Instead, what this chapter aims to do is provide an analysis of what made the man beloved, at least within his time at Raynesway.

As alluded to in the opening chapter, 'The Eagle Has Landed', Smith was a man who was gone from the game. Despite many of his closest sporting confidants enjoying their greatest years in the 1990s (Howard Wilkinson, Alex Ferguson, Barry Fry to name a few) Smith had decided that management had reached its climax for him. In his role with the LMA, he would instead look to improve situations for those who would be in the dugout on a Saturday afternoon, operating in their best interests with the knowledge he had gained across around 25 years. Disheartened at the way he had been treated in the game, Smith wrote, 'I was sickened … so much so that I looked at my situation and thought, do I need this anymore?'

Within the LMA he would find himself free of the abuse he'd have to take from supporters, away from the disrespect from board members and be placed in less stressful situations. Smith could begin to enjoy his later years. But if football management is a drug, the LMA was a temporary rehab. It's an obsession that simply won't leave many men who are well past retirement age. Take Neil Warnock as an example. Aged 73 at the time of publication, he had been a football manager for 42 years and still showed the same hunger, regardless of the location or the sleepless nights by the time of his retirement. Roy Hodgson too, 75 by the time this book is released, returned to the game merely months after seemingly retiring at the spritely age of 74. Consider the fact Smith was just 55 when Derby came calling, and it paints a similar picture of how difficult life can be for managers to officially call time on their responsibilities.

Jim's return to football was almost inevitable. Howard Wilkinson said as much, mentioning a desk job being as far from what triggered his enjoyment as could be imagined. And by the time he moved to Derby, that was made patently clear as he immediately found his way back into the hustle and grind of club management. This was as much in part to his ability to build relationships as to his managerial ability. When offered the job by Lionel Pickering in 1995, Smith was considered largely after a positive meeting between the two following a game years before, in which they drank copiously post-match. It would become a common theme across the years as the duo supped many a night away at the Yewtree pub, a location Pickering liked so much that he bought it.

It would be little surprise that the two would find common ground at Lionel's pub, as it was an establishment that would be as homely and welcoming to celebrities as it was to locals. Damon Parkin, who worked across Pickering's *Trader* publications before joining the press team at Derby, remembers one such incident: 'We'd go and have our Christmas parties there in the upstairs room, and then the summer parties in his garden which was about 50 acres. But I remember at the Christmas parties, you'd have "I Wish It Could Be Christmas Everyday" playing in the disco, then I came downstairs and Roy Wood was a regular there, Roy Wood from Wizzard. He'd be sat on his own having a pint; his song would be playing upstairs.'

'Jim was an old pro,' says Peter Gadsby, vice-chairman under Lionel Pickering. 'He'd managed [Robert] Maxwell, Jim Gregory. And he knew how to run a boardroom. Jim would come into a boardroom, and he'd go, "Mr Gadsby, Mr Chairman," and he knew everything in advance, because the late Keith Loring, who was the CEO, and him became quite close. So he knew everything that was going on. I said to Jim once in a board meeting [about selling a player], "You'd mentioned you'd already told the chairman a figure? When was that then?" "Last night in the Yewtree." Lionel had the pub, Jim was two miles away. Before every board meeting, they'd meet there!'

The duo would strike an immediate bond across their love of an evening drink, but it was their similar ages which would see them align in a working capacity and as close friends. Smith had experienced the worst fall-out in his coaching career when he was dismissed at Portsmouth in 1995, the young and inexperienced chairman Martin Gregory misleading him into a position which ultimately saw him removed from his position. At Derby, though, and with a nine-year difference, Smith and Pickering would share the same joys and grumbles in their later years and be able to share those same interests. As Smith simply put it, 'He was my kind of bloke.'

Neil Sillett would see the relationship in person. Having spent many an evening with Smith at Portsmouth and having eventually agreed to join him as a physio at Derby, he knew better than many the sort of mutual admiration Pickering and Smith would build with each other: 'I sincerely think that the age had something to do with it. Lionel came from humble beginnings and so had Jim, so there was that working class in common. They liked their cricket, Lionel liked his pub, and Jim would always accept a phone call from the chairman. But what he tended to do was go out and see him at the pub on a Thursday and have a couple of Guinnesses. And Lionel would ask questions and put his point of view over, but they spoke very openly. I found it really refreshing because it is difficult. They invest their money into the club so have every right to ask questions. Jim would evidence his decisions to him and, even then, Lionel might not understand or agree, but Jim would say why he wanted so and so, why the training ground needed this and that, why he wouldn't pick one of the chairman's favourite players. And Lionel would say to me, "Well I still don't bloody understand it but I pay him to do it!" They had a calm relationship and I never witnessed any volatility between them at all.

'Keith [Loring] definitely helped that because he took both of their frustrations, it would be directed at Keith and he was a good sounding board for both of them really. Lionel also, without being outwardly exuberant about being the owner or the main shareholder of the club, I soon realised that he was so humble. He was just wanting the best for the club and he never had an ego. And those things endeared you to him. To be honest he wanted to talk more about cricket to me because he knew I played, and he had a lovely way about him. It would be very difficult not to like Lionel. I've been in the game since birth and he is the best chairman I've worked with and just a nice guy.'

Across the six years they were together, the duo of manager and chairman would build a bond that has rarely been replicated at a football club in such a relatively short space of time. Pickering would find the decision to sack Smith ultimately gut-wrenching, wanting to offer him a role still within the club which would in time to be taken away from them both by external forces. And even amid difficult years for Pickering on a personal level, he would still find comfort in his friendship with Smith.

Without pinning it to one thing, the relationship between the two was pivotal in the success of the 1990s and it was something apparent across the club too, according to Dane Farrell: 'Other managers I watched come in and they had almost disrespect for the chairman, and I didn't like that because I knew how Jim would treat him. They would put Lionel on the outside, but Jim brought him in and Lionel felt part of the unit without being overbearing. Not being in the changing room, not wanting to pick the team, he had a lot of responsibility to Jim and Jim in return gave him a lot of respect and gratitude for his work. That was key because I watched other managers go in and they didn't have that skill or that gift or that understanding, and the knowledge of how important it was for a club. Lionel would be out socialising in the evenings, but it mattered and it made us for a better unit.'

The most simplistic way of describing how and why the two got on is a passage of conversation retold by Steve McClaren. The first time Smith and his assistant shared an evening with Pickering, by the end of the night Pickering was sat on his new manager's knee with a pint. Smith, nursing a glass of wine and a cigar, turned to McClaren and simply uttered, 'Don't worry, Steve, we'll be all right with this chairman.'

* * *

Smith, Pickering and Loring would become the holy trinity across the organisation, living in each other's pockets while the rest of the board and coaching staff would make progressions elsewhere, with the on-field play and new ground development. Their club wasn't exclusive though. One factor which had always been consistently important to Smith across his career was finding reasons to turn players into friends, and developing an ability to build relationships where typically they may not exist. It was a stance Pickering would also back, so much so that he would announce a series of annual pre-season squad bonding sessions at his Ednaston Manor home. The gatherings, designed to improve squad togetherness away from the training field, saw all staff members at the club invited into the stately home, with a barbecue held during the height of the summer. Even assistant groundsmen would get the invitation, Andy Croft one of those to be thanked for his service by the chairman. 'You could take your wife and kids to these barbeques, and Lionel and his wife [Marcia] would always do anything for you. We wanted to get some ice cream, so she went to her own fridge just to get some. Little things like that you remember,' said Croft.

As important as these days were, which allowed not only players to relax but also their families, it was the pre-season sessions which arguably had even more impact. Club holidays were not unusual in the game at this point – famously Brian Clough and his Derby squad became English champions in 1972 when on a post-season break – but there was an element of newness to the way Smith would look to do it. While earlier we touched upon the laddish culture sweeping Britain and subsequently a continuing drinking culture in the 1990s, Derby was a little bit different. Perhaps it was down to the influx of internationals around the side, but it was certainly first promoted by Smith himself. For all of his achievements and accolades in the game, they didn't hold weight compared to one other thing in his life: family.

The family element mattered more than anything else to Smith, and so it was something he wanted to preach to his side as well. Forming part of his overall assessment of a player in advance of their signing, Smith would relay a series of questions designed to build a character profile of a man before he would join the club. Family was at the forefront of this, as he wanted to anticipate the ethics which drove the people he would be managing on a day-to-day basis. His first meeting with Chris Powell went well because Powell was soon to become married. His relationship with Dean Sturridge would remain close because Sturridge was a caring father. By integrating the characters who best fitted himself, Smith knew he would be building a changing room of like-minded people.

And with the pre-season trips to locations like La Manga, it was Smith who would remain insistent on bringing families along as well. 'We would do maybe four or five days of pre-season training, but he always invited the partners as well,' recalls Paul Simpson. 'We would go over to La Manga and have these self-catering houses we would live in, where we'd train at 7am and 7pm and the girls had the whole of the time for a break. And it was Jim's way of saying, "Look, this is an early thank you for putting up with what they have to go through during the season. Because I will take them away places for overnight stays, they will miss birthdays and christenings and weddings because of football, so this is something back for you to say sorry and also to say thank you for what you put up with over the season." The girls ended up mixing all day long by the pool and we'd train at 7pm, get back to the house, get ourselves showered and changed and we would all go out for dinner together. It was a really good feeling among it all.

'It was probably a bit different to what it was under Arthur [Cox] because there were a group of players who all got on well together who went out drinking together but [he] didn't really involve the girls. But under Jim there was a really good feeling that if anybody was going out, there might be six or eight of the players with partners going for drinks and food, as opposed to a lads' night out where you go for a piss-up. There was a different type of atmosphere about it. And I had never experienced that before. Never had any of the partners ever been invited on any sort of training or games camps, so it was all new to me. If you're training at seven o'clock the girls could have a glass of wine with lunch, but the players were training. It was a case of us being really professional and, in fact, everybody was that knackered because training was really hard for that short spell of time, we tended to just sleep. Sometimes in the house, sometimes by the pool. We'd have a sleep rather than thinking about drinking. It helped create the atmosphere inside the club and the togetherness with everybody as well.'

Smith's willingness to adapt to new ideas on the training field stood him in strong stead, but it was away from football that his flexibility perhaps had its biggest impact. Ensuring his squad were able to bring partners into the inner sanctum of a football club was an ingenious tactic that made people want to give their all and more for the club.

Alongside his ability to appreciate the needs of families was also his own emotional intelligence when it came to the lives of others. To the outside looking in, Jim Smith was everything a traditional Yorkshireman would be: emotionally hard, physically tough, British and proud. And the three of those were no doubt true, but they were by no means what stood him out from others in similar roles. Where Smith demonstrated his very finest work was in his treatment of players. Though yes, he was a man with an undeniably short fuse and a wicked tongue at times, he was intelligent beyond the realms of fathomability. It was a matter sports psychologist Bill Beswick would become aware of early in his dealings with Jim, particularly when the two worked together on the emotional treatment of a young player.

Beswick said, 'He was a warm and loving man, and he generally would do the right thing. I remember one day at training and there was a young boy struggling, having a really bad day. Jim and I were stood watching and Jim said, "Next time they have a break, I'm gonna slaughter that lad." He did get very excited, very hot under the collar. So, I said, "Jimmy, will you do me a favour? Would you let me have first dibs at this kid?" I signalled a water break to Steve, and I went down to see the kid. The kid said, "I'm all over the place, Bill. My mum and dad split last night, they both want me to live with them, I don't know where I'm going to sleep tonight." I went back and told Jim and he couldn't have been better with that kid. He took hold of that kid, he walked off the field with his arm around his shoulder, took him to his office. "Right, let's sort this out, what do you want to do. Do you want to stay in the club hotel? We'll pay for it; you stay there and then let your mum and dad sort it out and then you take it from there. See me every morning and tell me what the state of play is. If you don't feel like training, you can watch." He was magnificent and a very kind man.'

An earlier iteration of Jim, certainly one who hadn't had Beswick at his side, would likely not have reacted in the same way. But with his willingness to bring psychology into the forefront of his club, he was able to build that greater understanding and deliver additional support on an emotional level. And it's not an isolated incident either. Former Rams defender Spencer Prior spoke of a traumatic incident in his life to which Smith aided his own personal recovery: 'For me, Jim and the staff were next level. We had some personal stuff that happened during my time at Derby and he gave me a couple of weeks off to do some stuff with my wife. At that time we lost a baby, and he had the emotional intelligence to be able to put the players' welfare first and that long-term relationship between the player and him was cemented. The way that he managed me and other players, he gave you space to look after family and put things first, so he was next level with that emotional intelligence as an older manager to be able to support.' Another player had a similar situation, Smith utilising his friendships with the non-playing staff to allow them to provide education on the issues they were to go through.

Such behaviours in those situations can be taught, but ultimately they can only be implemented from an empathic heart; Jim Smith was in possession of one. Similar incidences of Jim's kindness would appear throughout most interviews for this book. Even when kindness wasn't at the forefront, inevitably it would begin to lead down that route. Gary Rowett recalls a situation after being left out of the starting 11 for one match, saying, 'I remember going in to see Jim really angry because I felt I didn't deserve it, and I came out laughing. It was quite an unusual experience again because his man-management was so good. He knew what to say, he wasn't the sort of manager who would ask you to come back in an hour's time so he could pre-prepare. But he was so charismatic and he'd almost turn it on you and say, "Listen. You'll be playing next game, what are you worried about? Anyway, how's it going? How's your missus and your family?" And you couldn't help but like him, even at the worst of times when you kind of hated him for leaving you out.'

As it would with staff and players, Jim's kindness would stretch also to people he had never come across in his life. Ted Gascoyne was the disabled liaison officer during the mid-to-late 1990s and remembered one incident which still brings tears to his eyes when Jim comes to mind. 'One of my disabled supporters came to me one day and told me that when Derby were to play Man United in three weeks, it was his daughter Helen's 11th birthday. So I asked Jim about it [a meet and greet with players]. "Just for you Ted, yes. But she must sit in her wheelchair on the side of the pitch." So Helen was pushed down the players tunnel and placed at the side of the pitch. When the two teams came out players from both teams stopped and spoke to Helen, and when Gary Rowett and Christian Dailly came out they lifted her in her wheelchair and took her to the centre circle. The dear girl and her dad were in tears and, as she came off, supporters in the Main Stand applauded.'

In among these moments of care though, the most telling insight into Jim Smith as a man came across as a resounding theme. As part of this book, completely unprompted, almost all interviewees described Jim as one thing: a father figure.

* * *

Smith was many things to many people, not all of them good. But to his Derby County squad – and even his coaches – he was a dad. A father to three (Suzanne, Fiona and Alison) when he was away from the world of football, Smith knew what it took to build a family regardless of the situation he found himself in. And as a man of senior age, he found that his squad would look at him in the same way. Whether he was coaching an elder player towards the back end of his career, a youngster making their way into the first team or a South American trying to accustom to British life, Smith was always a man to lend an ear.

Youl Mawéné was one of those who Smith was there for, and one who – despite limited first-team appearances under him after signing from Lens in the summer of 2000 – had nothing but love for the Bald Eagle: 'He was very much a patriarch kind of figure, like a grandad or like a dad. He would think in certain ways, he would understand people's personalities and he would get the best out of players. It was a bit of a strange one because you parachute into it, and it's a big step for a 19-, 20-year-old as I was. I didn't drive and didn't have a car on site, then slowly but surely things got in place. The club helped us at the time, they had a deal with Toyota and for the first few weeks, when was Jim on his way out, I'd wait for him before Petaco [Horacio Carbonari, who signed in the summer of 1998] looked after me. Jim Smith was the one who would drop me to the hotel after training. I'd just be there waiting in the afternoon and then he'd say "jump in" and he had that fantastic Rolls-Royce car with panels inside and everything, so he would be talking to me, and I wouldn't understand a word he is saying. But that's where Jim was exceptional because in his man-management skills, he would get people involved, he had that knack of selling you the dream or the project and keeping you on board when you're not playing, and at the same time you wanted to be part of whatever he's doing, which was key.'

Paulo Wanchope, despite confrontations between the pair, would also experience the same level of warmth from Jim in his first days in England: 'He was sensitive, and he was human. He would always ask me how I was doing. "How is your house? Do you need anything? Just tell me and we will sort out any problems you have here."'

And it was the same too for Mart Poom, who joined Smith at Portsmouth before being picked up a second time at Derby: 'For me, Jim was a father figure. My father died when I was in Portsmouth. I had a difficult relationship with my father, we had our problems, and I was always someone who wanted to do very well and prove to my father because he was very demanding, which also Jim was. Off the pitch, he cared about his players. It's why he organised trips and get-togethers with players and partners. There were the end-of-season parties where Jim would always come to talk to your partner or wife, and he had a good heart and cared about you. Yes, he could be tough on matchday but he cared about his players' wellbeing.'

While Smith's emotional intelligence and caring for others was apparent in his treatment of many younger players, it was the same too for seasoned professionals and his own higher-ups in the boardroom. In the case of Craig Burley, signed in December 1999 at a time when Smith was urgently looking to rebuild a depleted squad in the midst of a £15m spending spree that brought in the likes of Branko Strupar and Georgi Kinkladze, he entered Derby on the downturn of his career. A league winner with Celtic and an important man in the Chelsea midfield under Ruud Gullit, his Derby years were tinged with relegation and a significant fall-out with John Gregory. But when it came to his recollection of his experience, there is one man who made it all worthwhile: 'I always look back having won a league title at Celtic, voted player of the year, playing in the World Cup, FA Cup finals and yet, I mean this with all sincerity, one of my proudest things is that I played for Jim.

'We always used to call him the gaffer, always. Working with some guys in the media, Don Hutchison talks about "The Gaffer" now as Howard Kendall, it's kind of that old school. If I'm talking about Glenn Hoddle, it's Glenn, but I always still refer to Jim as "The Gaffer". I hear some of the guys talking about certain managers and it seems to be an era thing. I used to message Neil Sillett and say, "How's the gaffer?" and he used to tell me how he was. We called Ruud Gullit 'Ruud', but Jim was always the gaffer. I called him a few other things along the way too!'

Even Smith's own coaches would see him in a fatherly manner. Both Steve Round and Steve McClaren would refer to him as father-like in the way they worked with him, while Sillett described him as simply a second dad. Assistant groundsman Andy Croft, too, would see him in the same manner, particularly in the way Smith would remember the birthdays of every member of staff across Raynesway. Whether dealing with a player who had got married, a wedding anniversary or a birthday, Smith would simply delve into his pocket and present the person celebrating with £20, adding 'get a drink on me'.

Because of the way his squad and staff would look at him with almost lovestruck eyes, it allowed Jim to get more out of his players than they knew they were capable of. It gave Dean Sturridge the faith to become a 20-goal-a-season striker and allowed Mart Poom to realise he had what it took to establish himself as a world-class goalkeeper. But it also meant that, above all else, they simply didn't want to let Smith down.

Plucked from the depths of non-league and handed a Premier League contract, Malcolm Christie would become the beacon of hope in the late 1990s for a Derby side seemingly intent on dropping out of the division. His goals in the 1999/00 and 2000/01 season were enough to keep the team afloat, but how much of that was talent and how much was belief instilled by Smith? 'Jim had an aura and a presence around him,' said Christie. 'I always knew with Jim I wanted to do well for him and perform, because I knew how disappointed he'd be if we'd not given it our all or not got the performance or result.

'When I say he was a father figure, it wasn't that I'd be crying on his shoulder or that I could talk to him about any sort of problem. It was more an authoritarian father figure, a headteacher kind of feel. You could go to him if you needed something, but you'd rather not. You'd rather try and sort it yourself, but if you needed to you felt that you could. I remember once I made a fatal mistake on a pre-season training camp and I was involved with the young lads but just breaking into the first team. We were having a game of pool, maybe Málaga or Marbella. So a few of the young lads got a beer, and I remember thinking, "No, don't." If Jim found out, it would be a problem. But a bit naively, we were playing pool so, "Yeah, get us one." And then all of a sudden, one of the coaches came in and he was like, "Oh, whose are these beers then?" The next day Jim pulled just me in because he wanted to keep me on the straight and narrow. "Right, someone has told me that you've been having a beer." You only needed to let Jim down once for the disappointment in his face. He'd given me an opportunity and a chance there, for the sake of a beer I wasn't going to do it again. That was my only time with him where I felt he was disappointed with me.'

Jim's authoritarian status extended to the media too, including Ross Fletcher. Then a fledgling young reporter with BBC Radio Derby, he would often be tasked to collect the pre-match interview with Smith at Raynesway and found that not only would he be provided with a typical footballing answer but also both an education and an unexpected respect. 'I was asking about a striker [to Jim], maybe Malcolm, and I said, "What's the one thing you really wish you could give a striker to make them consistently perform?" "Confidence. If I could bottle up confidence, I'd do it and I'd give a dose to my strikers every single day. It's all about confidence." And I felt very much at that point that he was teaching me. He didn't have to but he did, he was a real educator for so many. The fact I was given the respect by this seasoned, imperious, talismanic football manager that was so widely respected, it was huge for me as a teenager.

'My frame of reference for that was a pre-season, three seasons into the Premier League. We went for a big media event and there was myself, Colin Gibson, Ian Hall and Graham Richards. And I still felt like a bit of a pretender there that all these seasoned broadcasters were there and then me. But I remember at the end, Jim Smith came over to us and said, "Eh chaps, do you want to come into the suite next door and we'll have a glass of wine? You come along as well, Ross." Jim took us into his circle of trust and treated me just like anybody else.'

Very much a man of his time, a Jim Smith in the modern world of British football would be difficult to find. Bigger backroom teams, higher levels of scrutiny and less responsibility given to a manager mean the assets which made Smith, Alex Ferguson, Ron Atkinson and more so paramount to the English game are no longer exclusive to success. It's an argument for the game changing for the worse, Mawéné making the point: 'People like Jim I just don't think you'll find in the game anymore. The system promotes people who are really intelligent at certain aspects, but maybe that intelligence doesn't lead to an understanding of emotion or personalities, how to get the best out of certain people. And yes there are great coaches; you look at [José] Mourinho and those modern coaches, but those generation, their success was based on people interactions. Look at how Alex Ferguson managed over the years, without really being a master in tactics. Recruitment, he had to get the best for his team. So it's a difficult question to ask but, on Jim, I don't think you'll find many managers now who have just that desire and passion to enjoy the game.

'My late father always kept the newspaper, the local papers. After that first year, it said something like, "The recruitment at Derby, we don't have a huge amount but I'm after another Youl Mawéné." And I'll always remember my dad pinned it up, saying he's looking for someone like you, which was a massive thing for my dad as well. You cross over and go to another country, sometimes it can be difficult to be accepted for your differences, but for Jim to show as much faith as he has in me, I do owe him a hell of a lot. My career would have been totally different if it was with someone else and, as a matter of fact, when he left a lot of players just didn't have the direction.'

* * *

It was away from any footballing environment that Jim truly blossomed though. To the man, football was *almost* everything.

Because while any social situation would inevitably lead to tactical analysis, first and foremost it was a reason to forget about the tribulations of work. That included his time on the golf course with Rams fan and PGA professional Tim Coxon. 'I didn't know what to expect from him,' begins Coxon, 'because although he'd been around since the mid-70s, I didn't take notice of what he did because he wasn't involved at any of the local teams. He had a couple of lessons and just used to come in, buy his bottle of water or his three balls and sign somebody in because he would bring a guest every time and away he went. He didn't mix a lot, he didn't play in competitions or have a beer socially. [The first time I met him] he just walked into the shop with a cigar on.

'He was impatient, he swore all the time and he wasn't that great [at golf]. He didn't throw his clubs but he just used to hit it, wasn't interested in technique, didn't have a sporty figure. He just used to swear all the time! He just couldn't get why it was so difficult. And he would often lose a club, leave it on the green and be like, "Where's my wedge?" and he'd have to go back the next day. I remember I even gave Jim's wife Yvonne a couple of lessons on the course as well! You couldn't not like him, even when he was parking his car in the car park and people were like, "Whose is that fucking car over there?" You just think, it doesn't matter; it's Jim! He couldn't make you angry because you liked him, just because he was such a nice guy. He liked talking football, smoking, playing a bit of golf and a glass of Rioja.'

The first section of this chapter was about Jim Smith the professional. But this half is about Jim Smith the lad. For all of his kindness when it came to dealing with others, Jim's personality was complex. Because when it came to his life at Raynesway, it would rapidly vary between kindness, and maybe momentary rage before downtime. And what Jim got up to in that downtime was entirely of his own choice. Due to the strong relationship and understanding he had built with Pickering, in addition to the credit he had built up through his overachievements, what Smith wanted to do on a day-to-day basis was really of his own selection. With McClaren and Round leading on the training pitch alongside Billy McEwan and Dane Farrell, it gave the manager an opportunity to enjoy the finer things in life and catch up with old friends, safe in the knowledge jobs were being taken care of elsewhere.

Jim would rarely be seen on the training ground, instead spending time in his office enjoying a drink and a cigar while flicking through the newspapers, or simply meticulously planning his daily horse racing bets. One thing would always be certain though: he would welcome an audience. 'Everyone loved being in his office,' recalls Sillett. 'Big Ron [Atkinson] was a regular visitor, Sam Allardyce when he was at Notts County. He'd come over because he wanted a drink of wine. We had Ron who used to bring this singer in, Jasper Carrott [comedian and former Birmingham City director] would come in quite a bit. There was always someone rocking up who was a guest of his. TV people would always come and overstay their welcome like Andy Gray, and that. Jim used to do a lot of that because he used it as gaining information from other coaches.'

His ability to build relationships was important within a club, but it was outside of his employment that it paid the biggest dividends. Part of a golden era of English managers, Jim would count a generation of top-flight bosses as close friends: Harry Redknapp, Alex Ferguson, Howard Wilkinson, Ron Atkinson, Sam Allardyce, to name a handful. Even those who had moved outside of the game would spend their time with Smith. Redknapp recalled his visits to Derby in his autobiography *Always Managing*, remembering how in his Derby days Smith would always be found alongside Rams legend Dave Mackay when it came to drinks. It was the same for his scouting system too, largely built of long-retired players. At Derby he would work with Archie Gemmill on player identification, while it was Arsenal's ex-defender Bob McNab who would present him with stars such as Paulo Wanchope, largely because of the outside-of-football relationships he had built. Jim's ability to not just woo, but more importantly befriend agents, was at the forefront of the internationalism brought into the club during the 1990s.

Diane Wootton and Marian McMinn worked alongside Smith, long-time veterans of the club who both clocked over 20 years of service across first the Baseball Ground and then Pride Park. They saw first-hand how Smith would operate. Wootton remembers, 'At half nine, he gave me a list of other managers or agents he wanted to contact and on his drive in he'd give me a list of the contacts he wanted to speak to. And he would be right on the ball every day, no matter what time he went to bed or how many he had to drink, he'd be right there, and we'd then have his calls lined up ready for him.' McMinn adds, 'On a matchday at Pride Park, he always had the opposing manager in his office. If it was Manchester United and Alex Ferguson, they were in his office before the game with the racing newspaper, looking at the horses and everything. And that would be until very near kick-off.'

It wasn't Derby-specific in the way Smith would operate, but the older he got and the more connections he would build, the more his ability grew in the off-field management. Neil Sillett adds of those daily sessions, 'He liked to speak to his contacts in the game for a lot of time in the mornings. Alex [Ferguson] being one, he would call him a lot. Big Ron, Dave Bassett, Howard Wilkinson. And he would call them nearly every day to talk about football. He'd talk to my dad [John Sillett] as well. His morning was taken up speaking with press, with agents, any problems with players. And then there would be a circle of his mates that he'd call. Some of it would be nonsense but some would be, "You played them the other week, what did they do?" And they would talk football. Sometimes if they were playing each other, it'd be more of a fun call and sort of, "Who's injured? Oh I'm not telling you that!" A lot of that would go on and take up his time. But he would always, always be watching training through his window. Like Alex did at Manchester. And his dream was to have a balcony where he could rock up and watch training from his balcony down on to the pitch.'

Notorious as one of the strongest drinkers in the game, the two passions would occasionally find their way into the same environment, primarily when entertaining the opposing managers he called friends. One such time came in a late-1990s tie against West Ham, with physio, friend and drinking partner Sillett party to the pre-match shenanigans: 'Harry [Redknapp] knew that we liked a drop of wine and he invited us in when Dane Farrell was taking the warm-up. So Jim and I would go out to see what they were like, and Harry came up behind us and said, "Right lads, I've got a bottle of wine here that I've never tried it, but my man says it's different class." So Jim said we'd go in after the game. "Nah, I'm not hanging around after the game, come in now, I'm watching the race anyway." So we went in and watched this race with Harry, had these prawns and chips in there and a nice bottle of Chateau Musar, which is a Lebanese wine. So we have a plastic cup and a glass of Lebanese wine just in case anyone came in, and it was beautiful … so we had two bottles and then it was six minutes to three when we came out of Harry's office and everything was already said and the players were in the tunnel! It was a good warm-up for me and Jim!'

Smith's sessions with fellow managers were far from a rare occurrence, Ferguson writing in his autobiography, 'His hospitality would keep you there all night. When I did get home, my shirt would be speckled with cigar ash.' It also meant that for the staff entrusted to visit Jim's room following any manager, they'd need to battle through a fog of cigar smoke. Even Arsène Wenger, the great foe of Ferguson, would join Smith for a post-match tipple. In fact, Smith was the first Premier League manager to invite him for a drink, as the Bald Eagle retold in his book. He didn't quite convince Wenger to join him on his love of cigars, though.

'These were the days where you could smoke on an aircraft,' begins Dane Farrell. 'We were on a small flight, and I was pinned in windowside, he was there with his cigar smoking his way through the whole two-hour flight, and it was choking me. The other coaching staff were all having a good laugh because I'm known as the fitness guy. Don't drink, don't smoke, live a good, clean life, eat well. And there's Jim killing me off next to the window. But he liked his cigars! There were times where we would be in a restaurant and Jim was smoking his cigar, some restaurants didn't permit it. Occasionally he'd be asked by the manager to put it out and he'd go, "Yeah, yeah, fine," and then he'd light it up again. He wouldn't be told. I liken him to [Winston] Churchill with his powerful speeches and cigars.'

Drink and Smith went hand in hand, perhaps a little too much at times. Smith and Pickering would meet most often at the Yewtree pub owned by the chairman, leading to situations such as the signing of Fabrizio Ravanelli in 2001. The story, as told by Peter Gadsby, saw him and Keith Loring agree to a one-year deal on £38,000 a week. The next morning, Gadsby would wake up in horror at a BBC Radio Derby report announcing it as two years, after the duo had joined Ravanelli and his agent for a drinking session that ran later into the night, signing off on an additional season.

But that was a rare, if expensive, blot on Jim's record both in football and with a glass in his hand. Because when it came to Jim's ability to see off a drink, there were few matches in and out of the game of football. A connoisseur of the fine wine, Smith would become synonymous in the game for the selection he would present to opposing managers post-match, the proud owner of the finest bar in a manager's office across the divisions.

And to get along and on the right side of Smith, it would be preferable to join him at any given opportunity. Farrell was a rare exception of individuals who wouldn't drink alongside the manager, because all others would be encouraged, if not heavily persuaded, to indulge him at any given hour. Before his Derby days, Sillett remembers a trip to Italy during the days of the Anglo-Italian Cup: 'We were playing a team called Ascoli where Oliver Bierhoff was playing, and the owner of the club owned this hotel where we stayed and he wanted to meet Jim. So Jim and I went to this guy's house, and he had a wine cellar which was the biggest I've ever seen. Each bottle had a wax label on. Between six of us, we had 24 bottles and went to bed at 9am. Just as we were going to bed, Jim went, "You'll need to take the lads for a walk in the morning." I said, "Jim, it *is* the morning." And he went, "Well I'm not doing it so you'll have to get up at half nine." He was famous for one more bottle, was Jim. He let me choose the wines but he loved a Rioja and Châteauneuf-du-Pape was a favourite of his. He enjoyed saying it more than drinking it though, I think.'

It was just one of many, many memorable nights that Smith and Sillett would share together. The duo would remain great friends beyond just football, indulging in a series of evenings together with families both in the UK and in Jim's later years after he and wife Yvonne had bought an apartment in Spain. Sillett would have decades in the company of Smith, but others would not have that luxury and instead would only get to enjoy Jim sporadically, perhaps on a monthly or yearly basis. When they did have the opportunity though, it was something they would never be able to erase from their mind.

A natural storyteller and a man most comfortable when having an audience in the palm of his hand, Smith would spend many a Friday evening before an away game in a hotel with his fellow coaches. Sillett, Round, McClaren, McEwan and more would all be not just educated, but thoroughly entertained by Smith. Regularly up until the early morning, Smith's liver would be put to the test whenever the side had an overnight stay. Renowned for his knowledge of the wine world, most Friday evenings would start with a bottle of red, likely followed by another, before moving on to Glenmorangie. Staff inevitably would try but fail to keep up, falling to the wayside without an opportunity to disappear into the safety of their temporary rooms.

It would be apparent on some Saturday mornings too that the gaffer had made an evening of his temporary jaunt away from Derby. Craig Burley laughs, 'We would come down on the Saturday morning for a bit of breakfast and then be pencilled in for an 11am walk. I'd see the coaching staff and kitmen, they'd all be looking like shit. And the word always came out: the gaffer. "He wouldn't let any of us go to bed last night." So he's holding court at the hotel bar, smoking his cigars, he's on the red wine, telling stories and he's told them that if anybody goes to bed, they're getting sacked. Now he didn't mean that, but they didn't know that! You've got all these people at two or three in the morning, desperate to go to bed, trying to sneak off, then you come down the next morning and they're all hungover and struggling while Jim is fresh, full of life. That wasn't uncommon because he liked to get them all together. They wouldn't go to bed until the gaffer was finished, so they had quite a few late nights. But then sometimes Jim would come down to the team meetings and sweat would be running off that bald head of his, he'd be holding his teacup and saucer, the saucer would be shaking away because he had a couple of red wines too many. But that's the way he rolled. Deep down all the staff loved it, they really enjoyed being in his company.'

Even meetings with the club decision-makers, such as Keith Loring, would be conducted over a drink or three. 'If we had a drink, I'd feel like shit and he was in the training ground at 9am, I have never worked how he did that out. He used to get a bit silly sometimes when he'd gone too far, but apart from that he was just fantastic. We used to meet at quarter to nine and had a gin and tonic in the bar when we waited to go to dinner. Then we'd have a second. Then you got on then because you're relaxed. When he first came in he was a bit heavy. And anybody you ever went with in his company, all they needed to do was just sit and listen. Because you'll get the funniest night you've ever had.'

The same could be said too of standard evenings or celebrations with his squad. The difference between Smith and other managers though, as he himself admitted, was that everything came back to football. Steve Round says, 'At the end of a night you'd come home and just say what a great night you had with Jim. You'd go out for a meal with a restaurant with all the wives and, come the end of the night, he'd pull the staff off to one side and say, "OK, let's think about the team selection for Saturday. I'm thinking of playing 3-5-2," and all of a sudden you were back on football for the last 30 minutes! He always had one eye on it, but I think that's management in general, you can never step away from it.'

It didn't always revolve around football though. Jim had a love of many things in life which wouldn't immediately be expected. A man of his time, Smith was by all accounts, a gentleman. Devoted to his family and his wife Yvonne, he would find reasons aplenty to treat his squad to evenings of relaxation that he and his staff would enjoy, but he would also ensure that both he and Yvonne would get to know the staff and their significant others too. And they would pay huge and genuinely caring interest in the lives of others too.

Jim's assistant Marian McMinn remembers her own daughter's first-born, and how Jim and Yvonne sent an influx of thoughtful presents as a congratulations. Another moment where Jim expressed interest was one Christmas, when he and Loring organised complimentary turkeys for every single member of staff at the club. Diane and Marian would be responsible for the operations, with the latter laughing at the memory of an idea Jim implemented and left to the duo: 'They persuaded Lionel to buy every player and every single member of staff a turkey at Christmas, which was fine. But the logistics of giving out a fresh turkey to every single member of staff at Pride Park and the players and coaching staff, it had me and Di in the concourse in the freezing cold. We spent around three or four hours because Jimmy and Keith wanted to do something nice for the staff. I wish to God I could have gone home though, it was freezing, but that was Jimmy.'

That unity was important to Smith, and it was something he would preach when it came to the club celebrations. The one following the Crystal Palace promotion was one thing, but the situation where he would most come into his own was at the Christmas party. 'He always liked "Last Christmas" by Wham!' recalls Wootton. 'He used to ask the DJ to play it time and time again and, as he played it, he'd get me and Maz and he'd swing us both together so our foreheads bumped. The next day we'd both have bruises on our foreheads where he'd crashed us together!' It wasn't the only mark on the head, with the duo also recalling how Smith would end the night with cigar ash across his face from where he had obliviously missed his mouth entirely. One reason for that might have been the drink. Another might have been his fascination with Tina Turner.

It's a story I had to triple check in the writing of this, but on three separate interviews the subject of Tina Turner came up, including from Mark Robinson, who became the head groundsman at Pride Park. 'I was lucky enough when Jim had his 60th at Pride Park to get an invite. On a Sunday from 12–12, it was some party that was. All the top managers were there. Sir Alex, everyone. A fantastic day. Jim liked his rat pack and Frank Sinatra and that, so he had a great big band on in the afternoon and then at night he had a Tina Turner tribute and Jim was up on the table for "Simply the Best".' Not only would Jim be dancing on the table, he would also produce a wad of money to get her to perform the set all over again. The man truly knew how to amaze.

But all of the social functions and every glass of Rioja had a purpose. Whether it was a squad night out at La Villa, a Christmas party with the wives or a private pre-match drinking session with his coaching staff, they were all designed not only to give him a platform to entertain as he so enjoyed, but also to build harmony within the Derby County family. Though 1990s football marked major changes for British football with the launch of the Premier League and heavy influx of overseas talent, all of the tricks and tips Smith knew from his years in the game would still stand the test of time.

* * *

But when assessing the man Jim Smith was, one thing needs to be taken into account: temper. Not a negative in any sense; Smith's temper in the world of football was notorious and even a running joke to his close friends. In *It's Only a Game*, he made light of it himself: 'I have lost count of the number of times I have fallen foul of match officials. But in all cases I have to say that the men in the middle have been wrong. My big fault is I keep using the word cheat … but unfortunately my vocabulary does not stretch to coming up with another less incriminating description. Even my daughters have tried to get me to stop. "Dad," they said once. "Instead of calling the referee a cheat, just look at him and say 'Referee, how do you sleep at night?'" I was determined to take their advice the next time the occasion arose. I waited for him to come off the pitch after my team had been on the wrong end of another costly bad decision and said, "Referee, how do you sleep at night … you cheating bastard!"'

When it came to Smith around the club though, in his five years he would display many a bout of fury for differing reasons. Occasionally used as a way to keep his squad in check, Smith's high demands on a professional and personal level would become simply a part of everyday life at Raynesway, not that it made things any easier for some. Dubbed as 'like a kettle' by Sillett, Smith would regularly be difficult to calm. Reasons would range from the acceptable (a training ground incident, a wrongdoing or a poor performance) to the ridiculous (losing a horse racing bet). And though it was an accepted part of everyday life at the club, it still posed its own issues.

Perhaps the most widely rumoured incident came following a Premier League match against Barnsley in December 1997. After an abject performance by Paulo Wanchope, Smith took exception to – and his anger out on – the Costa Rican, with physical confrontation the final result. 'He went up to the pitch and walked next to him [Wanchope], all the way into the dressing room,' remembers Jacob Laursen. 'And when we got into the dressing room, it was all too much and he just wanted to hit him. But Jim stopped his fist just in front of his face and everybody started pulling them away.' Neil Sillett adds further context to the situation: 'We took Paulo off during a game and he came in and he'd got the hump, he got into the bathroom, and he'd switched the taps on in the bath, put the plug in and I think he'd forgotten. The floor was flooded, and Jim walked in in his new Prada shoes and got the water all over them. And he just looked at Paulo and went for him! You can imagine the scene, there were about 20 players and staff all rolling around on the floor with water going everywhere, trying to split them up.' Smith described the incident as 'tasty'.

In the process, Smith no doubt said many things. One claim he made during the brawl was that he was Yorkshire's boxing champion, an accolade he would reference on several more occasions over the years. It wasn't an isolated incident either, Smith continuously butting heads with his star acquisition over a number of seasons. 'At half-time in a match,' he wrote, 'I completely lost it with him. "Get changed and get in that bath." But the other players persuaded me to keep him on. "All right," I told him. "If I was in their shoes I'd be giving you a smack."'

Smith's temper could almost be perceived as a tactic though, designed to get the very best out of his players. Without caring what they thought of him as a person, he would look to turn the anger that was built up in his direction as a tool when out on the pitch. The added intensity which came from Smith's often purposeful remarks provided new incentive during the 90 minutes, and presumably provided a feeling of satisfaction for the manager too that his unorthodox approach had yielded results.

Though not ideal for the recipient, the outbursts aimed often at Wanchope or Mart Poom provided an element of entertainment for the rest of the squad. Then looking to break through into the first team, central-defender, club joker and Derby-born Steve Elliott struggled to contain his amusement at times: 'Jim could give you the hairdryer like no one else. Some players like Paulo or Poomy, he could push their buttons, he knew how to do it. If he was allowed, Jim would just have a fight with you. He'd just say, "Come on then, let's go outside and have a fight. Whoever wins is right." And he'd have a go at anyone. Even Paulo Wanchope, who is 6ft 4in, athletic as anything and Jim was trying to beat him up!'

As Elliott notes though, the true magic was in Smith's ability to change his temperament within mere seconds: 'But on that flipside, you knew when you had an argument with him that there would be no grudges held at all. There would be no repercussions. The next day it would all be forgotten about. He probably called him into his office and said, "You're playing Saturday, get your head right, here's a bottle of beer for when you get home." You knew where you stood with Jim and he was straight down the line to you, there was no sugar-coating anything or BS or lying; you knew where you stood with Jim Smith. If he didn't like it, he'd tell you as well. And that's what you want really. I played under a few managers where you were second-guessing and doing things they're not saying, but they don't tend to last that long in the end.'

It separated Smith from the good man-managers and put him in a category with the very best in the game. A man who seemed incapable of bearing a grudge – at least for footballing reasons – would know exactly the lengths he could go to when testing his squad and coaches, and he knew the right time to bring them back in as well.

Chris Powell says, 'I don't want everyone thinking he was just this big ogre, he was someone that we could relate to. He'd be your best friend after having a go at you in the same sentence, it was bizarre how at times he'd say, "What the effin' hell were you doing there?" and then he'd be laughing with you and you'd be laughing with him. That's a skill in itself, that you can have these players listening to you and getting all the bits from the game or the training session, but then he'd just relate to you in a way that you just had to laugh with him. And I think every player will tell you that.'

That element of treading a fine line with Smith was not exclusive to his squad. McClaren would bear the brunt of many fits of rage from his senior, as would Steve Round. Fitness guru Dane Farrell would be party to Jim's grumbles too: 'We all hear of him before starting there [at Derby] and then you meet the man and the man is just a wonderful all round good guy;

an incredibly firm but fair guy. If you stepped out of line, my God you knew about it. You wouldn't argue, and that goes with everybody. I've seen every individual, coaching staff, myself included, getting an absolute bollocking from Jim Smith. You accept it and you learn from it. As I've mentioned, he would never hold a grudge and is one of those people who would put his arm round not only players but also coaching staff as well. He was great at that.

'[It] was funny for everybody when we were not at the receiving end like Paulo, because it was funny watching somebody else get it! And I think that was all down to just keeping quiet and watching that person get absolutely nailed by Jim. When he went for it, he went for it, and it was good. Even on an aircraft, we had a pre-season tour in Chicago and Jim let loose at a particular player … no, a member of staff it was. And that was highly amusing. Jim had more or less sacked somebody mid-flight, and by the time we had landed he had reinstated that person!'

Like with the Wanchope incident and his claim of being Yorkshire's boxing champion, every element of fieriness was also sprinkled with incredible humour. Even when seeing red, Smith would find an anecdote, a quote or a simple remark to defuse the situation, whether he planned on it or not. Neil Sillett said, 'When we went down to ten men against Leeds once, he got so frustrated at half-time, he's got the board out and is going, "What we gonna do, Sill? What we gonna do?" And he meant to say "it's damage liability" but in front of everybody he said "it's lamage diability" and somebody corrected him and he went "SHUT UP!" He'd just come out with some things that would be so funny.'

Again though, it wasn't Derby-specific; this is just the man Jim Smith was across his entire career. Another such incident of finding humour in a dire situation came soon after he had signed Lee Chapman at Portsmouth, as Sillett explains: 'Within two weeks he was like, "What have I done?" I was on the touchline in a Simod Cup game at Oxford for Portsmouth. Chappy tried to control the ball and it went straight through his legs. I turned around and said, "Can we take him off?" And Jim went, "I've just fucking sold him to Harry [Redknapp]!'"

In those days on the south coast, another man who would experience Smith was Mart Poom. Leaving Estonia to join the club, not only would Smith give him an opportunity to learn the English game, he'd also provide him with a money-can't-buy prize – an English curse word lesson: 'I learnt loads of swear words from Jim! When I signed for Portsmouth, in the beginning it was really difficult to know if he was happy with you or mad, because he was using the f-word every second word. "You're fucking brilliant"; "fucking rubbish!" I wasn't used to that, is he happy or not?! He would rant and rave, but on matchdays you had to have thick skin for him. Swear words go with Jim's reputation though, and if you didn't handle or understand it, well I'm sure some players gave it back as well, but it made myself even more determined or angry to show him that he was wrong. But you had to take it from him. I knew from Pompey that he would swear every time he was praising you! You just had to get used to it.'

* * *

Above all else, when factoring in the temper and the kindness and the humour, Jim was simply Jim to the world of football and beyond. His is a legacy which will continue to be felt across the game, whether by players, coaches, supporters or casual observers. 'I still talk about him,' says Craig Burley. 'I work with Shaka Hislop and he worked with Jim at Portsmouth, we share stories. I regale stories that Neil Sillett used to tell me about Jim and I tell them to Shaka and he pisses himself laughing because he can see it. The guys loved Jim when he went down to Portsmouth and he was working under Harry. In fact, I almost went there because of him. Every now and again, Shaka and I will talk about Jim even after all these years, and every time it comes back around we just say, "What a character. Unbelievable."'

Bill Beswick echoes Burley: 'There are some men that you can love. I use that word carefully. They can be big, generous, fun,

warm, affectionate people. Jim was one of those. I became very …
not close to Jim because nobody was too close to Jim, but I became
one of the people he could share with. I was the person he could
talk about, sometimes when he was down, he could talk to me, and
I valued that relationship enormously, and I hope it was useful for
him. But I loved him. He was larger than life, a person of strong
emotions and basically a very kind and warm guy.'

What most impressed with Jim, though, was his brain. Because
for the perception he would give to the outside world, the mind
he possessed was a gift to football. 'In reality, there were two Jim
Smiths,' finishes Prozone's Ramm Mylvaganam. 'There was what
you saw on the surface and underneath all that there was a level
of football shrewdness that people totally underestimated. For Jim
Smith to be able to go and identify the players that played there
in the '90s … the World Cup in '98, you find out the number of
Derby County players involved, it was just frightening. To go to
poach AC Milan superstars like Stefano, to convince them to come
to Derby County for God's sake, there would have been thousands
of Italians thinking, "Where the fuck is Derby?" Underneath that
very unassuming exterior, there was a real shrewd tactician and a
business brain and knowledge that I had never seen before. The
more time I spent with him, the more I learnt.'

7

OLD AND NEW

IT WAS Keith Loring who had the honour of announcing that Derby County would be leaving their Baseball Ground home, five minutes before kick-off at a February 1996 game at home to Luton Town. He would proudly proclaim that the Rams would be transitioning into the 21st century at what would become known as Pride Park Stadium. The announcement was one of the biggest in the history of the club at that time and heralded the dawn of a new era for the city of Derby.

Loring was booed off the field.

* * *

The Taylor Report was a turning point for the world of British football and laid the foundations for a transition from a sport dogged in tribalism and city-centre brawling to transition into one catering for family friendly audiences. Following the Hillsborough tragedy in 1989 which led to 97 Liverpool supporters losing their lives, Lord Justice Taylor set about a restructure of facilities across the English and Scottish divisions.

Taylor's analysis was long overdue as British football culture increasingly grew prehistoric when placed in comparison to the continental divisions. Off the field, the English had become notorious for trouble across European competitions. Thirty-nine Juventus fans had been killed following hooliganism by Liverpool supporters prior to the 1985 European Cup Final at Heysel in Belgium, and English clubs were then banned from competing in Europe until the 1990s. Then there were racial issues across the country, with black players increasingly targeted.

Other grounds were failing too. The Valley Parade fire on the final day of the 1985/86 season was one of the darkest events in the history of British sport and left all clubs with a firm choice: replace any wooden stands in the stadium or move.

On the field too, England were lacking. Italia '90 had been the closest the national team had come to breaking a curse which still continues today, with the side then falling in the groups at Euro '92 and failing even to make it to the following World Cup in 1994. Growing an increasing reputation for not transitioning to the changing world of tactical analysis as well, English football was at an all-time low and needed monumental restructure, which would later arrive in the form (and money) of the Premier League.

Taylor's report, which called for set capacities on terraces, the removal of perimeter fencing and better policing when it came to the topic of controlling a crowd, would have been radical had it only sat at these points. But the consideration that all English football stadiums should become all-seater by a set time was the monumental shift in how clubs and supporters would operate in the future. It left all clubs in the top two divisions in England needing to adapt their stadiums by the beginning of the 1994/95 campaign, with the rest of the footballing pyramid following by the turn of the millennium.

Derby County, like many other clubs, would find themselves severely restricted. Attendances at the Baseball Ground would be capped at just over 18,000, less than half of what it had held during the 1970s. With failing fortunes and increasing trouble, most weeks that capacity was fanciful, as supporters began to turn away from the club. Stuck between knowing whether to renovate or simply move, Lionel Pickering first spearheaded a plan to press forward to a new stadium in 1993, with the board voting unanimously in favour. That idea would be scrapped, with the club stuck in a First Division rut. Instead, proposals were put in place for the almost entire redevelopment of the Baseball Ground.

The Pop Side would change in the space of 15 weeks, transformed from the all standing home it had been for its eternity into the lower tier of the all-seater Toyota Stand. By this stage, property magnate Peter Gadsby had been integrated into the board under Lionel Pickering, and with his extensive expertise he would be tasked with the redevelopment of the Rams' home. The ABC Stand was to be replaced; the Osmaston and Normanton stands would be demolished with new structure put in place. It was to be the Baseball Ground for a changing generation.

With the proposed development of a Main Stand alongside Shaftesbury Crescent, there would be opportunities for significant club growth off the field with themed restaurants, a mammoth club shop, brand-new dressing rooms and even a hotel, following the demolition of the Baseball Hotel. As quoted in *Pride Park: The Story of a Stadium*, Gadsby had remarked at the time, 'The Main Stand development is the most exciting element of the programme reflecting the quality, traditions and aspirations of the club. This will underpin the long-term financial stability of the club.'

With fans aware of the need for change and having been kept abreast of developments, many including club historian Andy Ellis were eagerly awaiting the progress. 'They demolished the Baseball Hotel on the corner which would have made way for the new Normanton Stand,' Ellis says. 'They'd got road closures done, they'd got some of the building equipment starting to be delivered on-site. They were within a couple of weeks of starting work.'

In fact, it was six days. Within six days of Gadsby's visit to the offices of Birch PLC on 2 January 1996, electrical circuits would be diverted from below the streets which surrounded the stadium. That day, consultant Arthur Burns would relay his plans for the coming weeks to Gadsby. Within a week, a multimillion-pound redevelopment would begin. In the meantime though, the vice-chairman had been crunching the numbers and keeping one eye on another area of land a few miles from their then home.

'So the Co-op [later known as Toyota after the vehicle manufacturer took over the sponsorship] Stand,' Gadsby begins, 'which was about 8,000 would go, and our capacity would go to 10,000. We were given an extension of 12 months and I was then asked to look at it, being a property man. Lionel said, "You better bloody do it. You've been on and on, moaning in my ear." Lionel didn't have any interest in progressing the stadium. He didn't want to know, but it was coming up on it. His interest was who was playing, what's the game, etc. So, we started to design the Co-op Stand with a local architect. All the cottages behind [on Shaftesbury Crescent] had to be bought, you'd have to buy about 13 to create the thing to go back with the gate.'

Despite leading on the development plans though, Gadsby maintained reservations on what would be the best course of action. During this time, it was a visit to Steve Gibson which would decide the future of Derby County. Gadsby said, 'By Christmas time I saw Middlesbrough's ground on the telly. The story was all about their new stadium, basically an old harbour that had been closed in the north-east. Middlesbrough opened up at the Riverside [in 1995], and everybody thought it was fantastic. I went up and met Steve Gibson, who was very helpful. A Derby County fan would not be going to Middlesbrough and vice versa, so you'd never lose any supporters. In business people won't, but they were very open and said it cost £18m and Taylor Woodrow were a building company of national repute and they said they'd build ten of these a year. So there was never competition for customers. I went back, told them and they thought it was ridiculous. Lionel said, "You'll get lynched. I've been at the Baseball Ground for 45 years, you'll be lynched. I'm not going." But I said, "This doesn't make sense. We're going to spend £11m to do one stand and we've got no car parking, no access. For probably £18 million we can probably move to a new stadium."'

And so, with only six days before a new-look Baseball Ground was put into operation, change of a different kind was afoot.

* * *

Middlesbrough's Riverside Stadium had opened in the summer of 1995, becoming one of the early adopters of modern concrete homes. Placed on a plot of land then unused, it had not just taken them forward from the archaic Ayrsome Park ground, it also provided opportunities for growth off the field too with commercial incentives. A club of similar stature to Derby, Boro found themselves able to implement hospitality opportunities with local businesses, sell corporate boxes and even attract stadium sponsorship from Cellnet.

For Derby, it became a learning opportunity. While they could look to take the stadium and build an exact replica hundreds of miles south, they would look to adapt some of the disgruntlements that Gibson had with his finalised stadium. Gadsby remembers, 'They took me round and asked what they would do if they could build it again and they gave me 22 variations. "First of all we'd make the press room bigger. When you arrive in reception it should be grandiose and in the corporate we have a wall. We should have had glass," and went through 22 things.' Loring added that, including small amends, 165 different changes were made at various points of the process.

Adjustments on paper varied from adapting facilities within the outside of the stadium to generate non-matchday income, to the corporate boxes facing directly on to the pitch, in contrast to Middlesbrough's misstep. Another section of the stadium they would look to amend was the press area, increasing the capabilities for journalists to convene and opening up more space between radio commentators and supporters.

That came in particularly handy for Graham Richards, the voice of BBC Radio Derby across three decades, who had found himself in hot water at times from nearby ears at the BBG: 'One of our problems at the Baseball Ground in front of us were the players' wives. We were slightly raised up at the back of the stands and everyone was sitting. So we'd be up here to people down there and these back two rows were reserved for wives or girlfriends.

And it was just my style that if a game was done and we were losing, Mrs Štimac would be the first up before half-time to go and get a cup of tea and cake. And I used to say things like, "Mrs Štimac's got a good lead on Mrs Simpson, now going down the stairs."

'Two things came up. One, they didn't like that I was doing it in a racing commentary voice, and secondly, the wives were busy telling the players and management what we had said on commentary because they had heard it! And they got the information about all sort of things that never went on air, including the second most embarrassing moment of my career. Colin Addison had been Derby County's quite successful manager and I had revealed that I really fancied Mrs Addison. I said something like, "Well Mrs Addison seemed to enjoy that goal. Mind you, I wouldn't mind enjoying Mrs Addison." And of course, Colin did exactly the right thing and he spoke to me privately about it later. He's now one of my great friends, I get a Christmas card from him! That's the sort of peril we had though.'

With differences in place and Gadsby spearheading a new direction, there was just one small matter to confirm upon: where would it be? For that, the vice-chairman had a clear vision in mind.

Over the years, Pride Park Stadium could well have been described as toxic, but it's a definition the land itself is suitable of. The area was formerly the industrial centre of the city, a 180-acre plot of land which had been integral to Derby's reputation as the industrial heart of England in the 1800s, housing the North Midland rail works. Gas works too would be a focal point of the site. But with a railway shake-up in the years following the First World War, the plot became less functionable. It would house a refuse tip and gas holders, but had largely lost its importance to the area and descended into simply an eyesore.

It wasn't only the eyes which would be damaged though. Through decades of work and the gas buildings themselves, below the surface saw the area literally grow into toxicity, with cyanide and tar making it a contaminated area. Known as Chaddesden

Sidings, the area which would eventually become Pride Park painted a depressing image of a bygone era for a city that was once so powerful.

It painted opportunity, though, to investors, and the most notable of these came with the launch of the City Challenge scheme. Launched in 1991, the multi-city competition would be used as an opportunity to regenerate deprived areas through a mixture of different funding sources. And while positioned as an opportunity to breathe fresh life into a distressed area, it also came with an eventual incentive which would see the successful area potentially playing home to what would eventually be known as the Millennium Dome.

By this point, the club had already expressed an interest in the land during their 1993 development plans alongside the combined Derby PRIDE Limited faction, only for the club to turn their gaze back towards the Baseball Ground redevelopment. Though it dealt a blow to the group, it opened up a new opportunity to bring the Dome to Derby. With work already ongoing to detoxify the area and reclaim the land for public use, Derby officially announced its intention to bid for the Millennium Exhibition, alongside interest from proposals in Birmingham, and London areas Bromley-by-Bow and Greenwich.

'Derby got £30m to completely take the stuff away and put a new road in, while creating this thing called Pride Park,' Gadsby remembers. 'The roads were done and I was quite well in with the local authorities and they told me they were going to win the bid for the Millennium Dome. It was between Birmingham, Derby and London. So I rang around a few people and they said it would be going to London, it won't go to Derby. But Derby thought it was. The council gave us ten weeks to buy the land and get on with it because of the Millennium Dome. I told them, "You've not got it," and they said, "Yeah but we don't want everybody else to know that, do we."'

And so with first Derby County and then the potential Millennium Dome turning down the land, the space threatened to descend once again. That's when Gadsby focused again on what was best for the club of the city.

Speaking in *The Story of a Stadium*, Gadsby added further insight on the ultimate decision to confirm on the Pride Park plans: 'What we were doing [with the regeneration of the Baseball Ground] didn't seem quite right. Many people have said to me that I must have known I was going to change direction – but I honestly didn't. Something kept telling me that if the Millennium Exhibition wasn't coming to Derby, something should be replacing it.'

There were additional plus points for Gadsby too when weighing up when to approach the board with his plan. The new Wyvern bridge had been developed and the Station Approach flyover was to follow. Then there was the additional TV revenue from the Sky deal, alongside the clarity that the club would be eligible for funding from the Football Trust. Within days, and after speaking directly with Derby City Council, Gadsby took his findings to board member John Kirkland, who agreed it was worth pursuing. Lionel Pickering would be the final hurdle.

Stuart Webb explained: 'When the idea of moving to Pride Park was mooted in 1993, I remember saying that ... this was an opportunity missed. Moving to a new site and having the freedom to build a new stadium – without the constraints we faced trying to redevelop the Baseball Ground – appeared to be the right decision.' The four-man board of Pickering, Gadsby, Kirkland and Webb had seen the first three give the thumbs up to the decision. Webb, who had been a custodian of the club since 1970, had looked at potential opportunities in previous decades, and he backed the call for a unanimous decision.

With two legitimate options now in play and a launch for BBG redevelopment just days away, the board moved fast. The speed of which was the following:

2 January 1996 – Gadsby sounds out Arthur Burns
3 January 1996 – Gadsby approaches the city council and then the board to explain a potential new direction
4 January 1996 – A full proposal is in place

Gadsby, consultant Arthur Burns, Pickering and Loring, who was taken from his own redevelopment focus on the BBG, ventured once again to Middlesbrough and confirmed on the changes they would want. The next step would see electricity plans put on halt at their current home, and following a full month of extensive project analysis and development which saw the decision-makers, construction firm Taylor Woodrow and architects from the Miller Partnership convene around a cardboard cut-out of a stadium, the decision was made. The renovation of their long-time abode was terminated officially in mid-February. Derby would be moving home.

* * *

'Ladies and gentlemen, the board of directors have a very special announcement to make. We believe you, the fans of Derby County, should be the first to know of an historic decision which was made within the last hour. After reaching agreement with Derby City Council and Derby PRIDE, we can now confirm that the club will move into a brand-new 30,000-seater stadium for the start of the 1997/98 season. The £16m state-of-the-art stadium will be build on Pride Park, close to the centre of Derby, and building work will begin in the summer. It will be one of the largest new football stadiums in the UK and heralds the dawning of a new era for the Rams. We want to thank you, the supporters of Derby County, for your patience and understanding during the negotiation process. Thank you.'

Keith Loring's announcement was brief and conducted five minutes before the start of a 1-1 draw with Luton, in which Darryl Powell scored a rare goal. Designed in timing to build on the excitement of the unbeaten run the club were on as Derby headed towards the top flight, it was always destined to be a bone of contention among the fanbase. For all, the move would mark the end of an era. One of the limited things which would be passed between generations, football at the BBG was all most people had ever known and to leave would be a crushing blow.

Supporter Ross Lowe was one of those immediately opposed to the news, despite being only a teenager at the time: 'I remember the first game [I went to] and there were about 17,000 at the most, but it was the first time I had seen that many people in one space and I thought the Baseball Ground was like Wembley. I stood up every time Derby went forward and this old boy behind stood up, put his hands on my shoulders and shoved me down. We were in the Normanton End and then we were in the Normanton middle with season tickets. It was a marvellous place, especially night games. When Derby first announced they were moving to a new stadium, I was against it because I was like, "How can you move us out of that place which is perfect?" OK, it's wooden, if it catches fire we're fucked, but for me it was the character of the place, the amount of things that had happened there in the past, the history there.'

There was contrast though. 'The Baseball Ground had this uniqueness,' says supporter Jamie Allen. 'I mean, with the terracing, people would go down to the front and have a piss because they couldn't be arsed to go to the toilet. The facilities were a joke, and it wasn't very family friendly, so I really wouldn't have took my kids there. And the walk up to the ground could be a little bit naughty. So watching Pride Park rise up was quite exciting, and it made a change that something decent was actually happening in Derby. We'd always played second class to Nottingham all the time. Our shopping centre was always crap; if you wanted anything decent you went to Nottingham. But for a change we had got something decent. And it made the crowd big, people wanted to go. It was the best decision they made.'

There was one hitch following Loring's announcement which would need to be addressed before progression, with the board needing to reassess exactly where the £16m for the stadium was to come from. 'Lionel had put a lot of money into developing the team when he first joined the board,' wrote Gadsby at the time, 'and again, when it came to the financial agreements … he was prepared to put his hand in his pocket. Several such key moments were moved on by the stroke of Lionel's pen and it's a measure of the man that this has not been publicly recorded. It would have been very onerous to continue without Lionel's support.'

Therefore, when prompted by Pickering, each member of the board would commit to putting in a certain amount themselves to top up the funding to the tune of £2.5m. A £2.75m Football Trust grant was in the works too. Additional funding from Banque Internationale a Luxembourg and Lombard North Central had the budget in place and, with the temporary setup of an additional company named Derby County Stadium Limited, Taylor Woodrow moved in.

At the time looking likely to pursue a plan based on the Riverside but without two of the corners filled in, the firm had built the Middlesbrough equivalent and saw the opportunity to do the same in Derby as relatively straightforward once the exact plot of land had been confirmed upon. The first concrete pillar would be installed on 2 September 1996, weeks into the first Premier League campaign that the club would embark upon. And while the timing of the move would never have been perfect, with Derby seemingly two months from promotion and comfortably in the top two, it was the best it could have been.

It could have been disastrous though. The idea of a new stadium was largely built around Premier League football and had things gone askew on the field it would have had the same result off it according to Gadsby. 'I think if we hadn't got promotion we would have had to sell players,' he bluntly says. Promotion they did get though, and the over the course of their maiden Premier League voyage supporters were treated to a monument rising from the ground: Pride Park Stadium.

* * *

Though fans were able to take in the progress of the stadium by turning up and watching from a distance, it was the development of the Pride Park Visitor Centre which would prove the biggest driver of supporter excitement. In a cabin on the grounds of Pride

Park, visitors would flock to get a sense of what home would soon look like thanks to a virtual reality (at least a 1990s version) of the projected finished product.

Loring was the man who drove the centre, an idea which generated over 70,000 visitors during the development as supporter intrigue increased closer to the finalisation. He said, 'The whole philosophy of Pride Park changed from the BBG. You could bring the family with you because the facilities were there for them to deal with. They could walk in and see the stadium they want to use. And we sold 18,000 season tickets in our first summer. That's a year later from when we opened to 9,000 people. Eighteen thousand people, then maybe five from the away crowd; 23,000 people. I know that not every one of the 18,000 comes to every game but you still have them coming. You can see how you build that crowd.'

The centre would officially open on 17 November 1996 and was marked with the unveiling of the foundation stone by Lionel Pickering. Months later season tickets would be put on sale, with the club launching three-year tickets as anticipation grew and the Rams continued to perform strongly in the top flight. Corporate boxes too would sell out rapidly, as Andy Dawson, later the commercial manager at the club, would find out: 'We were still at the Baseball Ground and Keith needed some help because they were creating a visitor centre that was going to be where Pride Park Stadium is now. He needed some support and he offered me the job. It was a big decision at the time because we'd just had Daisy, my youngest daughter, but we rented a place for a little while and then moved in with Jim and Yvonne [the Smiths, Andy's parents-in-law] for a little bit, then got a place of our own.

'You remember at the Baseball Ground there were zero facilities. There was a little players' room and another lounge, a little bit of sponsorship but not many commercial opportunities at all. Ramtique as they called it was not generating a lot of money away from matchdays and Pride Park enabled a huge opportunity with a vast amount of hospitality facilities, a huge superstore and a number of other commercial opportunities. So it was a really good time.'

Hospitality boxes, available at £20,000 per year, would sell out within weeks, as local businesses realised the new facility was one they wanted to be involved in, a sharp contrast to a Baseball Ground which was not high on sponsorship priorities. It would lead in part to Pickering's decision to install the north-west corner housing further boxes and the famous Baseball Bar & Grill. '[It] was my project and I'm proud of it,' the chairman said years later. 'I've got a lot of time for pubs and it didn't give me any pleasure to buy the Baseball Hotel and knock it down. Before it was closed I noticed this beautiful mahogany bar and the bar mirrors ... it was great to be able to incorporate them in the Bar & Grill.'

The bar would be located in the soon-to-be finished corner and would be one of few Baseball Ground references in the final construction. And while Gadsby does recall the club were perilously close to naming the stadium as 'The New Baseball Ground', Pride Park Stadium was the final decision.

With the squad travelling down to oversee progress when not performing minor miracles at grounds up and down the country, it was at the moment that the turf was sown in May 1997 that the realisation officially began to set in. It left psychologist Bill Beswick with a panicking Jim Smith to deal with: 'We were at Raynesway and Jimmy said, "Come and get in the car, come with me. They've laid the turf at Pride Park, I wanna go and see it." So we got into his old Jag, went to Pride Park and it was just being completed. We walked on the turf, and he said, after about five minutes of looking at this turf, "Fuck me Billy, we're gonna have to pass." He went back to Raynesway – because at the Baseball Ground nobody ever passed the ball because there was too much mud – and Jim was shouting, "Pass the ball, pass the ball!" Darryl Powell said, "Gaffer, we've not passed it for years."'

Coach Steve Round recalls the session as a whole: 'We were quite worried actually about leaving the Baseball Ground which was a really tight, tense, intimidating place with an average pitch which literally would level the playing field. I'll never forget we were training on the pitch and it was right towards the end of the season, and we were moving into Pride Park that following year. And I think we had one game left, and we decided that the game plan in this game was defending a little bit deeper, hit this team on the break, go a bit more direct, just because of how they set up. We would use Paulo Wanchope a little bit more. So we were working at the Baseball Ground, and the session was on working deep and transitions into a fast attack, countering and penetrating, a few diagonals for Wanchope and Sturridge who would play a bit wider. And Jim said, "Look, I can't make the start of the session because I've got to go to Pride Park and look at them laying the pitch, they want to check the dimensions."

'So he's not back for training, we start it and start the game plan, Steve [McClaren] is coaching and I'm watching at the back. He comes running on to the pitch, Jim, and he stops the session and pulls them all together and says, "You can forget this long ball, I've just seen this pitch at Pride Park. It's the most beautiful pitch you have ever seen, from now on we are going to pass, pass, pass. We are moving into this new stadium and we have got to up our game, up our style, change the way we do things. We are going to be part of something special." So he had a bit of humour in there with a really strong message. And it was inspirational to move to that stadium, but there were issues and we did have worries about certain things, like anybody does when they move to a new environment, but it was a move that the club needed.

'It had the wow factor.,' contunues Round 'We had been up to look at Middlesbrough's, which was a very similar design, and I remember Jim coming back and saying, "I think we can do better. We can improve this." He got a meeting with the architect that afternoon, but when we walked into Pride Park [for the first time] it was magic really. You could feel that the club was moving forward and moving in the right direction. It was sad to see the Baseball Ground [go] because of all of the history and tradition, and what you felt it had been for the club over the years, but we needed to step forward and to take a move towards the future and this was it.'

It would become a reason for many a sleepless night for Round and the rest of the staff. For decades, Rams sides had been accustomed to working in spite of their Baseball Ground surface, more reminiscent of a monster truck arena than a football one. Ironically, monster trucks did come to Pride Park in 2011, but then so did the Brazil national team a few months earlier, so the two counteract each other.

For the surface, they'd call upon Mark Robinson, assistant groundsman at Sheffield Wednesday, who would move to take senior leadership on Pride Park's grass: 'My next-door neighbour was a Derby fan, who spoke about how they were building this new stadium and said, "Why don't you go for the head groundsman job there?" So I did, thankfully, and I was up at the Sheffield Wednesday training ground one day when David Pleat, the manager, came out and said, "Have you applied for a job at Derby? I've just had Jim Smith on the phone asking about you, so I think you might have a good chance." I started in the June as Pride Park was opening.'

Robinson would oversee the creation of a playing surface the likes of which the BBG would never have seen. Utilising five different rye grass seeds meant the grass would not be damaged altogether should it succumb to any issues. Though he took his learnings from his own experiences and training, he'd also be supported by those of Andy Croft, who had worked his way up to be assistant groundsman and spent too many weekdays to count desperately trying to turn the Baseball Ground into a playable condition.

Croft said, 'You were just fighting a losing battle. I started in '91 and the renovations back then were really basic. It was a scarify spike, 100 tonnes of sand and seeding, job done. Renovations these days have the whole pitch ripped up and everything. You start from scratch every year. But it was a really, really old pitch and if you actually sat in the home changing room you could see the pavement outside and you could see people's feet and ankles from the windows. The actual pitch sat lower than street level on Shaftesbury Street, so the water couldn't even get away from the pitch. It was knackered and it had been knackered for years, and there were stories from the previous groundsman about how he'd put plastic cups in the drains to stop the water going away and to stop the opposition playing football. There were all sorts of stories.'

The ground staff duo would need to balance three areas together by the time Pride Park opened, with Raynesway's boggy surface and the Baseball Ground's now reserve team base testing their limits. 'It changed massively,' continues Croft. 'It took me out of being almost a semi-professional groundsman to being proper, this is professional. You've got something to work with, but before you could do nothing with it. Mark Robinson came from Sheffield Wednesday when the stadium opened and he was head groundsman before me, but he brought in loads of practices that we would never think to do. He played a big role in educating us on what we should and shouldn't be doing.'

While considering the new focus on more possession styles of play on the carpet of a pitch, there was also one potential negative which had everyone a little concerned. For the benefits that would come in moving stadium, a major worry was the loss of the intimidation factor that was apparent at the BBG. No longer would fans be contained in compact spaces, and no more would they be within touching distance of the players. For a stadium which had built a necessary hostile atmosphere for visiting teams, it posed a worry.

One such worry came in the mind of supporters, including Ross Lowe: 'The season I was in the Popside, I remember Notts County had this awful tartan strip and a guy in the crowd shouting to the guy taking a throw-in, he shouted, "What the fuck are you wearing?" and the guy with the ball just turned round and went "dunno". A woman in one game, I remember a guy went to take a throw and she just got her umbrella and poked him up the arse with it, because she could. There is no way you could do that at Pride Park!'

Even the great Igor was wary of what could be lost between stadiums, saying, 'Before going there we were having pre-season somewhere. We had to do a test before going to Pride Park to find out what the most important thing was for us that season. I remember my answer was adapting as soon as possible and making it our home. I knew how big a challenge that was going to be because playing at the Baseball Ground and enjoying that atmosphere, that feeling there, it was going to be different. We were going to a proper stadium which might have just made us feel like we were playing an away game. You need to get used to it because it's a new home. You need to learn how to feel good at that ground because everything is different now.'

Therefore, with the squad themselves wary of losing that fear factor that the Baseball Ground contained so well, it was the task of Bill Beswick to mentally prepare the players for making Pride Park their new home in their own mind: 'I had time in my job to do the research about previous occasions when it had happened to other clubs and the lessons. The Baseball Ground had been very traditional, evocative and there was a lot of love for the Baseball Ground. I knew the players and the staff to some extent would be intimidated, so I ran a series before we moved in of day visits where they would get things like a questionnaire. They would arrive in reception at Pride Park and get a list of questions. Where is the creche? Where is the press room? Where is this and that? And they would have to tour the stadium and find these things. And slowly we made it home. We went to practice there a lot more. We started to move practice to one day a week, two days, three days. We did a very good job of making it feel like home, and some of the foreign players just said they thought it was marvellous because the Baseball Ground was a bit ... really? But we made that move very well and everybody adapted to it very well.'

Above all else, the move of stadium was to lead Derby into the 21st century. When Jim Smith was appointed, members of staff such as Marian McMinn and Diane Wootton were working from typewriters as the club hadn't purchased computers. Marian remembers 'rats behind the wall in our office and in the cupboards' while Diane only recalls dark corridors in the depths of the ground. Pride Park was in a different world though. 'There was a sadness about leaving the Baseball Ground,' says Wootton, 'because we'd had good times there. But then when you went there to Pride Park and we had a whole influx of new staff with different roles, [whereas] there were only eight of us at the Baseball Ground and we did everything. If we got through to a big cup game, my husband would have to come and help in the ticket office. He'd be answering the phones, and he was a policeman really, but he was roped in.'

From a skeleton staff at one stadium, suddenly Derby County as a company would grow beyond belief and become a seven-day-a-week operation. Catering would increase, the club shop was to become a focal point of income and events for businesses would be made available. It was a stadium fit for royalty.

* * *

Unfortunately, Queen Elizabeth II was unable for comment as part of this book. If she had had been, she would probably have been doing the foreword. I jest, as she wasn't approached for this. Much like she wasn't approached to open Pride Park Stadium, yet she did end up doing just that.

'To put it in easy terms, the Queen would never come and visit us and at Pride Park she came and rode in an open top car with Jim and did a lap of honour. That's how big it was,' Steve McClaren puts it bluntly. Whether you're reading this as a royalist or not, and whether you were one in 1997, the question you will have is the same: why did the Queen open Pride Park?

Even she would be left mystified when delivering an answer. Because Her Majesty had never before and never since opened a football stadium. Her Derby experience was her only one. Which either means she knew she couldn't possibly better it, or it was more than enough. We'll go with the former.

When planning a stadium opening, it was Gadsby who would lead on the operations for a royal seal of approval: 'The Lord Lieutenant came to see me one day and said, "The Queen would like to open the stadium." We would have wanted a royal and we went to him; he said he'd find someone, maybe Prince Charles. But for whatever reason, the Queen came.'

Already set to visit the city in July 1997, Queen Elizabeth II's organisers were looking to pin a major event to her day in Derbyshire, and the opening of the stadium seemed as good an opportunity as any. Leaving Gadsby to ensure the stadium would be completed in time, the ask was then on Loring and his team to plan a day which would be fit for her arrival.

But this was the 1990s, and the '90s was a different time. In 1997 alone – the year of the opening – Britpop was raging its way through the UK singles charts with Blur and Oasis battling it out. Yet you also had 'Barbie Girl' and the Teletubbies hitting number one. But amid these four titans of music, they couldn't hold a candle to an international force that had just cracked America: the Spice Girls.

Derby had hit the motherload in gaining the agreement of Her Majesty to open the stadium, but seemingly they felt that maybe they needed something else. Would she sell out 30,000 seats for the opening? How would she get the crowd popping? It had been years since 'Bohemian Rhapsody' (apologies). What the club decided they would need was pop music's biggest name.

Unfortunately, they couldn't get them, so they settled for a lookalike tribute band from Nottingham and a parade of seven-foot-tall Disney characters. Looking back at 1997 seems a lifetime ago in both time and culture, but Derby's choice to pair royalty with youth-focused entertainment would provide a prolonged day of entertainment and historical value.

'I remember asking Peter Gadsby, "Well who have we got to open the stadium then?"' remembers Marian McMinn. 'So I was guessing and then it was announced as the Queen and flipping heck, she's quite high up. We had Jeanette in who still works there, and she was in charge of sorting everything out for when the Queen came from the special toilet paper to what sort of tea and coffee, the list of things you've got to do.'

Led out by Lionel Pickering following the first glimpse of the players in the stadium, the royal visit would receive the first of many large roars from Rams supporters over the years. With a crowd made up of fans and 10,000 local schoolchildren, the morning as a whole ran into the early afternoon as a collection of entertainment turned the day into one that continues to be spoken about 25 years later. It wasn't without a hitch though.

First, Jim Smith and Prince Philip were left alone together. Not breaking protocol by any means, more of a worry in terms of what the two would be conversing about. As Smith recalled in *It's Only a Game*, 'Her Majesty did not say a lot but her husband was very chatty. "You have a lot of foreign players here. You obviously like them a lot." I continued to point people out to the Duke, among them a group of our young apprentices. Quick as a flash he retorted, "Well they haven't got much hope here with all these foreigners, have they?"'

Secondly, Pickering left the Queen alone, a major unbreakable rule. The chairman had momentarily forgotten his duties and left his guest to converse with members of the 1946 FA Cup-winning squad. In his absence, Gadsby would take up position of introducing her to the current players. Only upon taking position, Gadsby was presented with one of his players who he didn't recognise, the newly signed Jonathan Hunt. 'I almost got in deeper trouble as the next player in line was Mauricio Solís and I would have struggled with his name too, but by that time Lionel and Jimmy had caught up again,' he remembers.

Thirdly, although preparations had been put in place, the first members of the squad offered their hand. It resulted in Her Majesty needing to shake the hands of every single member of the playing squad, who were on the field in the 1997/98 kit. But they were minor details in a day which was more about the individuals of the city than anything else.

Kerry Ganly, then a teenager, was one of those individuals who the day had a lasting impression on: 'I've got the photo in front of me and it is bringing back memories. The club invited lots of local schoolchildren in Derby and Derbyshire and my mum was a cleaner, and still is, for Ripley Junior School. Being a Derby County family, she was asked for people to chaperone so me and my mum went to look after all the schoolchildren. There were a couple of double-decker buses that the school had hired out for the day, it was a really big occasion, lots of buzz around the city and the county.

'We made our way with hundreds of other buses into Pride Park, walked down the stadium and you could hear all the cheering going on. You had the Spice Girls who were so big, their tribute act with a flyover and we sat in the North Stand with all the kids, and it was just a real carnival atmosphere. There were local football clubs paraded around the pitch, there were lots of Toyota Corollas being driven around the Pride Park pitch, you had Jim Bullions and Reg Harrison with the FA Cup and then the Queen and Prince Philip. She wore all yellow and looked beautiful and it was just a really happy day.'

The day was memorable too for another young supporter, Kelly Dreuitt: 'When Pride Park was built, my dad popped down one day to renew the season tickets and, fortunately for him, he knew one of the stewards so he basically went in the ground and picked his seats. He saw his mate and he said, "Oh it's open, come with me, I've got a pass." So he went and picked our seats and we've sat there ever since! My dad never believed it until he actually went into the stadium and he couldn't believe he'd actually watch football there. You couldn't believe it was going to happen until you had your season ticket there for the first match. Even then we felt like we shouldn't really be there.

'[The first time] would have been the opening. It was so noisy that it was unbelievable. The concourse was massive compared to the Baseball Ground [an amend specifically requested by Pickering], you would go through these massive turnstiles, then walking up the steps and walking in, it was just amazing. A massive beautiful green pitch which the Baseball Ground never had and it was just ginormous. It felt like Wembley. And I was 21 that day! I was in my first year as a student nurse and it should have been my last day of the first year, and I had my 21st party that night, so I had to pull a few strings with my tutors to get the day off because I should have been at college. But my personal mentor was a friend, so he let me go.

'I think there were a group of us because we sit with some friends at the match and my best friend came with us. She came with it being my 21st birthday, she bought me a brick so I have one of those bricks outside Pride Park where we go in, which is by pure fluke. She showed me where it was going, although they weren't laid out by that time I don't think. She gave me the certificate and everything, and she said, "Oh, you're gonna be at Pride Park forever!" Then I had my party that night, so it was a big celebration all day really. Seeing the Queen and the Duke of Edinburgh, at 21 I didn't properly appreciate it at the time but, thinking back, it really was a great day and I had the Queen there for my birthday!'

And while it was a day for celebration, the opening of Pride Park also provided context as to what being a supporter is about at the heart of football fandom. As important as the sporting side is, take away the people around you and you are left with little of the pleasure a Saturday afternoon can bring. It's a message Ross Lowe is quick to state when thinking back to that day: 'That summer of '97, my mum and dad broke up. My dad was my absolute hero growing up, we had a season ticket at the Baseball Ground for nine years, we were totally Derby County through and through, and I fell out with my dad when he left my mum. For the opening day at Pride Park, [he] took me and my sister and it was the first time I'd seen him since he left. The only thing we would talk about would be Derby County. We'd get really animated about it, but as soon as we finished talking about Derby, there would be nothing else to talk about.

'It was tricky because my sister was still making a real effort with my dad and it had hit her quite hard, but I was determined just to enjoy this day because I knew it was historic. We just went into default of there being this elephant in the car, but we'll talk our way around it with Derby County, and we both knew that was the safe ground. Talking about the side, the new Puma kit, what our hopes were for the team, Christian Dailly, Robin Van Der Laan and the fact the Queen was going to be there. Maybe that day in a way was the first steppingstone if you like. Every step we took we came back closer. Six years later, he died of cancer in the Nightingale opposite the DRI. It was the start of building that back together, so by the time he passed away, I was able to tell him how much I loved him, and he told me how proud he was of me. Even when he was tanked up on morphine, we were talking about the fact [Brazilian striker] Junior had signed and had scored the week before. It was the still the thing we went to. Derby County holds everything together.

'It's this indelible thing that Derby County has on me that is very much connected to my dad. As frustrated as I get with Derby, it's in my heart and I love them. When it can hold a family together when everything else is going wrong, that's powerful.'

* * *

At the time of publication, Derby County have made Pride Park their home for the past 25 years. Largely unchanged as a stadium, the area around has vastly grown. The area of Pride Park houses a wide range of businesses, evolving from a wasteland to the epicentre of the city. Over one bridge you have the Wyvern retail park and a series of fast-food restaurants. Directly across from the West Stand you have car garages and a newly opened service area. Towards the south-west corner, the unmistakeable curves of the Derby Arena. It's an area which has grown year on year, with the ground acting as a central hub for all around it.

Derby today is a modern club, largely due to the stadium. It's worth sparing a second to consider just how modern they would be if they had gone ahead with their initial plans to just adapt the Baseball Ground. Because for all of the trauma that they have endured since their move to the stadium (record points lows, administration, the threat of liquidation), life at Pride Park has been progressive.

One of the main concerns for supporters ahead of the move was how that Baseball Ground atmosphere would be recaptured and, put in layman's terms, it hasn't been. But for what Pride Park lacks from the BBG, it has made up for it in multiple other ways. Had Pickering and the board opted to go forward with their plans to redevelop, there still would have been a likelihood that the days of the stadium remained numbered. And had they gone ahead, would it even have been the same stadium at all?

Today there is little indication on the site of the old home that league championships were won there, or that it was the location of the city's heart. A solitary statue is the only remnant, and only the stronger memories recall that walk down Shaftesbury Street. It's not to say that it is forgotten though; far from it. And that is why the biggest move in the history of the club evoked such powerful emotions then – and why it still does now – as the club faced up to life in pastures new.

Rams fan Dan Walls was one of the thousands over the years to set foot inside the Baseball Ground, his first footballing memories coming at the Rams' former home: 'I remember my first memory of it being the atmosphere, [which was] something else. It's loud in the South Stand now but the Baseball Ground was crazy and I remember the song, "We Are Derby, Super Derby", and it seemed to go on for 20, 25 minutes. It just felt forever. The whole crowd singing it was just unreal. And just being so close to the pitch, players would come over to take a corner and you could literally touch them. It was surreal to see your heroes that close, especially when you're in the Premier League days and seeing some of those players.'

The early days as McClaren and Smith adjust to their new surroundings – Image by Andy Ellis

The duo who sparked it all.

The Man. The Moment.

Robin Van Der Laan and Dean Sturridge pictured with fan (was how Derby Telegraph *captioned this back in '96).*

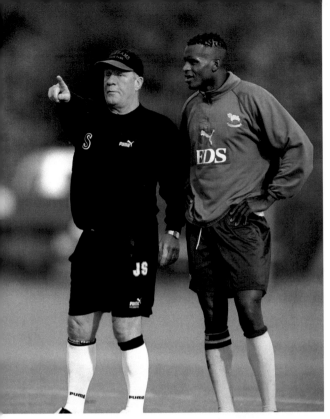

Jim Smith with cult hero Darryl Powell. Prada shoes not pictured.

Who's the real leader? Smith was the authoritarian off the field, but a suited Igor Štimac would not be afraid to put team-mates in their place.

The intimidation factor of the Baseball Ground would be a huge loss.

But they had the excitement of Paulo to come. Here he'd just done the greatest thing in human history.

A proud day for a proud Derbyshire man as Pride Park opens.

Before darkness descended – Image by Andy Ellis

An inspiring duo, Steve McClaren and Bill Beswick took their philosophy to the highest point in English football.

The Bandit and The Maestro.

Where the magic happened. Prozone, bowling greens and ingenuity at Ramarena.

The huddle. What is now commonplace in football began with Derby County.

Rare shot of Taribo West not praying, being in Milan or wearing a trenchcoat. When he played though, he transformed Derby.

The last big addition.

The closeness would be missed, with supporters and coaching staff wary of losing the intimidation factor which the Baseball Ground and so many older stadiums boasted. Ross Lowe's tale of the supporter with the umbrella could be told by countless fans from over the decades. And the fact that Derby County had to find a new way to adapt to a carpet of a pitch would be daunting too. But the nostalgia was the sticking point for most as to why the move would be so feared. It represented a change for the city, and a cutting of the ties on what generations of family members would have in common. No longer would Derby County play at a stadium which boasted former league champions; it was a new beginning that took significant getting used to.

The same could be said for Jim Smith and his squad when faced with the reality of a club evolution, but most of the squad embraced what was to come, not least Chris Powell: 'It was new because the infrastructure wasn't there like there is now. There was just this one basic road in and road out and there was always talk there might be a training ground to there, but eventually they bought Moor Farm and have a brilliant training facility now. We had a pitch and a half and he [Smith] just felt what we needed to do was train there a lot initially, which was right because we needed to make it home. We knew that almost double the fans we had at the BBG was another thing we had to take on board.

'"Just make sure we get everyone on side," Jim said and [we] really mucked in. He did some things in the local paper because I'm not too sure websites were up and running then, but we did make it home and the fans embraced it. The first year you always miss your old ground and your old haunts and pubs, but the fans knew it was long overdue. In many ways we were quite fortunate we were one of the new clubs with the new style of ground, and it was looked upon as forward-thinking. And you know, we embraced it. Whether you're a young British player signing or a foreign player, you come to a new stadium and that can sell it for you.'

While nostalgia is set for life, former Rams executive Don Amott puts a rational thought together: 'It was our home. And all the atmosphere, it was good at the Baseball Ground. It was where you went with all the terraced homes you walk past, on a Wednesday night the fog would come over the Ley Stand and I was quite sad when they decided to move, and I was in the majority. But when you did move and I remember going to the first game against Wimbledon, I thought, "Bloody hell, this is brilliant." I don't think anybody likes change and, if you speak to supporters my age now, they will say they didn't want to move but it was brilliant. We all loved the Baseball Ground because it was all close knit, you had the Normo [Normanton] End and Ossie [Osmaston] End and all that. But if you had the chance would you go back? No.'

And that was the clincher. For the talk which still continues today, Derby County immediately made their new house a home with a long unbeaten run settling the nerves early into the 1997/98 campaign. And while the floodlights at the BBG could still be seen from the highest seats at Pride Park, the yearning to return dissipated as Smith and his squad continued to achieve. It was the perfect antidote to the biggest transition the club would ever have to face.

The move wouldn't necessarily signal the end of the love affair with DE23, with a new generation of youth players plying their trade in reserve games at the stadium which remained in operation for a few more years, albeit in a state of disrepair. A young Malcolm Christie would begin his Derby venture there, recalling, 'I didn't even know the Baseball Ground still existed. But we did a pattern of play there, so I thought it was just our normal training facility now! Inside was a bit more old school with the wooden panelling and everything in the back areas, but it was good to use that as a facility to go and take ourselves away from the Ramarena and use a neutral sort of area where we could just lock up. It was sad that it had to be knocked down, but the fans remember it. Chris Riggott used to tell me how he would go in the stands and watch the matches when he was younger.'

The first team would also share training responsibilities between Raynesway and the BBG, utilising the full-length pitch and an improved surface to emulate matchday situations. But that run would be fleeting though, and with the long-discussed development of the new training facility in 2003, the bulldozers moved in.

The club provided supporters with a chance to bid to play in the final match there, a farewell for a handful of fans who had grown up in this second home. George Glover remembers the day fondly, including going down in the history books as the final goalscorer in the stadium: 'There was this advertising and media campaign that there would be the last game at the Baseball Ground, which was a good few years after Derby had played Arsenal. So they put it out there to bid online and the money would go to charity. I happened to bid £50 or £60 to play left midfield in the second half for the team in black or something like that. So we got to the ground, got changed and I think there were teams managed by Roger Davies and Roy McFarland.

'After about 20, 25 minutes I was absolutely shattered, but we were 5-1 up. And by sheer luck I was on my right foot, so I faked a shot and fooled the defender who brought me down. So I took it [the penalty] and scored, somebody else scored and somebody else, and with about 15 minutes to go I found myself up front, pointed where I wanted it, took a touch and clipped it into the nice big goal at the Normanton End.' Glover is even referenced in the Wikipedia page for the ground, a constant reminder of what £60 can get you.

And while Glover could play on the pitch, another fan was presented with a rare opportunity to have the stadium to himself merely days before it became a patch of land. Stephen Newman's dad owned the contract to demolish the ground, and it opened up the opportunity for him to tour every area of the place he had spent many happy Saturday afternoons over several decades. 'You don't realise how much they needed to move; it was a wreck,' he bluntly puts it. 'You walk round and there was water coming down the walls, I went in Brian Clough's old office which I don't think had improved since the '60s. The players' lounge looked like the local labour club in there, everything was like that. The changing rooms were ... rubbish. The local school changing rooms would have been better, then they had the big baths. I used to play rugby for Derby and we had these big communal baths we used to sit in, which they had. And then there were still bits of clothes around. I took out a few pictures which were just lying about. A goalkeeper shirt which was just lying there. The press box was actually quite OK, but I didn't realise overall what a tip it was. I know that they were knocking it down but I didn't realise just how bad it was.'

But for the criticisms, Newman found himself in his element as he got an opportunity few others ever would have done: 'I couldn't wait when my dad said I could have a look around. It was a boyhood dream. I could go wherever I wanted to, but the best room was the chairman's office. The manager room was my favourite, but it was crap. I'd want something a bit better. These are football men though, it's the pitch they were interested in. Paintings were on the wall, I've still got a couple. It was just ... could you imagine being allowed to walk around Buckingham Palace? It was a bit like that because the BBG was a bit like a shrine for us. To see all these things was quite incredible. I'd walk into the dressing room and you'd have the board on the wall where they'd put their tactics and you could actually feel who has been in there. Charlie George, [Kevin] Hector, all of those. And also the players from the opposition who had been in there; it was quite emotional and I didn't want to leave. I went to the manager's office three or four different times. I only thought of Brian Clough being sat there, his sarcastic self.'

By the time this book is published, the Baseball Ground will have been gone for almost 20 years, and it's a quarter of a century since the last time first-team football was played there. And though it doesn't exist in a physical form, Derby County will forever continue to be closely linked with their former home. Not least because most of the days at Pride Park so far have paled in comparison to the glorious 1970s.

Not all at Pride Park has been underwhelming though, and as the Rams made the switch from home to home, their first years in DE24 threatened the dawning of a new era for the club under the Bald Eagle.

8

A PROFESSIONAL ZONE

THE A5111 in Derby is known for a few things to locals. A base of Rolls-Royce for one, the dual carriageway is a stretch of road which also boasts easy access to the A52 and the M1. It's a motorist's paradise and the recent addition of a pub and a McDonald's on the roundabout leading north only solidifies it as one of the ultimate roads in the centre of Derby. Put down the *2022 AA Roadmap* though, because the serenity of a national speed limit road linking Spondon and Alvaston is well and truly over. Because along this road, in the 1990s, it was a footballing fast lane.

You'll be relieved to read that the car-based analogies end there, because I drive an automatic Corsa and don't really know anything about motor vehicles. But in a convoluted way, it was along the A5111 that football, and not Midlands football or British football, but *global* football, took a leap into a new era. Jim Smith's Derby County side were genuine world leaders in football thanks to three key innovations. We've done fitness and psychology, now it's time for performance analysis.

* * *

While the general rules of the sport are the same as they were 25 years ago, almost everything around the actual premise of kicking a ball into a relatively big goal has changed. Finances have made the game indistinguishable from the one of the 1990s, as has increased media coverage, though that has been brought about due to the former. Atmosphere around football stadiums is largely different, with the '90s lad culture largely reduced into a sport focused around family attendance. These are all off-field changes which don't impact the actual professionals, but on the pitch there are significant differences too. The game is played as much away from 90 minutes on a Saturday as it is on it, statistical analysis focused upon at every club by armies of performance analysts. It's a relatively new phenomenon in the grand scheme of the game, and understandably perception is based around the larger clubs integrating it into their game plan early on; which they did.

But it didn't begin with a Manchester United or a Liverpool. Not even an Arsenal side who under Arsène Wenger were perceived as the driving force behind the changing face of the English game. The integration of performance analysis began on the A5111 with a man whose name was only ever suitable to take him to one place. 'My background is that I worked for a large international company called Mars,' begins Ramm Mylvaganam, the brainchild and inventor of performance analysis in British sport. 'My background was as a business development manager, and I helped set up Mars businesses in several places around the world. Japan, Latin America, several places in Asia. But I hit what you would call the proverbial glass ceiling and decided to leave in 1996 and I was looking for an opportunity to do something else – I didn't know what it was. All I knew was I didn't want to sell chocolates anymore.'

Mylvaganam isn't a name you'll recognise when it comes to the global changes behind the sport. Has name hasn't been attributed to anything like a Jean-Marc Bosman has been, because he isn't one for the limelight. That's probably why he ended up at Derby's Raynesway in the first place. During the course of the mid-1990s, though, Mylvaganam founded Prozone, the performance analysis programme which would go on to change the entire makeup of football clubs across the world. The first team to use an element of Prozone in 1996 was Derby County Football Club.

Ramm said, 'One of the projects that I was asked to look at first were therapeutic chairs. They were developed by a professor in Finland, and they used a soundwave to tone your muscles. What they wanted to do was to sell these chairs in volume, so I said, "Look, this is a whole new concept. The only way that you are going to be able to do this sensibly is if you can show that people who are famous are using it and getting the benefit out of it. And the guys who seem to break down quite often are elite athletes. So, if there is a way we can get elite athletes using it regularly and getting a benefit from it, that will help with sales of these chairs."

'According to the professor in Finland, the worst thing that happens with people is they have soft-tissue injury and you tweak a muscle, tweak a tendon. That usually happens because you're not finely tuned. So what is a travesty is you spend all this time finding the right player, training him, developing them into an elite athlete. But the guy tweaks a muscle from over- or under-training. If somebody tackles and breaks a leg, there is nothing you can do. It's a throwaway injury, just sod's law. Effectively what this professor had done is worked to show that using sound therapy as opposed to traditional massage, which uses pressure points, soundwaves penetrate the skin and went through the body to improve the flow of nutrients to the damaged parts. Your body heals itself by providing nutrients to the damaged parts. If you can get the veins to supply the right nutrients more efficiently, it will heal better; that was the theory.'

Prozone would start as an idea not built around performance analysis though, more about maximising the performers' fitness themselves. That was the basis of what Mylvaganam first presented to the coaches at Raynesway. 'I met Jim Smith and Steve McClaren through a football agent who I used to play golf with and presented this case to them, saying, "Would you be interested in trialling?" because they'd just been promoted to the Premiership. I said, "This is what we've got, do you guys want to give it a try?" They had a squad of 25 people, what they should do is buy 25 chairs from us and it would cost an arm and a leg. "You are currently training in a glorified garden shed, there is no room to put it in so you'll need to build a building to put this bloody thing in." And the board was really enthused with it; they couldn't throw enough money at me,' he says with a grin before adding, 'Or like hell they were, they said, "Bugger off!" very politely. So, I said, "Look, I think there is value in this. What happens if we invested in installing? What you don't have now is a room where you can talk to the players sensibly."'

Working with limited space at the 'glorified garden shed', as he calls what became the Ramarena, Mylvaganam became serious about his project and the impact it could have on this newly promoted Premier League club. It was he who worked with Portakabin, funding the centre himself for the design and installation of a new temporary building on the training ground site, one which would factor in the addition of 25 luxury chairs. A prototype would be developed, but the club were reluctant to invest in something without proven pedigree in the game, not offering a fee to Mylvaganam. 'Let's do it,' he told the coaching staff, 'but one condition: you guys have to use this room every day. You've got a squad of 25 people so I'm going to install 25 chairs, this is going to be your war room. Jim and Steve, you guys are going to do all the presentations and your tactical stuff, whatever you want to talk to the players about, we'll have a presentation screen.'

Ramm added, 'There would be all kinds of gimmicks in there. We set up a computer, I taught Steve and Bill Beswick how to do PowerPoint presentations, Bill would come and give me some topics and I'd put a presentation together for him. So we had it all conceived as this all-encompassing idea. And it was going to cost us X thousand pounds to build this room, because Portakabin would design the room, the outside of it, then we built everything inside as we wanted. We connected all of the chairs into a computer, and you could manage the treatment of each chair separately. Someone would have a hamstring issue and you would have a different treatment to a guy with a back or shoulder issue, and we called it our Tardis. There was this garden shed

[Ramarena] and then there was this Prozone room, which was computers, networks, PowerPoints, screens, access to videos where players would lie there and watch them. All I wanted was for them to experience the room and use it as much as they could. The more you used it, the better they got; that was the concept.' But there would be a financial incentive to at least recoup some money – any player who failed to make it to the room by 10.30am would be fined £50 that would go directly back to Ramm.

'Some people don't realise exactly how Prozone came about,' mentions Chris Powell, 'but we were introduced to it at Raynesway where we would sit in these vibrating chairs after training and it was meant to help us recover and help us prepare for future training sessions. And then what happened was we started to see our stats from games on the screen. And I think it was short for Professional Zone or something, and it got shortened. But we were the prototype, we were guinea pigs, but we loved it because no one was doing that and looking into player stats, no one was looking into these vibrating chairs. We used to fall asleep because they said it was good for us.'

His defensive colleague Gary Rowett adds, 'We were one of the first clubs in the country to have Prozone; we had the big room with the massage chairs, and you'd sit in front of the screen, and they'd show clips and show stuff, we had all the stats and it was all new to us but very, very forward-thinking. There were so many things that we did in terms of our preparation that were ahead of the game.' Players would dedicate more hours to Raynesway, including Igor Štimac, who would spend an hour there prior to home matches.

The Prozone chairs, though an early integration into what football would become, did have their cons though, as forward Lee Morris, who joined in 1999 from Sheffield United, remembers. 'They'd have the massage chairs on the go, which were really nice and relaxing, but at the same time they would be trying to do tactical meetings with it on the big screen. You'd be sat there and the low whirring noise of the chairs, 30 chairs on the go, they'd be sending you to sleep. But at the same time they'd be trying to have this serious tactical meeting and you'd be nodding off in the middle of it. It was like, a well-thought-out room but having the massage chairs there as a meeting room, you do it before without the chairs and then go to sleep, but they were trying to do too much with it. But I remember thinking at the time it was a space-age kind of thing that not many other people had.'

For Steve Round, then the reserve-team coach, he too was not entirely sold on the chairs at the time but could see opportunity: 'Players always moan about having too many meetings, but that's all part of it and they loved it. We had the chairs in and I wasn't too taken on board. I thought maybe that was a bit gimmicky, but it did give us a room where players could sit down, feel like they were given some sort of recovery from these chairs, and it gave us an opportunity while they were doing that to show video, present stats, talk to them about performance, and that room itself was a real plus.'

Ultimately, it was a first step into what Ramm and his team could offer, and though the creation recouped relatively little financially for him, it provided a trial base for the area of behind-the-scenes development he truly wanted to delve into next.

* * *

Towards the dusk of our Teams chat in mid-2021, Mylvaganam trawled through his computer hard drive, intent on showing a clip from his formative years at Derby. To the untrained and unfamiliar eye, it looks simply like what he serves up is a grainy footage of 1990s footballers. And it is. It screams '90s, in fact. Transitions with an element of pre-Adobe sci-fi to them, a subtle techno backdrop, a few boyband-esque curtain haircuts. The VisionRams – the club's in-house media production arm of the time – clip begins with media man Damon Parkin outside what looks like an old makeshift school mobile facility. Up three short steps and there on the door is a small sticker simply saying Prozone. 'I'm not a scientist and I don't know the ins and outs,' explains Steve

McClaren to camera, 'but we've only had about one or two strains, which is remarkable. It's been a great benefit in our build-up to games. And the other way we use it is as a meeting room. We have a big screen at the front where we can put videos on, MTV or music. And it's a great way of presenting things to the players in a professional manner. And it's very useful for me in analysis of games, of individual performances, of feedback to the players. Feedback is the breakfast of champions.'

Phase one of Prozone was the chairs, but both Mylvaganam and Derby County's coaching staff were looking for something more than a place to relax. In an article with The Athletic's Phil Hay in 2020, the Sri-Lankan born Mylvaganam remarked that football was 'late to wake up to data. Other industries used it and understood the value of it, but football was new to it.' And this focus on data, not on recovery, was what would become the next focus in the Portakabin.

Football in the 21st century is played more off the field than on, at least at an elite level. Visit Manchester United's Carrington or Arsenal's London Colney and you'll encounter a performance analysis team which would be roughly the same size as an entire backroom staff of the 1990s. Life is numbers and football is no exception. Signings are based on fitness insights, positioning and so many more hidden details previously unavailable or overlooked to the human eye. It's the same for progression of youth-team players and weekly squad selections. An endless cycle of numbers that three decades ago would not have even been worthy of conversation.

Blame Derby County for bringing it into the chat. As Prozone developed as a way to sell Finnish massage chairs, the ever-curious McClaren was working behind the scenes on the type of content an assistant manager rarely would at this stage. 'What Steve used to do was to have two video recorders and a television screen,' Mylvaganam laughs. 'He was stuck in a little broom cupboard, copying interesting events from one video to another so he could then show it to the players. "Steve, how come you are spending all of your time doing this?" Steve said, "It's very simple, Ramm: I'm the only one who knows what is good and what's bad. That's my job.'"

McClaren himself recalls the process of meticulously going over individual performances with two VHS tapes: 'I remember once with Marco Gabbiadini, he got taken off and he wasn't happy, didn't agree with the decision. I was up all night and I had to go tape to tape. I tape to taped his clips of the game and the next morning I pulled him in before he was going to see Jim and just said, "Have a look." He couldn't believe that I'd done the clips, but I had to do it tape to tape. One tape with the game and the other recording. It was all, "Stop, there he is. Record it. Stop, next clip." I showed him that and, after five or six clips, he said, "Yeah I understand now why I was taken off," and it just showed me the power of coaching a player and actually showing a player what he did, and feeding back. Just like we're talking now, I'd be talking with players. "OK Marco, what did you think of that?" "Yeah I gave the ball away there." They think they are doing well, but you show them the clips and they weren't doing well. So anything that is easier than going tape to tape, and me taking all night for one player.'

Fun fact: Giles Barnes mentioned in *Pride* that Billy Davies would do something similar during the 2006/07 campaign. Davies, however, would opt to do it overnight before venturing into Moor Farm 'looking like he hadn't slept'. Performance analysts existed at this time.

With McClaren able to see the importance of individual analysis not only for his own coaching but for his squad too, he and the equally promising Steve Round would begin to exchange thoughts on their ideal scenarios. Round said, 'Initially myself and Steve McClaren were cutting videos just using reels on a VHS, editing the game and then showing the players an edited version so they didn't have to sit through an hour and a half. We showed them what was relevant, what was right, what we thought was very important to learn from for the next game.' Round, a connoisseur

173

of American sports following years in the USA, was able to see how American clubs were integrating analysis into their team sports, particularly within the NFL and NBA. Together, he and McClaren would brainstorm. And all would come together once Mylvaganam joined the conversations.

'[I said to Steve] but what would happen if I took a video and tagged all the videos for you?' Ramm adds. 'You could say "show me all the corners" and bam, it shows them. "Well that would be amazing Ramm, could you do that?" And well, I said, "I don't know but it would be better than the way you're doing it right now!" I'm an engineer by training, it was an engineering solution I was looking for. And I found a company who had done that.'

English football hadn't opened the door to many of the ideas that its European counterparts had. While AC Milan, Ajax and Juventus dominated the continental scene with distinct styles of play and cute interchanges, England was lacking. Dinosaur tactics of 4-4-2 remained the weapon of choice for around 75 per cent of the top flight, while the idea of professionalism to an English player was polar opposite to that of most Serie A, La Liga, Eredivisie and Bundesliga sides. Professionalism in England was not having too many beers the night before a game; professionalism in Italy was rarely having beer at all. Therefore, it's little surprise that Mylvaganam's first foray into the actual sporting analysis came when discovering a French company who said they could deliver the service: 'It would consist of getting a video from a game and finding a way of tracking all that was going on in that game and providing Steve with that information set. And I bought a percentage of that company for a lot of money. Unfortunately, what the company sold me was smoke and mirrors, they couldn't do it. So I then went and created a team. When these guys said they could do it I set up a business in Leeds and they came, installed the stuff at Derby County, tried to get it going but it didn't work. So I just kicked them out of the office, said bugger off, I never want you guys here anymore.

'But I knew it could be done. I then recruited a whole new team and started from scratch to develop Prozone, which we called because the name comes from Professional Zone. The idea was that in here you behave like professionals. And the rest is history I guess!'

* * *

It wasn't an immediate implementation which saw statistical performance analysis be brought into Ramarena, but the growth was quicker than at any other club in Britain. Completing the Prozone room and installing the massage chairs in the later months of the 1996/97 season, it was in 1997 that the statistics work would fully begin, before being finally mastered one year later. In that time, Jim Smith would oversee a side who would consolidate a Premier League spot before moving towards the cusp of European football. The analysis played a vital part. Comparatively, Sunderland – who finished above Smith's Rams in the 1995/96 promotion campaign – were immediately relegated, struggling to accustom to the demands of the top flight.

Fitness coach Dane Farrell was one of the many who would benefit in his day-to-day role through both the Prozone room and the analysis: 'We used it superbly well on a Monday morning after the game, or on a Sunday, where we would go into a Prozone room and look at the analysis, the players' movement, the speed, how much ground they had covered. I don't think we used it as well as we could have done though, because I didn't have the time or the technical gift for it. But I thought it was brilliant. I don't think Derby County are acknowledged enough for it.'

Though McClaren is primarily hailed as the brainpower behind the introduction of Prozone in both its forms to Raynesway, it was much more than a one-man operation. In combination with Steve Round, the two were able to work together to bring the idea on board, and the manager. McClaren said, 'Jim had heard about this Prozone initiative being the new way to analyse matches, and that's really the start of the whole analyst movement we have today. Nobody else was doing this sort of stuff, so he said, "Right Steve, I don't really understand using a laptop but I know you do. So here is an opportunity, I'm going to link you with these guys, get on with it and I want to see something in the next three months." When it was presented to him, he went, "Love it. Get on with it, do it, deliver it." And he would then support that with his own style, his own brand, his own way of doing things. The mixture of old-school and new technology worked quite well. So Prozone came along and met with us, Ramm and Barry McNeil, who was very prominent at the time. They had this idea and we latched on to it straight away, so did Steve, and it was, "Right, we can start measuring players on the pitch, put these cameras around the stadium, we can see how far and how fast they run, we can start getting the physical data, which Dane Farrell was really interested in.'"

Like all good things, it would take time to fully develop though, with Mylvaganam recalling the first version he presented to Jim Smith: 'We needed to find a way to make this data into football, so football could understand it. I still remember showing the first database to Derby and to Jim, he looked at it and said, "This is nothing like a football match I've ever seen. I don't understand it, I don't want to understand it." I was barking up the wrong tree because I was doing the classic *Hitchhiker's Guide to the Galaxy* of saying the answer is 42. There's the computer, which looks for the answer of the meaning of life, and it comes back and says it is 42. And there was a need to contextualise the analysis and convert it.

'That's when I recruited a bunch of smart sport scientists. Those guys did all the work because they understood football, they were able to convert it into information. Also, each manager needed something different. For each club we provided our own analyst. The club didn't have any, we provided our own and charged them a monthly subscription for installing the cameras, doing the analysis, giving them an analyst and helping convert it to reports they understand. It was a great business model for us because it's a recurring revenue. I think Derby and I probably instigated it.

Derby helped facilitate the process but there is a whole load of people below who did all the technology, the software guys who were smart enough, the image recognition and tracking, how to then do the mathematical transformation of what was effectively 3D data into 2D, then validate all that. It's not a question of saying someone ran 10km, prove it to me. And we had to validate all that. We got a university to validate all our datasets and all that contributed to launching the business.'

Round continues, 'At the time we didn't know really what the information meant, but we just wanted the information and thought we would put some structure to it after. And then let's try and integrate it into a strategy, and it was a trial-and-error process at the start of what was good, what didn't work, they would come to us and tell us what we would need to know from the information. What can we deliver to the players that affects their level of performance and ability? So, it was sort of a work in progress in those initial years and the product became so good that they could then sell the rights, tap it out to all the clubs and make sure everybody had that equal playing field, because initially it was very much a "let's see what we can get from it".

'You're trying to deliver high levels of information within the least amount of time, because time is so important when you're playing Saturday-Tuesday-Saturday; you've got to prepare off the Saturday what was not done so well, individual meetings, team meetings, and then you've got to flip it instantly on the Monday for the opposition analysis, this is what they do. It's about saving time and being more efficient because the more information you get, it's then about what can be accepted in the least amount of time.'

You had the Portakabin and the general analysis, but within the training ground and the stadium there was more to be developed to allow Mylvaganam's new team to get the most out of their newly developed product. He said, 'We set up around eight cameras, which would depend on the shape of the stadium. So effectively what we did was place the cameras in such a way that every part of the pitch was covered by three cameras, and then it was almost a voting system. If the first camera said it was Ryan and the third said it was Ramm, it was probably Ryan, then you stitch it all together afterwards. Now it is a lot more sophisticated but when we did it we didn't even have computers large enough to put all the data into one disk. We had eight disks, one for each camera and we couldn't transfer it over the internet because it was too expensive, so there was a biker waiting at each stadium to pick up the disks and he drove like mad to get it to our office so we could then do all the analysis. We had a horde of people in our offices, about 150 workstations and we just did games, one after the other.'

And as it was used to develop the squad, Mylvaganam was also able to show Round and the coaches how it would become beneficial in their pursuit of the next Igor. Ramm explained, 'If you are looking to recruit a forward, it is like recruiting a key operator in a company. You would have a job description, analyse all the competencies and that's what we did at Mars. I did in football what I had learnt at Mars. If you find good people, you develop a good product. If you develop a good product, you make good profit. But they lacked the ability to use data to write that job description. "This is a forward I want, so go and find me a guy who can do A, B, C and D." To be able to do that you need to be able to analyse the game and that's where the Prozone came in. It was not just tracking to see how many corners. We played in two disciplines almost. One was sports medicine because suddenly you could decide what the body was because you knew what you expected the players to do and, therefore, how do you train this guy so he doesn't break down? The other was sports science. What do you need to do to make these guys play the way you wanted to play? How do these two disciplines work together to create that elite athlete? All that couldn't have started without Prozone.'

Though the cost-free agreement of Prozone had significant plus points for the football club, Derby weren't exclusive to the option of analysis. Their agreement allowed Ramm and his team to welcome management from across the country to experience one of the cogs making the Derby County wheel turn so ferociously.

Ramm said, 'We then got agreement that we could use the Prozone room on a Friday to present to the opposition. You go back to the late '90s and football was like clockwork. Home game, away game, home game, away game. Every other week the away team came and stayed at a hotel not very far from Raynesway and I would invite the opposition coaches and the manager to come there, put some food on, couple of beers and give them an opportunity to give them a look at Derby County as Prozone. And we tried to sell it to those guys.' Such was the reluctance to accept change, not a single club that visited Raynesway took Ramm up on his offer.

Mylvaganam adds, 'The agreement with Derby was that we would use them as the beta site. We would do all the development work and they wouldn't pay us for it. They were our marketing suite, everything happened at Raynesway, which was a good mutual agreement. Even when I left, they didn't pay for us. But they would give us seats in the directors' box, after a game I would have a glass of wine with Jim, he would introduce me to various managers who came in there and it was just truly mutual.'

In time, he would have takers, some of whom would pay actual money for his services (Derby would pay a small fee for setup, but it was outside of Raynesway that Prozone would make their money). When McClaren moved in the spring of 1999 to Manchester United, the soon-to-be European champions, he did so with the idea of taking elements of what he had experienced at Derby to Alex Ferguson, beginning with Ramm himself. A 1999 *Guardian* article waxed lyrical about how McClaren had changed the face of football: 'Derby have become the first club in Britain to develop a preparation chamber for their players. Situated in a portable building, it resembles a space-age cinema with 22 Prozone seats resembling dentist chairs, facing a large screen. When operated, the beds vibrate gently and oscillate to send pulses through the players' bodies and relax muscles. They have increase [sic] flexibility by 17 per cent, and the proof of the pudding is Derby's injury list – 70 per cent better than the corresponding time last season. Before and after every training session, Derby's players have a 12-minute warm-up or warm-down with the vibrations sending whale sounds reverberating through the chamber. McClaren was the man who initiated the use of such hi-tech facilities. On site he leaves behind his own editing suite where he produced motivational films of sporting icons such as Michael Jordan, or footage of recent games to discuss tactics.'

Arsenal would follow, then Sam Allardyce became an early adopter. Within the space of around three years, Prozone had gone from sci-fi nonsense to an integral part of any elite training ground. Ramm's gamble in leaving confectionery had paid off: 'On 25 May 1999, we had two clients – Derby County and Manchester United; neither of them paid us. United said they would pay us at the end of that first season and I persuaded them to give us some money retrospectively and then onwards. I couldn't quite get them to pay three times as much for winning three trophies, but it was a thought which did cross my mind. We negotiated a contract with David Gill and then suddenly I got a call from David Dein at Arsenal saying, "Hey, we want this," and it propelled from there. Then we signed Sam Allardyce at Bolton. He was in the First Division, Sam and Phil Gartside wanted it and installed it, and then those two guys won the play-off against David Moyes' Preston to get into the Premiership, which gave us another massive boost. Then we worked with Clive Woodward and England rugby in 2000, all the way through to the World Cup and Clive dedicates nine pages in his book to us winning the World Cup!'

But though Prozone would go on to play heavy roles in trophy successes of clubs not only across Britain but across the global game too, Round reiterates that it should never be forgotten that everything started in a Portakbin, five minutes from the Wyvern: 'It was just me, Steve, Billy McEwan and Steve Taylor. But then we sort of realised the amount of information, data and visuals we were getting from it, the images, we needed someone to come in. Prozone provided us with a full-time analyst, which was a massive step forward because it gave us more time to use the information for practical application of the players, and we got a few really good guys over the course of two or three years that really put so much time and effort in. It was the birth in this country of analytical responsibility. And it is massive now.'

9

FORZA

CONSOLIDATION IN the top league. It's not a bad thing, is it? Offer it to most professional clubs across the pyramid and it's little more than a pipe dream. But Derby County under Jim Smith did not fit into the bracket of most professional clubs. Armed by an owner with a wallet designed to support only the football club he owned and with a contact book that would make Pablo Escobar raise an accompaniment of choice in appreciation, the Rams had an idea of where they wanted to be, no matter what level of optimism it reached.

It wasn't greed to aspire. It was greed to get promoted so quickly. Anything that would follow was riding on the back of the unexpected wave. And so after a steady first season, attention would immediately turn to the next stage: top half and, subsequently, a European adventure. Not too much to ask for, right?

'I remember going on a Christmas do,' laughs Gary Rowett, 'and it was fancy dress. Some of the foreign lads were wondering what the hell had happened. I remember them meeting us in the pub in fancy dress and, honestly, you should have seen some of them. Four of the foreign lads came as Teletubbies and, oh my God, it was the worst night of their life.'

For the initial influx of internationals (Igor, Asanović, Wanchope, Laursen, Willems, Poom and Solís), integration into the Derby side had the prospect of being daunting. New area, new lifestyle, new traditions and a new language would be enough to leave a nagging doubt in their head of just what they had taken on. But of the six mentioned above, almost all settled in within the space of a few weeks. Only Solís struggled, returning to Costa Rica a little over a year after joining, having found himself out of Smith's plans.

'They would still muck in,' continues Rowett. 'They might not come for drinks – or they might come for a couple – but they would muck in. They didn't have the same cultural expectations as some of the British players but it seemed to fit together really, really well and you could see it because the synergy on the pitch was really superb.'

That mucking in aspect of life at Derby was successful in considerable part due to the external factors the club had put in place: club cars, salsa music on the bus, efforts to integrate families in as well as players. And what those relatively small tweaks did presented Derby as the multicultural example of a late-20th/almost 21st century footballing side that we see across English football today.

But what Jim Smith embarked on during the summer of 1997 was one beyond just identifying up individual players from foreign lands, or promising young sensations like Wanchope. Having picked up the taste for leading British football away from the doldrums of 4-4-2, hoof ball and a terrace-wide attitude of 'bloody foreigners', Smith dared to return back to the table of greed. What followed were arguably the two most dynamic additions he would ever make.

* * *

Going back to an earlier point, the Bald Eagle trod a fine line when it came to fashion; somewhere between style icon and elderly man on Skegness beach with a handkerchief on his head is the best way of describing it. When referring to the latter, you need to picture a man who would turn up to training with Puma shorts above his belly button, with a shirt tucked in and socks past his knees. From all accounts, it was a sight to behold. But for the former, when he turned up in Milan for the coup of all coups, he could easily have taken a break from negotiations for a photo shoot in front of Duomo di Milano. Aperol Spritz at the ready for that man, please.

Dressed in his finest suit and having packed a single pair of recently purchased Prada shoes for the occasion, this wasn't any standard transfer deal that Smith was looking to pull off. He was heading to the sacred capital of European football to complete the signing of an Italian international, an AC Milan regular and a Champions League winner: Stefano Eranio. 'I remember him going to Italy to sign Eranio,' reflects Steve Round. 'Eranio was that impressed because he was wearing Prada shoes and a nice suit, and the way that he courted Eranio and convinced him to come was exceptional.'

The Italian great laughs at the notion of Smith's Prada-based persuasion, but there is no doubt that if his fashion played a part, it was what Smith could offer to Eranio that persuaded him to take a chance away from San Siro. 'It wasn't an easy choice,' begins a man roundly considered to be one of the greatest to ever wear a Derby shirt. 'When you play in the best team in the world at that moment, everything would be less about the club. The opportunity was to go to France, and to Porto and England with Derby County. I watched many times the Premier League so, for me, the football was there. In that moment, the club was planning to make the new stadium [and] to do something good. For that reason, I chose Derby. When I spoke with Jim Smith I saw a good man in front of me.'

Eranio's signing was different to the rest. Boasting eight major trophies and having starred alongside everyone from George Weah to Marco van Basten, this wasn't a bit-part player who Derby were keeping tabs on at the European giants. Eranio had made 30 appearances in the season prior to his capture. Three fewer than Roberto Baggio, six more than Edgar Davids, two of his Milan colleagues. Eranio was a heavyweight capture and like nothing Derby had ever dared to even pursue before.

He said, 'The big change was the sports centre. You're used to training in Milanello with seven pitches. And Milanello was one of the best facilities in the world. But when you are a professional footballer, you have a ball, a pitch and two goals. That is enough to play football. For me I just need a ball and one pitch, it's enough. You can't use two pitches at the same time, so [Raynesway] wasn't a problem.'

Even if he says it slightly tongue in cheek, the notion of switching the palatial Milanello for the Ramarena is only a microcosm of the changes Eranio would encounter upon arriving in Derbyshire.

'I didn't understand the words because in that time I didn't speak any English. Even when I should do an interview with the TV, I tried not to do it because my English was really very poor. And even in Italy my life was a normal life. Playing in one of the best teams in the world, I could walk in the town like a normal person, I just played football in San Siro! But in all the places where I would go in Derby, everybody would see me!'

Then you have the stadium. While ultimately a deciding factor in choosing Derby over Porto, Pride Park would be a far cry from the tower of footballing history that is San Siro: 'When I moved from Genoa to Milan in 1992, season tickets were all sold, 80,000. Every single game the stadium was [kisses fingers] full. Nobody from outside could come to watch, just season tickets. And they would help us to win any game. All opponents, they would play 11 guys all the time in their half of the pitch. Nobody could shoot once in our goal. It was just a great time because every single game we would set out to destroy what was in front of us.'

Derby would inevitably be different. And that's why as important as Eranio was as a footballing addition, the capture of a man as comfortable on the left wing as he was at right-back meant Smith was almost bringing in an additional member of his coaching staff with the Italian. Eranio would be used for multiple reasons in and out of football, and would find himself as almost the one man who Smith would never take issue with, because he saw the game from a different dimension.

Eranio would work with chef Mark Smith and fitness coach Dane Farrell to transform the diet of the players, leading on what meals would get the best out of himself and, therefore, those around him. Farrell remembers, 'Nowadays all players are professionals, have a good diet and a healthier lifestyle. When I joined, players were regularly down the pubs getting pissed the night before and it seemed to be an acceptable thing because it came from the England captain Bryan Robson who would do that and was successful with it. But one cap doesn't fit all.'

Eranio, too polite a man to ever turn down an opportunity to pass on his wisdom to those in need, would be the epitome of gentlemanly in Derbyshire. His aura, his wisdom and his naturally developed on-the-ball ability caressed the hearts of supporters, players and, in Farrell's case, even coaches: 'I met him for the first time in La Manga and from the moment I met him he was a big character and a wonderful person. A real gentleman. Footballers tend to have this mentality of turning up late, and I came from a disciplined background with the forces and that sort of attitude. But Stefano was always early, always on time, very, very respectful and knew the families. My family and Stefano's wife and children all got on well, they all bonded well together. He was just a great professional and on the field he would perform to his best ability. He would get a little frustrated that we would do things slightly different to where he had previously been, but he was a wonderful, wonderful professional. I know he got frustrated in terms of certain things, so how the team would play, the format, the plan of action. But he mucked in and always gave his best. One thing which always stood out about Stefano Eranio was he was always respectful of others, respectful of all the players and his colleagues, and his coaching staff.'

It also meant that even as Steve McClaren and Steve Round progressed, they themselves could learn from a player in the prime of his career, and it even allowed them to take a backseat on the bowling green of Raynesway.

'I tried to [coach them],' continues Eranio, 'with Štimac's help because he was speaking a little bit of Italian, so he could be a good translator for me when I started being there. And I was maybe the oldest player there with Štimac, so we were the experienced two. He was in the national team and the captain, I used to play in AC Milan where we won all there was to win. For that reason I tried to learn very quickly the style of their football. But in the same time I tried to help the boss to change something on the pitch because when you have the experience you can try to help the young players. Because the team was very young. Adjusting through the training session, when there was something from my point of view I would call straight away to Štimac and say, "Igor, please stop the game." And we would try to adjust what was wrong in that moment. The boss would then try even to help me because I think that he thought that I was a good man and, in that moment, it was important for him too to have a guy that could help the team to improve.'

Over the course of his four years at Pride Park, Eranio would find fortunes fluctuating as coaches and players eventually left. But remaining ever loyal to Smith – re-signing for an extra year at the insistence of the Bald Eagle, despite that emotional farewell at the end of the 2000/01 season, then requesting his release upon the boss's departure – Eranio struck up a connection rarely seen between player and manager. Physio and long-time friend of both, Neil Sillett saw the bond on a daily basis: 'I [think] Jim would say that Paul Walsh [at Portsmouth] and Eranio were his two best signings. Eranio was unbelievable. I could not believe how good he was. I just had never seen anyone do what he was doing. He went around the gym when I had six injured lads doing a session inside in the old gym at Raynesway, and he went around the whole gym without dropping the ball, bouncing it off the wall. Sometimes 20 yards away and it still wouldn't drop. I just sat the six lads down. There's videos of him now when he came back a couple of years ago doing the same as well. That was a different dynamic that he brought to the club. He taught people like Carso [Lee Carsley] and Darryl Powell tricks with the ball, and people go on about coaches, but they wouldn't even entertain those ideas before he was brought in. And hats off to Jim because he let that all happen.'

The most important signing since – or even including – Igor? Peter Gadsby may say similar, 'Eranio, just a beautiful, lovely man. I remember we were changing the side around and after a game or something on the training ground, Stefano said to Spencer Prior, "Spencer, why you kick ball in stand? No players in the stand, no players!" And Spencer said, "If I could effing trap it and kick it like you I wouldn't be on these wages!"'

* * *

While business in the summer of 1997 was minimal, it was decisive in administering the touch of class that Smith continued to aspire to bring in during his first two seasons. Eranio, courted over the course of three separate meetings by Derby hierarchy, is historically the most notable, but he was just one on a shopping list of Europe-wide talent that Lionel Pickering was more than willing to financially back his manager to bring in.

Having made efforts to bring in Toto Schillaci and Emmanuel Petit (with the latter famously opting to join Arsenal instead), Smith found himself with a decision to make when it came to the forward line. Despite an 11-goal return in his maiden Premier League voyage, Dean Sturridge found his attention ever so slightly wavering, with Arsenal keen on his signature for a reported £8m at the time. With that threat hanging over him, Smith made efforts to secure a potential replacement – or – an additional option.

The first, and most draw-dropping, name to be included in his thought pattern was one of the greatest forwards to ever play the game. Roberto Baggio (owner of the greatest nickname in the game – 'The Divine Ponytail') was a team-mate of Eranio's in Milano, and six weeks removed from the midfielder's departure he had not only alerted Smith to the prospect of what would have been the most jaw-dropping signing of the 1990s but he had also set up meetings with the man himself and his representatives.

Agreeing on a potential deal of £4m and a weekly wage of £30,000, Smith was confident enough to take the story to the media, describing the likelihood as '50/50'. But with escalating hidden costs and, as Stuart Webb wrote, 'Both Milan and his people were trying to get him a better deal elsewhere and he signed for Bologna,' Eranio would be used as mediator for another of his friends: Francesco Baiano.

'Who the fuck are these two then? Are they jockeys?' Another Webb anecdote in *Clough, Maxwell and Me* recalls the first take when Lionel Pickering welcomed Baiano and his agent into the grounds of his Yew Tree pub. The diminutive forward standing before Pickering measured at 5ft 7in, a far cry from his most recent forward recruit of Wanchope. But while he didn't have height on his side, what he did have was a pedigree that saw him appear alongside Diego Maradona at Napoli and most recently make over 100 appearances at Fiorentina.

'It was important to have somebody who could help us in front,' Eranio admits of his early weeks. 'And in that moment it was Baiano. I said to Jim, "Boss, I have a very good player who has finished his contract with Fiorentina. I can try to call him and give him the chance to come here." It was very difficult to convince his wife though. It was a very big job because when you live in a great town like Florence, it's one of the best towns in Italy. The food, the history, everything, the lifestyle, the shops. It was difficult but I tried to say, "Listen, Ciccio doesn't have any other choice. He has no contract. They can offer you a good contract, so you can try for two or three years here. But for you, if it is enough, you can stop and move back to Italy."'

Baiano settled into the Rams' way of life quickly, even if English would never fully follow. Another who matched the right mentality of the squad and the gentlemanliness of what Smith would hope for in those around him, it was another success for the staff in highlighting not only a footballing star, but an amenable person. McClaren would later in the season tell *The Ram*, 'When we buy players we are not buying just their footballing ability but the person too. We always look for good, honest people.'

Eranio's powers of persuasion were enough and, as he welcomed in a friend and a compatriot, a clear vision formed in the mind of the coaching staff of how this side could look going forward. A glint comes to McClaren's eye when thinking back to when he first realised what the newest recruit could do for their squad: 'There were some players we'd only see on video, but Jim trusted agents and they would never bring him a bad player. I always remember the Baiano signing. We'd not heard of him but seen a few clips. He came with his curly hair, earrings in and he looked like a right bandit. Small, he looked tiny and looked ... well, not like a footballer. But I remember we had a practice match on Pride Park and we put him in that number ten position. I came off at the end, and I think Jim was away in meetings somewhere. But I just said, "Where the hell did you get him from? He is unbelievable. He'll score goals, play people in, he is just this tough player." A right assassin; I used to call him the little assassin. And him and Eranio, we just surrounded them with damn good players. These were all players who were used to being looked after very well and that's what we did to get the best out of them in the twilight of their careers really.'

Baiano would adapt to English football like few others ever have done. An astonishing strike rate of eight inside his first eight games settled him into the game remarkably well, and with Sturridge eventually remaining at the club, the side would soon have a base of four strong forward options comprising of Sturridge, Wanchope, Baiano and another new addition, Deon Burton. The Jamaican international was the final piece of the attacking puzzle that Smith was after. A young, powerful forward who was able to hold up play and bring in Wanchope and Baiano around him, Burton joined Jim's revolution after playing for him previously at Portsmouth, where he now found himself out of favour.

'My agent called me and said, "Oh Deon, we're going up to Derby tomorrow." So I just said, "Why, what's up there?" Jim Smith wanted to sign me, and I couldn't believe my luck. Obviously having not been around Portsmouth in what is now the Championship, to go to the Premiership with Jim Smith ... I couldn't believe my luck. So we drove up there the next day and he just went, "Hello son, are you gonna come and play for me again?" And I was like, "You don't have to ask me twice – I'll go and get my boots!"'

And so with the four, opportunities presented themselves for change in the shape of the side. A two would easily slip into a front three as Smith moved from a more conservative approach into a pacy, fluid attacking unit that put the emphasis on moving forward at speed. Sillett reminisces, 'Me and Choppy [Wanchope] go back through the goals and smile and laugh because it's beautiful football. There are goals where you've got back-heels going on, Baiano against Southampton with about three back-heels, [where] it was like watching Brazil. People also don't really realise that Jim was also clever because big teams struggled against Derby. Manchester United, Arsenal. It came because we high-pressed them and went with three up front of Paulo, Deano and Deon. Deano in the middle, the two aerial guys marking their full-backs. It would stop them throwing it out to their full-backs, so it was kicked straight down our throat, and then when we had the ball we'd have two aerials on Lee Dixon and Nigel Winterburn, or [Gary] Neville and [Denis] Irwin. We had an immediate out to put them under pressure. And it wasn't long ball football, but it was to our strengths of Deon and Paulo. They were touching things in behind slow defenders for Sturridge who was like a whippet to race on to. And nobody said it was bad football, it was thoughtful and clever.'

Though it did at times put more of a pressure on the defence, even for Chris Powell, the Jack Stamps Trophy holder was willing to bear the brunt: 'We had to accept that they may not do the defensive work but what they gave us going forward with creativity and their passing and scoring ability, I think Jim knew the sort of British-based players would do the work and the running, and it was a great balance. And we accepted it and got on with it because we knew we'd win games, we knew that we had a really good balance and it really worked.'

Smith would have to wait some time before he could get the best out of his squad though, with early season injuries forcing him to play a scarcely believable front line of winger Paul Simpson and defender Matt Carbon at Blackburn Rovers on the opening day of 1997/98. Still, after the dress rehearsal against Sampdoria, at least everything would be fine for the first competitive match at Pride Park a few days after the visit to Ewood Park.

* * *

It's no secret that life hasn't gone exactly to plan at Pride Park Stadium. There's been buy-outs, misvaluations and, at the time of writing, a bald man is holding it ransom because he made a series of horrendous financial decisions over the years and would like something to cling on to. But I digress. Because for all of the pomp of the visit by Queen Elizabeth II and the general buzz around the football club in advance of the official opening, the fever pitch levels would dissipate in the space of one August evening against Joe Kinnear's Wimbledon.

'It's something I've never been involved in, ever,' Chris Powell bluntly states. 'It was really strange.' What occurred at Pride Park on the evening of 13 August 1997 should never be forgotten, as much as all those involved would like it to be. The first competitive game at the new stadium ended in an abandonment due to a floodlight failure. Mere miles away, visible from the place now called home, the old home could be seen. A Far East betting scandal, as some suspected? Nope. Misjudged preparation? Ding, ding ding.

Speaking in *Pride* back in 2019, Peter Gadsby looked back on the evening: 'It was a disaster. The mistake we made was not testing it for a half-time. Apparently the peak time at Christmas is 3.10pm when the Queen comes on and everybody puts a cup of tea on. All the stations have a surge. But we hadn't tested for half-time, which is the same.'

'It's pretty basic but if you don't realise that at some point the electrical load is going to be massive when you turn on heaters and water heaters and all this, then somebody has dropped a clanger,' laughs broadcaster Colin Gibson, who was left in the dark pitchside that night.

Should it have come to an abandonment though? Communications manager Jim Fearn recalled in *Pride Park: The Story of a Stadium* of the evening. 'Right, you're the communications man, go and talk to the referee. Buy us some time,' Fearn was told. But having overheard the exchange, Wimbledon boss Joe Kinnear and Dons captain/general terrifying man Vinnie Jones stormed off after him into the centre circle, accusing him of being 'Jim Smith's man' and attempting to pressure Uriah Rennie, officiating his first Premier League game that night.

Gadsby continues, 'I went in and knocked on the Wimbledon door and said, "Excuse me, please keep your players warm, I'm assured we'll be playing again soon and the lights will be on." Joe Kinnear said, "Is that it? You can fuck off." They had changed and they were going, they didn't want to play.'

Colin Gibson also remembers the irate Kinnear, content for a postponement with his side 2-1 down and outplayed, 'We put out Joe Kinnear's press conference where he was effing and blinding about it, but I interviewed him in the tunnel and he was playing the classic football gamesmanship. You've got Uriah Rennie saying, "Right, we'll give it 20 minutes. You get them back on in 20 minutes otherwise it's match abandoned." Ten minutes later and Kinnear is already starting in his ear, "Ref, you've got to call this off now." And the only reason he wanted to call it off was because his team was losing, which is pretty obvious. Eventually they can't get it sorted and it was match abandoned. So then with Kinnear, I interviewed him afterwards and we said we'd put out his press conference, but we had to stop it because of the language.'

Having survived the Sampdoria test, the blame for the power failure was mixed. Gadsby attributed it to failing to test, while an additional lighting system to highlight the club badge on the Toyota Stand took the stadium setting past 160 amps. But with the stadium setting only set at that minimum, anything above was destined to put additional pressure on the capabilities. And without turning up the nozzle, disaster was almost an inevitability.

Abandonment meant Ashley Ward was stripped of the honour of being the first scorer at the stadium (he was also the last Rams scorer at the Baseball Ground), with an Eranio penalty against Barnsley later putting him in the record books as the Rams bounced back from two away losses in what were now their opening matches. Not that there was any panic involved, because life was very, very sweet in those early months at Pride Park.

Eight games into the season, Derby sat sixth with 15 points. Two games in hand on those above them meant they could easily have gone second with a quarter of the campaign gone. So when Igor Štimac admitted in the 18 October copy of *The Ram*, 'I believe qualifying for Europe is a possibility this season … and we are capable of winning a major trophy in the next two years,' he wasn't bluffing. Such was the quality of the squad Smith had built that even Asanović found himself out of contention, his inclusion curtailed by the three non-EC players rule in place at this point. He would leave the club mid-season.

Making a wondrous start at Pride Park which would last long into the season (no Premier League defeat on home soil until February), it was Smith's side at their true finest. Wins at Sheffield Wednesday – the iconic 5-2 – and a Baiano-inspired 2-1 at Leicester, plus a victory at Spurs in the League Cup, were tonics to the home form that saw all comers dispatched. Manchester United had to scramble for a point after going 2-0 down; Everton, Coventry, West Ham and Southampton were easily seen off. And then there was the stupendous 3-0 win over eventual champions and Double winners Arsenal at the start of November, their first defeat of the season. In potentially the finest

Pride Park performance of all time when considering the calibre of opposition, Wanchope's double was supported by a deft chip from Sturridge for a comprehensive win. The Rams were truly firing.

But it's important not to only dwell on the attacking positives though, because there were unsung stars across this side. Perhaps less fashionable than those further up the pitch, Darryl Powell had proved his worth over the previous two campaigns and was now ably accompanied by the increasingly impressive Lee Carsley. '[Powell was] the guy who knitted everything together and always put his heart into it,' says supporter Jamie Allen. 'He just seemed to do a lot of the ugly work, break up play and give the ball to other guys.'

Powell's value was noted by supporters and teammates, and the same can be said of Carsley. Dean Sturridge was especially keen to emphasise the overall improtance Carsley had on the side around him. There's a reason he would go on to be an integral part of a Champions League-qualifying side with Everton in later years. A hardman with the footballing capabilities to back up his inclusion, the duo progressed from the streets of Birmingham to be part of one of the most exciting young sides of the 1990s.

'I have to give Lee Carsley a mention as well,' Sturridge proclaims. 'I remember him at the time saying, "I don't need Bill Beswick. We're Birmingham boys!" We had a certain DNA, so we didn't feel we needed the help. But Carso's the same in that he may have had a little bit of help in certain times from Bill and he realised it was a strength as well to show that vulnerability. And what a career he's had. He is one of the best players to come through the youth ranks, for me. Sold for good money, played for his country on numerous occasions. He doesn't get the credit he deserves, because he isn't mentioned enough in terms of Derby County and what an important component he was. They call it the [Claude] Makélélé role over the years, now the [N'Golo] Kanté role. But he was doing that, and he broke the lines with his passes. He knew that role, then made that role his own over the years at Derby, then at Everton. I think he really deserves a big mention in terms of the history of the club.'

Powell, too, was pivotal. A cult hero in the truest sense, the Jamaica regular was the easy scapegoat for supporters when things weren't going quite so well. Less comfortable on the ball than those around him (because those around him were often Eranio and Asanović and, frankly, they are two of the most comfortable men in the history of the sport), what Powell brought to the side cannot be ignored. Alongside his ability to break up play and dispense to those more comfortable going forward, it was his midfield leadership which was another underlying factor to why Smith's sides were so successful.

And so, considering all the components above and the defensive displays from individuals including Christian Dailly and Jacob Laursen, it's bittersweet to assess the first season at Pride Park as, ultimately, European football did not follow. Struggling from February and having succumbed to their first home loss, PPS would feel less like home as the campaign wore on. Five were conceded without reply against Leeds, then four inside the first 15 minutes against Leicester. A final-day win over Liverpool would be too little, too late, leaving the side in ninth with 55 points. A single win (or even a couple of draws if we're not being picky) anywhere else in the campaign would have elevated them to seventh and therefore Europe. But for a team who never dropped outside of the top ten from September onwards, and having had to deal with the magnitude of moving to a new stadium and still be relative top-flight newcomers, maybe it's fair to contain that greed again.

Because not aided by injuries to key men over the second half of the season including both Italians and the by-now injury hampered Igor, Smith was willing to settle for a top-half finish. 'I will understand the disappointment if we don't make Europe this time,' wrote Smith in his final programme notes of the season. 'But we have achieved the target of improving on last time's points total and if we make the same level of improvement during 1998/99 we will qualify for Europe.'

10

WHAT HAPPENS AT RAYNESWAY

DERBY COUNTY Football Club were sporting leaders in the 1990s. The Rams boasted the first analysis system in the form of Prozone, they had the only sports psychologist in professional football and with Dane Farrell leading a fitness revolution, the trifecta was complete.

That isn't simply enough though, and it doesn't begin to tell the story of why Jim Smith's side beat all comers in their first years in the Premier League. Had Derby possessed one of the above three then it would have been impressive, and three bordered on greedy. But their impact could only go so far if they weren't supported by the relevant footballing brains to both capitalise on the innovations and directly impact what was happening on a Saturday afternoon.

What Derby could boast alongside this was arguably the greatest assistant manager of the 1990s in Steve McClaren. The man who would push on the integration of the three, he became synonymous with a changing time in British football during the second half of the decade, partly responsible for dragging the ideology of club football in the country forward. But he wasn't alone.

Steve Round was next in line. Still in his 20s after a career cut short by injury, he would work alongside Smith and McClaren and mould his own coaching style, a style that today has him as the assistant to Mikel Arteta at Arsenal.

Then you had Billy McEwan. Largely responsible for the development of the reserve team, which would go on to secure Premier Reserve League success in consecutive seasons, he was the older head in the backroom staff. Steve Taylor, another younger man, would dutifully support and remains closely associated with the club today. And don't forget arguably the greatest goalkeeping coach this country has ever seen in Eric Steele. A man who developed everyone from Mart Poom to David de Gea is a giant of his profession. Smith, McClaren, Taylor, Round, Steele and McEwan were probably the core six. But they were far from alone.

Peter Melville and Neil Sillett would head up physiotherapy and become integral to the cohesive unit that was the coaching staff and playing squad. Then you had the legendary figure of Gordon Guthrie, who did everything there was to do in Derbyshire and is rightly remembered today with a corner named after him at Pride Park. A young Jon Davidson, still kitman to this day, was his protégé. There were more, plenty more, and I apologise for not naming every single person within these last few paragraphs. But every individual at Raynesway played their part in the progression of Derby County, dragging them from the depths of the First Division into the visionary world of the new-look top flight.

This chapter is dedicated to those people who made this happen.

* * *

As every successful football manager needs, Smith had an element of luck from his time at Raynesway. One such stroke came in the fact of the working relationship and eventual friendship he built with Lionel Pickering, who afforded the trust in him to build a coaching squad he felt would best reflect what he was trying to achieve. Having been out of the managerial game for months, Derby represented a fresh start for Smith in relation to who he would look to bring into his setup.

McClaren was his first call, the man who 'knew how to pour a glass of wine' as he was humorously referred to by Smith. Today, a coach would be expected to arrive with his own backroom staff, and in Derby folklore it almost resulted in the premature departure of Billy Davies in 2006 when he was unable to bring in trusted assistant David 'Ned' Kelly. But 1995 was a different time, and Peter Gadsby remembers: 'We had him [McClaren] for somewhere on very little money. In fact, we had great difficulty getting the board to accept Jim wanted an assistant, it was quite silly in those days. I think it was less than £20,000.'

McClaren was one cog in Smith's machine, and considering the deterioration after his departure in the spring of 1999, it's not unfair to others to say he was the main one. What would become of McClaren after his time at Derby is often forgotten, and as decades pass his name is associated away from his biggest successes and instead – at least away from Derby – used disparagingly. Hit podcast *Athletico Mince* has a section dedicated solely to McClaren, and a Google search will swiftly throw up the image of him with *that* umbrella. But McClaren's achievements are long and his value in the game is criminally undersold. Because to his accolades, the man has:

- Been a part of Manchester United's treble-winning staff as Alex Ferguson's assistant
- Won Middlesbrough's only major trophy
- Managed the England national team
- Coached overseas, winning the Eredivisie with FC Twente

It's no bad résumé, even amid some roles which haven't gone exactly to his own plan. Among all the successes though, it was the partnership he built alongside Smith which set him on his way and hinted at a long, prosperous coaching career ahead. 'He was a very talented coach,' admits Bill Beswick, a long-time working colleague of McClaren's at United, England, Middlesbrough and more. 'Jim had very cleverly recruited Steve. He had gone to Oxford for a meeting, looked out of the window and saw this under-17 youth coach putting cones and bibs out half an hour before practice, and thought, "There's a real professional." From that he recruited Steve to first-team coach, a brilliant move.'

The coaching duo both shared the connection of Oxford United, where the recently retired midfielder had moved into the first elements of coaching. Demonstrating a unique insight into his sessions and a kindness that instantly adhered him to Smith, McClaren's integration into Derby provided the learnings he adapted throughout his coaching tenures. Given the never easy role of appeasing Smith, McClaren found his first weeks under the Bald Eagle as an education from the master.

'I always remember the first day,' laughs McClaren. 'Jim came in the office and he said, "What are we doing today, Steve?" And I had it up on the chart, I'd spent a long time pulling it together. So, we'd start with this, do this, do this, do this and he just went, "That's rubbish, Steve. What else have you got? It's rubbish, you better change it." The next day I came in and he said, "What have we got today?" That, that and that. "Rubbish Steve. Have you got anything else?" I turned over the page and I went, "Yeah, we've got this." "Ahh, that's a little better. But I don't like that, and I don't like that." So I turned over the other page and went, "Well, we could do this and this?" And I think I wore him down and he went, "That'll do, do that." I learnt to have plan A, plan B, plan C. And I tell every coach [to do] that.'

Never an easy man to please and certainly not one who would compromise for anything less than perfection on the field, Smith taught his protégé a series of valuable lessons, not least one key message: Jim is in charge. Academy product Marvin Robinson described Smith as a sporting director as opposed to a manager, responsible for the general overseeing of the club, making signings and taking a back seat where he knew his coaches were able to implement his wishes on the squad. And it's a suitable label when looking into the roles and responsibilities Smith himself would take on.

The duo would build up the basis of their relationship in a hotel together early into their time at Derby, mulling over tactics, personnel and ideology over a glass of red wine. For McClaren, he was provided a footballing education, yes, but also one into the magic of a glass of Rioja from perhaps the finest connoisseur in the game. Those evenings allowed the two to better understand what they wanted from each other, and with the gradual introduction of the trilogy of new ideas, McClaren would be further trusted by his mentor. 'Steve McClaren was ahead of his time,' says winger Kevin Harper, a signing from Hibernian early in 1998/99. 'When I look back and think about what Steve McClaren was doing then and Steve Round and Billy McEwan as well. Jim as well. The whole culture at Derby was very forward-thinking. Jim was an older manager but he let Steve do most of the work. You only really saw Jim on a Monday when he was either talking about the game or having a joke and a laugh, and then you'd see him on the Thursday and Friday. But it was a really, really forward-thinking club and for me it really opened my eyes to doing things right.'

But for the trust Smith would place in McClaren, the assistant would be left in little doubt as to who wore the trousers in their partnership. The duo would very quickly develop an approach that would allow McClaren to run most of the sessions during the week, with Smith soon trusting that things would run smoothly on the training pitches. The process would see the assistant run sessions from Monday through to Wednesday, with Smith largely only becoming involved when building the shape later in the week for the Saturday matches. And that would often throw up significant headaches for McClaren and even the players.

Dean Sturridge laughs at the memories: 'I have never seen anything like it. Steve would do the training on Monday and Tuesday, then Wednesday [would be] off. Thursday the gaffer would come out and just tear a strip off Steve; just hammer him. And us as players would be thinking, "What is going on here? How are they arguing like this in front of us?" Steve would take it on the chin, then whisper quietly to certain players, and he definitely did to me, "Just let him have a go for a minute, we'll be all right." We became accustomed to it and we just got used to it. Sometimes we'd do things tactically on a Tuesday and a Thursday, but on that Thursday he would throw it all away and start again, and maybe we'd go back to the original plans but Jim would have to have his two pennies' worth as a manager.'

The topic of those encounters at Raynesway was spoken about heavily for the research stages of this book, so over the next few paragraphs I'd like to take you a little further into them, beginning with McClaren himself: 'Some things can go wrong and if Jim was on the field things could go wrong. We used to do Thursdays and 11 v 11, and it doesn't always work. And I used to say to him, "Everybody has about 80 attacks at the opponent, and they might not score a goal. So, in training we might have 80 attacks and we don't score. That's what happens in a game. We can't score on every attack." But he expected because of the coaching to score on every attack. And for it to work.

'Eventually we got to the stage where Thursday we would play 11 v 7, or v 8 to make it work. And I used to have to say to the seven or eight, "Look, can you just make it work? I'm not saying not try, but just allow it." Because if we didn't score, it was wrong. It was right, but we just didn't score. And I'd say to Deano or Marco, "Just please, please, please put the ball in the net. Don't think because it's just a practice you can try something and whack it over the bar, you can't." So we worked around, but he set the scenes, set the scenarios, he set the team and the tactics and we fed off him. He would always used to drive down to the Baseball Ground every Thursday and I'd think, "Oh no, this is my worst day, this.' So sometimes we'd play 11 v zero and we still wouldn't score! And he'd go mad; he really used to go mad. "Get that Sturridge in my office. Whacking it over the bar." But it was always entertaining.'

McClaren would bear the brunt of Smith's momentary anger, and at times would find himself growing increasingly frustrated as long-thought-over plans were ripped apart in seconds by the manager who had only seen a handful of minutes in a week-long plan. Gary Rowett adds, 'Steve would build the confidence up all week and Jim would take the Friday session, the shape session when you were working on what to do in the game. The first person to make a mistake would mean Jim's hat would go off, he'd be kicking it across the pitch, effing and blinding and would be demanding standards that way. You look back, though, and it was such a good dynamic that it felt almost at the time quite comical. Jim would take the session and he'd get angry, go red, he'd start stomping around and shouting at people, but you look back and you don't know how deliberate some of those actions were because Steve was quite thoughtful and methodical, technical. And Jim was such a good leader, such a knowledgeable guy and a lot of his interventions and strengths would come on matchday in the heat of the battle when he'd make big calls and big decisions and what not. The first person to cross the ball over the keeper and out of play you knew was getting it off Jim a little bit, and Steve would be pulling his hair out on the sidelines. But it was a great, fun dynamic and it worked fabulously well.'

Comical is one word to describe the scene, though at times it would border closer to farcical for some players, including Spencer Prior: 'It was his [Jim's] one session a week where he got out on the grass running a session. And it was fucking chaos at times, but it was something that he wanted to do and as players we responded how we needed to and made sure we could still get up for things on Saturdays. Everything we had done in the week was just gone. That was his session. You knew what to expect so as players you just went with it, so it was just a case of, "Get us back to Raynesway so we can get on that bowling green and have a five-a-side," to clear our heads of everything we'd done on the Thursday! I don't want to be disrespectful, the sessions were more enjoyable when with Stevie Mac. The sessions with Jim were a frigging nightmare, confusing as hell. You really looked forward to working with the other coaches and as a manager, but Jim was so comfortable as a manager that he didn't want to make it the Jim Smith show.'

And to round off on the relationship on the pitch between the two, a word from Paul Simpson, 'He would tear into Steve and anybody else who got in his way as well. Really his main day was Friday. When we've gone in to do our 11 v 11 work on Friday where he would name a team, on quite a few occasions I've seen him stop it and send somebody out of training just because he wasn't happy with them. "Right, that's it, he's not playing," and he'd change the team just because he wasn't happy with something they'd done in that session. I say to this day that him and Macca are the best team I worked under as a player, but I still describe Jim as horrible in the way that he went about it with us! He was horrible … but he was absolutely brilliant as well.'

It's a tough word, but no doubt Jim could be horrible. The difference between him and other managers in the 1990s, though, was that he was loved across the training pitch, finding the perfect balance between hairdryer treatments and father-like figure. For his players, it was almost impossible not to fall in love with the man, such was his affection for his squad and his astonishing ability to display a genuine care for those around him. That is why things worked so well, and why McClaren and Smith built up the prosperous relationship that they did.

The tough love instilled on McClaren on a daily basis was – if anything – a commendation for the faith Smith had in him. The clearest inclination of this is when assessing the fact that Smith would allow multiple new footballing ideas to be used in the sessions, because he trusted his right-hand man. 'At that time you couldn't tell what Steve was going to become,' recalls Igor Štimac, 'but for us who worked under him, I could say immediately that he was making a difference. His training sessions were fabulous. They were practical, different, they served us to improve our game. He was always trying to motivate us in changing exercises and all that, never to keep things the same or become boring, he would talk a lot to the players and that was making a difference. And you have to attribute that to Jim.'

Smith's mastery came in recognising the abilities of those around him as well as himself. Later in his Derby tenure and following the loss of McClaren, he would be required to take on more roles across the training ground as a succession of coaches came and went, unable to find the same formula that McClaren did. It was a situation which caused significant issues, Smith being taken away from his priorities, away from the football and instead having to balance focus over more elements of the day-to-day squad preparation that previously would have been done for him, changing his job significantly from what it had been during his Rams heyday. But that's for the end of this story, because for the time the two worked together, they struck coaching gold.

As alluded to by some of the players, they could sense the occasional furore Smith gave his assistant was done from a place of love, including Danish international Jacob Laursen: 'On a Thursday morning you could just see him for the first time. He would come out in his shorts and [with] his cap on, throw his cap and scream "NO NO NO". And you could just see all of the players get nervous about what's happening. It happened 90 per cent of the time that he would come out on the Thursday, make a bit of a change. But from his perspective, he knew that Steve did a really good job and I think he did it just to keep us on our toes.

'If you had a hidden camera, you'd see some of the players panic and be unable to pass the ball. You could hear him. At Raynesway we had the club house and the terrace, with five or six steps down to the pitch. Most of the time he never got to the pitch before he had thrown his cap and was shouting at somebody.'

Lars Bohinen was another who would be taken aback and, though he settled into the Derby side, he was able to see how a Smith rant could affect some of the players less accustomed to the treatment: 'I remember at one point, Steve McClaren, Steve Round and Billy McEwan had to sort of tell Jim to stay inside when we had those match preparation sessions because, when things didn't work out, it could work out negative. So the other coaches convinced him to stay inside during those sessions, so he was watching us through his window in his office. It lasted for a while and they actually found out that when we were practising the first 11, if we didn't succeed in what Jim wanted us to do [before he was inside] we got so stressed and nothing worked.'

The same can be said of many others. Lee Morris, at the time a club record signing, was one of those who didn't reach his potential at Derby, struggling to deal with his manager's anger. Another regular victim was Darryl Powell, although the Jamaica international used it to his advantage and found the best of himself with Smith at the Rams and Portsmouth.

And while McClaren had to deal with the Smith outbursts, a key component of his position would come when picking up the pieces from players who had been on the receiving end of a Yorkshire-made tirade. Paulo Wanchope would often be the recipient of such a lashing, most notably with the physical meeting the pair had following a match against Barnsley. Another who would take the brunt was Mart Poom. Poom, who had experience of Smith following a short spell with him at Fratton Park, was the most singled-out individual on the training field, as any effort which found its way past the menacing stopper resulted in Smith pointing an accusing finger his way.

The often-harsh treatment caused significant concern for McClaren, who after one particular week realised that the anger was having a detrimental effect on the man who would go on to become one of the greatest in Rams history: 'We had to educate Jim, and an example was [with] Poomy. Every goal that went in, he always blamed Poomy. Steeley [Eric Steele] worked with him and I used to say, "Jim, you've got to be careful because Poomy's losing confidence. He's losing belief." So eventually we came to the point of, "Don't kill him after the game, let me go through the game, have a look and on Monday I'll tell you whether you can kill him or not." And that's the agreement that we had. Let me and Steeley have a look, and on Monday morning he'd be waiting for us, saying, "Right, can I kill him or what?" It became quite a bit of a joke. "Yeah Jim, he was quite a bit at fault for that." "Right, get him in my office!" But many times we saved Poomy from goals that weren't his fault.'

Poom continues from where McClaren left off, adding, 'It wasn't easy because he was always the first to blame the goalkeeper. He was old-school because he had such high demands, but I wanted to always show him that I could play at the top level. Steeley or Steve had to stand up for me because the goalkeeper is the easiest target, so I had to be on my toes with him. But he set high standards for all of us and they push you on, because he just wanted to make us better. He would get emotional very quickly and say a few words, just because he got so emotional from football. But if we had arguments, and normally he'd calm down and watch the video again, he'd ask me into his office and say, "Sorry Poomy, I was a bit over the top there!" But he had a good heart.'

And for Poom too, that was the clinching point. Though Smith could be as harsh as anyone, it came from a place of knowing he could get better out of his players: 'He hated it when goalkeepers would parry the ball; he thought that the rebound would always lead to a goal. In training I'd just hear, "Catch that fucking ball!" and he was always shouting at us. And he always wanted his goalkeeper to come for crosses and dominate, but sometimes he went silly with it. He wanted me to come for every ball, and I knew that in England you had a lot of balls coming into the box, it was an English characteristic. And he would always demand his goalkeeper comes off his line and dominate the box – in a way, he demanded it from me and it became my strength by the end. I had to work a lot on the pitch for it and in the gym as well, and then also mentally because it would need to be a quick decision when reading the cross. I remember in afternoons he'd bring the second team in and say, "Look, you can all do whatever to Poomy, just pull him around," and I know that was because he wanted me to dominate. In a way I was grateful that he demanded that from me.'

Ultimately, the mention of emotion in the former paragraph is also pivotal when assessing the mentality of Jim Smith on the training field. Though his hours on the Raynesway pitch were limited when he had McClaren beside him, it was that emotion which drove the burning desire Smith had for success. 'Jim being like that was Jim and we did not want to stop that,' admits McClaren. 'We call it tough love and he was very honest, very direct, didn't mind conflict and that's how we coached in those days. Players had to deal with that. They had to deal with Jim and they did do. You knew if you'd done something wrong, you were going to get in trouble. So he was consistent with it, which is important.

'How some of the players took it I do not know and it ended up, as you say, he is a like a second dad to me. He used to kill some of them every time, but it was tough love. But he would come in, give you a kiss on the cheek or whatever and the next minute he'd be killing you, but the players accepted that. And we had good staff around Jim to deflect that and to cope with that. We had the tools to be able to deal with the criticism because players have to do that with managers, coaches, 35,000 fans who don't like your performance.'

It's important at this stage to ensure it's not a negative light which is painted on Smith, because the man drew adoration from almost all players who spoke for *Groundwork*. And when he did come on to the training pitch, it wasn't only anger that he served up, just like it wasn't only eye rolls that would come from McClaren when his sessions were interrupted. Smith would also serve up hilarity on a daily basis, whether it be through passing remarks such as 'I was Yorkshire's boxing champion' or by opting to take one-on-one sessions when the likes of Eric Steele were away. Poom recalls one such day without Steele, when a suit-wearing Smith opted to play the daily role of goalkeeping coach, ruining his suit and brown leather shoes in the process.

Fashion was also another Smith trait that could draw both admiration and disturbed looks. Known for dressing to the nines when the moment called for it, that suited session was a rarity. For the squad, the way they described the manager's outfit choices points more to Fred Dibnah than Fred Perry. To get the Jim Smith look, you'd need a cap. Any cap, branded or not. Ideal for throwing at a player. A pair of short shorts. No, shorter than that. Pulled up over the belly button, blocking half your T-shirt. There you go. Maybe long socks too, depending on the weather. With that, you have adopted the Jim Smith look. Go well.

Gary Rowett laughs at one fashion-focused memory: 'I remember one pre-season John Harkes walked in late into the dressing room and Jim would go, "Harkesy, Harseky, what are you doing? You're effing late, what are you wearing? You've got shorts on!" And Harkesy turned around to him, "Look Jim, am I sweating?" And Jim was there with his shirt stuck to him, he had sweat pouring down his head and he went, "Yeah, good point."'

Away from Smith's fashion, though, and back to McClaren, and it would do a gross disservice to only focus on how he managed Jim Smith, because what he achieved was so much more. His decisions to bring in psychology, analysis and fitness rightly earn chapters of their own, but it was in his tactical work where he had the most telling impact at Raynesway.

Beginning his sessions more often than not with an integration with Dane Farrell, the duo would meet the afternoon before to plan out what would come the next day, meaning no two days would look the same, a rare accomplishment in a British side of the 1990s. Farrell says, 'We'd stay behind and discuss what we were going to do, which players needed certain coaching that was lacking in a game before and looking at what we could do with that player. So we'd work out in the morning that we'd arrive and I'd warm them up. Twice weekly I'd do a speed and power session with small groups of players in small pockets, and then put them back in with the football coaching. And then afterwards we'd do something else in terms of speed and endurance at the end of the football practice. So there was a good cohesion there. And we always kept the players guessing, not knowing what was going to happen next. But with the coaching staff we had a good work plan, knowing what we would do each time.'

Farrell, like Bill Beswick, had free rein over how he could get the best out of the players, but both experts would build their training with McClaren, who would oversee every aspect of the session, fully trusted and supported by Smith. Farrell continues, 'We all had our own individual selective practice and an inner belief with each other and a trust. I'd go straight into the physio room, see which players are up for playing and how the rehab guys are getting on. Then I'd move from there into the coaches' room and Steve would then tell me which players we have, who needs a little extra away from the training side. So I was the one who was moving all over the place, I was a new person there and I was finding myself. But I was seen as an asset, I'd like to think, in terms of how we can get a player out and do a bit of work on them. As a unit, we worked really well together.'

And off the back of these fitness sessions, the rest was left to McClaren. With a variety of sessions designed to both improve and mentally stimulate the squad, it quickly became apparent that the £20,000 or so it took to hire him was the best money Lionel Pickering could possibly have spent. Whether it be overseeing the switch to a five-cum-three at the back that facilitated Igor, or being able to get the very best from Sturridge and co., the work done by McClaren was only truly appreciated after his departure from the club.

* * *

But the future England manager wasn't alone. We've already touched upon the impact of Dane Farrell within this chapter, the same with Bill Beswick, who both rightly earn further analysis elsewhere in this book. But there are some men who haven't received the same coverage and should be focused on within the rest of this chapter. The first of them is Eric Steele.

Steele is a rarity in the game of football in that he is a known goalkeeping coach. It's the member of a core coaching team who is most anonymous to the outsider, as they only have an impact on one-11th of the side. But Steele transcends typical coaching knowledge to the everyday supporter though, largely due to the way he has taken the profession by scruff of the neck over the past 30 years. A goalkeeper in his own right who made a career at Derby, Brighton and Peterborough, it was in coaching where the footballing world took the most notice.

'I still call him my guru,' beams Mart Poom, who instantly comes to life at the mention of Steele. 'He is the best goalkeeper coach I have ever had and he helped me a lot to establish myself in Derby and to develop. He helped me to have the career in English football.' The duo worked together after Poom was highlighted for signing by Alan Hodgkinson from the Scottish setup. The Estonian couldn't have found a better mentor than Steele to find his feet in the British game.

Poom said, 'It didn't matter if you were number one, two, three, he set everybody different targets and helped everybody. He was very modern and was thinking with a holistic approach and not only what we'd do tactically but also physically with the fitness coach, being position-specific and also the mental side as well. We had Bill Beswick, and we would phone him on Sundays after the games to see how the game went. Eric was a great coach and his trainings were very good as well. Intense, but I have to give a big thank you to him and we still keep in touch as well.' Even Igor, with his vast career across a number of clubs and countries, is quick to say, 'He is one of the best goalkeeping coaches I have ever seen.'

And while Steele was listed as a goalkeeping coach, the dynamism of the coaching setup meant that he was not tied solely into working with the keepers. Part of the outfield sessions alongside McClaren and working closely with Farrell as well, he was part of a series of routines that would benefit forwards too. Rather than it being a goalkeeping-specific zone for his work, he would bring in attackers for shooting practice, including the young hopeful Marvin Robinson: 'Our goalkeeping coach would have his own schedule that involved us for shooting practice, but in effect it was goalkeeping practice, which would be part of my development then. It was really profound.'

Steele's work has not gone unnoticed over the years, largely seen as the giant in his profession for his work in developing the next generation of goalkeepers. At Derby, he brought through Lee Grant and gave Poom the tools to become one of the greatest stoppers in Rams history. Away from Derby, he was the man who helped Manchester United's David de Gea settle into British football after a difficult beginning, while he has also been involved in the England setup and created his own coaching business in his spare time. Not only this but in his time at Derby he was responsible for working on cuisine with head chef Mark Smith, having had a career in restaurant management.

Steele, McClaren and Farrell were important, but so was Steve Round. 'I had been at Derby County ever since I was nine,' begins the now Arsenal assistant manager. 'There was a guy called Richard Williams and Gerry Summers who signed me up as an apprentice at 16. I did my two years on a YTS scheme, signed a professional contract, and then got into the reserve team, and this was all under Arthur Cox at the time and Roy McFarland. And during my journey towards the first team, just as I emerged as a potential first-team player and made a few appearances, I got a bad injury which I wasn't able to recover from. I ruptured all my ligaments in my knee and had extensive surgery to try and get back; couldn't. And during that transformational time with my injury, I was also working in the school of excellence for Jerry, coaching the under-12s and the 14s, coaching three or four nights a week and taking a team on a Sunday. And it was something I was really interested in, regardless of my playing career.

'So I took my FA badges at that time while I was injured, I took my UEFA A Licence, and actually I think I was the youngest ever to get it at that stage at 22. And just as I had to finish, Jim Smith had come to the club. And he had watched me coaching with the school of excellence and said, "Your knee's not going to be good enough, is it? I've been really impressed with what I've seen on the coaching side, have you thought about going into coaching? There's an opportunity for you here next season. Come in, take the youth team and I'd like you to do a bit of work with the first team and let's see how it goes from there." So I finished playing, I came on the staff with the under-18s, the 16s, 15s, 14s, and I was also doing little bits around the first team on certain days.'

Round's move into coaching may have come in sad circumstances after his dream of professional football was cut short, but the environment in which he found himself proved to be a blessing in disguise. At an age where a career had been robbed from him, finding himself under the tutelage of Smith sparked a passion that has taken him to the very top of English football. First working under David Moyes at Everton and Manchester United, it's with Arsenal and Mikel Arteta that he has become the standout second-in-command as part of a new-wave of young Gunners talent.

Bill Beswick has nothing but pride when looking at where his two Steves went to in their careers: 'Steve Round is my neighbour so the morning coffees with the discussions about Arsenal at the moment and the clubs he's been at before still continue. Steve Round and McClaren have two things in common really. They are both very tough characters and they are both great learners. Roundy since our work at Derby has gone on to take a master's degree and has done really well. At Arsenal I think some of his work replicates what I was doing at Middlesbrough and Derby. He's assistant manager and is picking up the human relationship side, and that's what absorbs us when we meet and talk over coffee. It's fascinating to see their progress and Derby was the basis for that. Something happened at Derby with Jim, Steve McClaren, Steve Round and me, something clicked and we took Derby forwards to become a more modern, progressive club, we did things in a different way, and that was the launchpad for those people to go on to other clubs.'

Round, who would go on to join McClaren at Middlesbrough after he opted to make the move from under the wing of Alex

Ferguson in 2001, would begin his days working with the youth sides, but through seasons of slow integration into first-team sessions (in which he could observe McClaren) it meant he had the necessary tools quicker than was expected to be able to fill an eventual void following the switch. So prepared was he that when McClaren left Derby for United, Round would soon make a step up into his position, even in his mid-20s. One man who went the other way from McClaren was Danny Higginbotham, who said of Round, 'Roundy would set you goals and he'd set you aims for the season of what he wanted you to do. He'd pull you to one side and just tell you about certain aspects of the game.

'I remember at the end of my first season, which ended finishing well for me, we got the result at Old Trafford [a 1-0 win in May 2001], playing in the back three, some of the games before then. He just sat me down and said, "What did you think of your season?" and I knew it was really difficult at first because I had to adjust, understand, respect and appreciate that my whole game had to change. And then at the end he said, "We'll go through some clips and that. What did you think about these situations?" and he'd show me clips where I'd made last-ditch challenges and everything, and I was really proud of them. And he was like, "You know what, they're great. No, no they're not great." And this never left me for the rest of my career. "You're doing last-ditch challenges. The reason you're doing them is because you were out of position in the first place." And I got told this at 22; I'm 42 now and I still remember these things. He was really good with the details and explaining things.' Another plus came with Round's age, younger than some of the players and therefore directly joining in with elements of the sessions, such as the long-distance runs.

But just to hammer home, it was Derby and Jim Smith who first recognised something in a youngster who has gone on to become one of the leading coaches in the country. Round says, 'I had mentors everywhere. I had Jim to look up to to see how he handled the environment, the media, the arena, how he dealt with discipline, how he worked with the players, with families of players and how he looked after them off the field, how he dealt with selection issues, dropping players, how he recruited and brought players over and convinced them to come and play. It was just a massive learning curve. And I'd got Steve McClaren that was on the grass, to learn and watch him work and see how he was innovative with his tactical coaching, his technical work, the sessions that were put on, the learnings he would deliver, the presentations. I'd got Bill Beswick who I could tap into from a psychological aspect and look at the bigger-picture thinking. It was just a massive learning curve and was so influential in everything I do. At the time and I still do, I couldn't thank Jim enough for giving me an opportunity and for allowing me into that inner sanctum and helping me develop as a coach.'

You had Steve Taylor too, another man whose own playing career was cruelly shortened by illness in 1990, one year after being named the club's young player of the year. Like Round, he would progress through the ranks, spending almost two decades at Derby in total in various coaching positions, including assistant manager through to 2005 under George Burley. Taylor, who had played alongside McClaren years earlier, would be the sticking point across a series of managers, beginning with Arthur Cox. Now a manager in his own right, Taylor was instrumental in the day-to-day running of both the senior teams and the youth sides as well, overseeing the progression of players from Chris Riggott to Tom Huddlestone.

And then you had the late Billy McEwan, another manager away from Derby who would operate across the Raynesway pitch alongside McClaren and Round during those main years, before eventually going on to become a caretaker manager following Smith's departure in 2001.

That was the core of the coaching, but it is a lost opportunity to not go just a little further, starting with Jon Davidson. Another man who progressed through the youth system to become a professional at Derby, where all others have departed, Davidson has stayed. Again and again and again. Three decades later, the kitman (and so much more beyond this) remains at Pride Park, having worked under a plethora of managers across two stadiums and two centuries.

'I think there's a couple of the ground staff who have been there a long time as well but I'm certainly on the football side the longest,' he reflects. 'Maybe a couple of people in maintenance but that's all I'd say. Nobody that long as the footballing side! On my side now as kit manager, I can remember when we were apprentices, you had to clean the boots of the players. I had Steve McClaren's I seem to remember when I was an apprentice! When he came back to the club for his second stint as a manager, I said, "For Christ's Sake gaffer, this is the fourth time now I've had to clean your boots!" and he laughed about it. Four bloody times!'

Davidson would likely pass up the mantle of Mr Derby County, though, if it was handed to him, because that belonged to the man he considers to be his mentor – Gordon Guthrie.

During a staggering six decades at the club, Guthrie did as much as a human being is allowed to do; reserve player, physio, trainer, before finding a permanent home as a kitman, beginning under Brian Clough and working across every manager since. A constant presence across the club, the number of personnel he saw come and go would easily reach four figures, with one of those being Steve Elliott: 'Gordy was a strong bloke. He was getting on a bit but he was as strong as an ox because he was in the gym every day doing sit-ups, press-ups, bench presses, out-bench pressing all the young lads, and what he said went; you didn't want to get on the wrong side of Gordy.

'But he really liked me because my grandma and grandad lived on the next road to him in Allenton. So he knew them and took a bit of a shine to me, so I couldn't do anything wrong, not that I did, but he always took it a bit easy on me as he knew I was a local lad and he knew I was a massive Derby fan. So Gordy was a character and you would not want to mess with him. He was like a sergeant major.'

The loss of 'Gordy' as he was known in 2016 was a sad day for the club, with the ever-popular stalwart still appearing at Pride Park on an almost weekly basis. Former players, including Štimac, Higginbotham and Chris Powell, all spoke of their love for Guthrie, with the kitman regularly becoming a coach in his own right during the Smith years. Primarily assisting with the goalkeeping training alongside Steele, Gordy would go beyond the expectation of his role each and every day, demonstrating a love and a passion for Derby County that would rub off on many of the players and staff he worked alongside over more than 60 years.

* * *

What is perhaps most surprising isn't where the coaches went on to or what they achieved in the game beyond Derby, but more how they were able to do it. Round, McClaren and co. undoubtedly had talents and a knowledge of the game which was destined to take them to the pinnacle of their profession. But although they had a perfect upbringing with Smith, it was almost counterbalanced by the environment they had to perform in: Raynesway.

To those who have only ever known Derby's training base being the secluded acres of Moor Farm, you are privileged beyond words. Because Raynesway was as ramshackle as Moor Farm is perfect. Situated across the road from Rolls-Royce and within litter-throwing distance of the A511, Raynesway was for decades the not-so-hidden-hub of Derby County during their later years at the Baseball Ground. Drawing sharp contrast to the new training centre they would move to in 2003, there was an endless list of differences which would be rectified with the move, the first of which came around access.

Not only was the base fully viewable to passing cars and lorries, but it was also open to all. Supporters, journalists, anybody who wanted to head there to observe the players in their natural surroundings could simply pass through. Spies with binoculars were not necessary.

'It was just an old wooden hut,' laughs Andy Croft, who progressed from cleaning bathrooms at the BBG to working alongside head groundsman Mark Robinson after the switch to Pride Park. 'When I first started [the players] used to turn up for training, have a shower and go home. I was telling my mate today how, when I first started, the lads would be training and the incinerator would be right next to the Ramarena. All of a sudden it was going all day and, if the wind was blowing in the right direction, all the smoke and everything would be blowing over the pitch and the players would just be carrying on training. It's mad when you think of it! You could barely see them through the smog.'

Seth Johnson would go a step further in his memories, labelling it a 'shithole'. He said, 'When I turned up I was thinking, "Bloody hell, Crewe's training ground is better than this. The changing facilities and all that were rundown."'

But for all the criticisms the training base would face, Raynesway and the Ramarena had a homely feel for the players. 'The showers were always grimy,' remembers Lee Morris. 'It always seemed to be cold there no matter what time of year and, any sort of rain, the river at the back would flood. The fields were always not the best but, overall, I loved going and training there. It was like an everyone together kind of atmosphere, whereas if you go to Moor Farm it's clinical and very, very professional. Raynesway was all about being the underdog, gutting this one out and matching the atmosphere.'

International signings would not be welcomed to the Ramarena at first, with initially the BBG and then Pride Park being the scene for grabbing signatures before the grand reveal of where Monday to Friday would be spent. And though it did come as a shock to some of the overseas talents (Mart Poom spent equal amounts of time training at the David Lloyd gym; Stefano Eranio would escape as soon as sessions were over) it did become a home and a place the squad would enjoy their days.

And while the football was the focus, the Ramarena was also vital for that overall build of the squad. For physio Neil Sillett, he was part of the wider team who would double their working roles with an oversight on how to bring cultures together: 'We had a big cricket thing going on in Raynesway. Houlty [Russell Hoult] was decent, Rory Delap could bowl at 100mph but wouldn't know where it was going, Chris Riggott had an option to join Derbyshire and was a very good player. Davo [Jon Davidson] and Roundy used to play. Two security guys, Pete and his brother Jim, would be in there. And the lads would pretend they were bowling with a tennis ball and then get a bloody cricket ball out. Darryl would say he wasn't the worst but he was a bit crazy with a cricket ball, and he certainly wasn't of the West Indian ilk when it came to cricket. Peter Gadsby would have a game once a year as well, but then with the different nationalities some of the boys had never seen cricket before and didn't have a clue what was going on. They thought it was some form of crazy baseball.'

The setup on site would see a pitch and a half that would be destroyed on a daily basis, the ground staff left to fight a losing battle on a surface located six feet below the river level. But the pièce de résistance was the bowling green, the specially protected part of the training ground which would be in pristine condition for actual football before matches. Head groundsman Mark Robinson said, 'It was an old green and we put boards around it which were three foot high. We called it Mini Wembley. They didn't use it a lot, maybe on a Friday morning for a six v six and they used to love it on there. The ball would just keep in play, bouncing back.'

With the bowling green being the late-week advantage, it brought in the more technically focused players. But for homegrown British players, the overall pull of Raynesway came in a familiarity with what they had experienced growing up through local leagues themselves. Danny Higginbotham may have come from greatness at Manchester United, but even he recognised the allure of the Ramarena: 'The majority of my time [at Manchester United] we had been at The Cliff, so you got changed at The Cliff and then travel over to Littleton Road and that had a real close-knit feel about it. And then they moved to Carrington, this huge training campus-type thing at the time, one of the best around. But for me to then go to Raynesway where there was the changing area, the little dining area, the bowling green where we would always have a five-a-side on a Friday with the young v old. Then the little Portakabin where you'd watch the videos and a little indoor area and then the training ground – I loved it.

'It's bizarre but I love those type of things and even further on into my career, when I was at Stoke, at first we'd get changed at the stadium and then have to drive down to the training ground, which was just a field, then we ended up with Portakabins from Aston Villa. And then it ended up being at a beautiful training ground. But I loved the closeness of things and everybody being together and things like that, I just thought it creates a real good togetherness, so I had no issue whatsoever and, if anything, I just embraced it and loved it.'

The Rams would leave Raynesway in 2003, and the site remained derelict thereon after. Travellers moved in, travellers moved out, the place swiftly becoming a target for arson in a grim visual metaphor for what would happen on the football field. And while Moor Farm has gone on to house the brightest talent in the UK in the years afterwards, for those passing by the A511 on your way into or out of Alvaston and beyond, it remains a place of hope. The patch of overgrown land that Derby County called their Monday to Friday home for decades.

11

CLOSER

WITHOUT BEING rude, watching a World Cup as a Derby County fan is something of an innocent pastime. You definitely won't have someone you support 38 afternoons a season in the England squad, it's unlikely that any of the representative players will end up at Pride Park anytime soon and you're probably not there in person watching. So all that is left to do is drink through it, enjoy it for what it is and breathe a sigh of relief when the first pre-season shots come through.

But 1998 was a different time. With a World Cup in France and the Eurostar still very much an intriguing novelty, there was a closeness and, for all the anti-France sentiments no doubt bubbling inside some of you reading this right now, it felt pretty close to being a home tournament. But that's an irrelevance. France '98 was a special, special tournament for Derby County supporters because they were able to see several of their own players rock up in the colours of various nations.

For Croatia, there were the inevitable faces of recently departed Aljoša Asanović and club legend Igor Štimac, who both played a part in taking the country to a third-placed finish on their World Cup debut. Representing Scotland was defender Christian Dailly, with Jacob Laursen in Denmark colours. And as for the Reggae Boyz of Jamaica, the duo of Darryl Powell and Deon Burton wore the yellow shirts. To put it into perspective, in the long, prestigious history of the tournament, only 11 current Derby players have appeared at a World Cup. Five of them were at France '98.

Burton – who led the line at the age of just 21 for Jamaica – found himself in a group with not only Argentina, but also Croatia themselves. He recalls, 'I was at Portsmouth when I first got into Jamaica's team, then Jim gave me the green light to go and represent them when I was at Derby. But he'd always say, "As soon as that final whistle goes, make sure you're on that first plane back because we've got a game at the weekend. And it'll be a bit better if you can score as well." But it was good because at the World Cup I played against Igor with Croatia. To be up against my club team-mate on the biggest stage and knowing about him, yeah it was good. We had a bit of friendly banter during the game and I remember missing a sitter header. He ran past me and tapped me on the back and went, "Oh, you'd have scored that if it was on a Saturday." But it was surreal to play at the highest level at the World Cup. It's every boy's dream.'

Burton was no stranger to the international stage, and over time became the most capped international in Rams history. What is often overlooked, though, was his involvement ahead of the France '98 group stage draw, where he appeared for the Rest of the World XI against a European side. 'I was with Batistuta, Ronaldo,' he proudly lists. 'We played the game and it was on the telly, then you had to get changed into your suit and they'd call you out one by one by your name and country to come and sit in your groups as they'd pull the balls out. When I came back [to Derby], Jim went, "Bloody hell, you were a bit scared weren't you! I didn't even see you break a smile, son. I could see the sweat pouring down your brow!" He took the mick out of me a little bit on that occasion.'

Ideally, Burton and his fellow internationals would have looked at their foray on to the global stage as a welcome taster of the type of attention they could achieve on a weekly basis with a Rams side continuing to grow. The same can be said for the pre-season visit of Barcelona to Pride Park, who brought Luís Figo and Rivaldo – among others – for the star-studded extravaganza.

That evening allowed a look at the only two summer additions that Smith opted to bring in too. While Stefan Schnoor would arrive from the relatively local depths of Germany and perform solidly over his two years at the club, the more notable addition of Argentine defender Horacio Carbonari was the headliner. A then record signing, Horacio from Rosario would immediately become an integral part of the side until the drop out of the top flight. Opting to respond over email, he simply wrote of his time, 'The most important moment for me (apart from scoring goal [against] Nottingham) was when in a practice that we played for [the] FA Cup, Jim asked me if I wanted to be captain of the team. I said no because I didn't know the language well, but I will never forget that moment in my memory. The club was always available if I needed something and I am very grateful to all the people who work in the club because they always treated me and all the players with respect and admiration. Derby is a fantastic club, the fans are the best [and] always in my mind.'

Scouted first by Archie Gemmill and then Bobby Roberts, both reports stated mobility to be a potential issue. Physio Neil Sillett says, 'When he first came, he nearly went home because we couldn't get him fit. He was one of the nicest people that I've met in football, an absolute top guy and I see a lot of him. But he was at full health to stay with his head above water at Premier League football. To perform he found it difficult but he adapted. And when he was fit and playing well, he was fine. He played with passion, which is what the fans loved, and they loved the fact he could score a goal out of nothing. You had the goal at Notts Forest where he went crazy when he scored it, it went a long way towards his cult status at the club. He scored the winner as well at home. And he was great fun, all the lads loved him.'

But it was the outgoings which raised a little more surprise than those coming in the door. Robin Van Der Laan dropped a division to Barnsley, with 1995/96 player of the season Dean Yates moved on after a torrid spell with injuries. Mauricio Solís would leave after failing to fully break into the squad too. The biggest eyebrow raised came in the departure of Chris Powell, which caused the most alarm considering his importance on the left side of the defence. 'I always look back and wish I was there longer,' confesses Powell. 'Sadly for me I moved on but I suppose the biggest accolade is that Jim said, "It was a mistake we let you go. We got money for you and brought someone in on a free but I shouldn't have done it." That's always a proud memory for me with Jim.'

And despite another strong campaign, the loss of Powell for seemingly budgetary reasons was the first inkling that this Rams side couldn't compete financially for a great deal longer. Derby hadn't lost a genuine starter for quite some time, and opting to allow Powell to depart to newly promoted Charlton Athletic would be the catalyst for subsequent losses over the next 12 months. There was also some discomfort on the additions as well, with Igor questioning the addition of another central defender: 'I remember that I had three great seasons, a great World Cup winning bronze, but I came back and the only player we had signed was playing in my position. I was a bit surprised to be honest. They spent £3.5m on Horacio; I didn't feel good about it. It's not my business to get into that, but I didn't see any logic in that move.'

The course of the early season did see a couple more moves made, namely Spencer Prior and Kevin Harper. And with young Rory Delap consolidating his spot in various roles within the starting 11, a slow start was swiftly put behind them as Derby charged up to second in the Premier League. Smith even cheekily wrote in programme notes ahead of the October Tottenham fixture, 'I know you [the supporters] were disappointed we didn't hit top spot last weekend but we don't need to get carried away this early. I'll start to get excited if we're top by the end of March.' They wouldn't be, that Spurs outing the first of several games without a win that took them to the more mind-sustaining mid-table region.

Taking an eerily similar style to the campaign previous, Derby would never find their consistent level of form over the course of the season, not helped once again by injuries and poor form in front of goal. Igor's bad back kept him out for weeks at a time, while Messrs Sturridge, Burton, Wanchope and Baiano only managed to contribute nine goals combined by the turn of the year.

It's not to say there weren't highs, they were just a little fewer and farther between than they had been in the previous campaign. Perhaps the most notable high of the season came at Anfield, sparked by an early goal from another capture in the form of ex-Hibernian winger Harper. 'That was my first-ever start in the Premier League,' relives the Scot. 'But it was strange because I felt like we were gonna win, there was just an air of togetherness because we had so many injuries for that game and we had a lot of players playing – myself included – that if everybody was fit wouldn't have played. The goal itself, I think if it had been Alan Shearer who scored the header, everybody would have been going crazy for it. But for me it was just really, really an exceptional feeling playing for Derby in the Premier League against Liverpool, scoring and showing that I genuinely felt that I could live and breathe and play in the Premier League.'

And while new faces like Harper and the 'Bazooka' that was Carbonari would step up in importance at times over the campaign, off-field shenanigans would keep the unit together. Raynesway was the hub for all behind-the-scenes life at the club, and with an updated menu and a family feel continuing to develop, the squad would find themselves spending more and more time there out of personal choice.

'We had a big cricket thing going on in Raynesway,' Neil Sillett recalls. 'But we would have golf days in Mickleover. We had our days out and we stayed at Cambridge, where we then took them to Newmarket and then we played golf as well as a group. It wasn't easy, though, because a lot of the guys had different cultures and it was difficult to get your Eranios and Wanchopes to play golf. If Eranio worked hard at it, he'd have eventually been flicking it up with his club though. We were always looking to get the boys together though. We did paintballing over Nottingham way.'

It's not quite the perception you'd have of a 1990s football team though. Little drinking, no wild nights, nothing illegal. As Jacob Laursen says, it was actually unusually serene: 'We didn't go out eating a lot because we were a very serious group of players – for us it was more like we needed to train really well and be focused on that. I know it sounds funny but David Lloyd's in Derby gave us free membership. And us going there on a Sunday for a warm-down built our togetherness more than going out. We were a bit different as a group compared to others. I've played in the national team with a lot of Danish players who were in England, and they were like, "Oh we did this, we go out," and we didn't. Some of the young players, on a Saturday they would have their fun and that was accepted because everybody pulled in the same direction. That's just how we did it.

'We didn't have any fallings out or stuff like that. You could have the odd striker being jealous of the other, but that's natural. There was never anything which ruined our focus or the team spirit. Because he brought in foreign players, I was spending a lot of time with Lars Bohinen and Stefan Schnoor; I spoke a lot to Stefano. But we all had to speak English at the training ground. It wasn't the Italians speaking Italian, me speaking German, it was always English. He [Jim Smith] made sure there were no cliques either, we would all mix.'

* * *

Even among a start to the season which saw a two-month spell that warranted just two wins in ten (including the Anfield victory), there were still hints that European ambitions would not be fully extinguished. Sat in 11th at the midpoint of the season, by matchday 28 Derby had found themselves in sixth spot with ten left to play.

Mart Poom says, 'I look back at it as a "what if". We were always underdogs, but we'd always do better than pundits and people were expecting and fighting against the odds. Seventh, eighth, ninth. We were always around European places and there during the season, and that is a credit to Jim.'

So much better than pundits predicted was a theme throughout Derby's time in the top flight and a notion that Smith was quick to pick upon when exceeding expectations. In one edition of *The Ram* a season earlier, Smith wryly mocked pundit Mark Lawrenson's prediction of relegation, while a run through *It's Only a Game* sees the manager take pride in proving his doubters wrong.

The run of two wins in ten was immediately followed by a contrasting one of six victories in the same amount of games, putting the Rams' European hopes well within their own grasp. In among this, Smith – always one to hammer home the importance of the FA Cup, had his side in the quarter-finals ahead of a mouthwatering tie at Arsène Wenger's Arsenal side at Highbury. The afternoon would prove a reflection of what was about to happen in the league season though, an 89th-minute winner from Kanu curtailing cup ambitions once again.

In the league, things took another unwelcome turn. One of the strongest defences in the Premier League shipped eight against Leeds and Newcastle. And while Carbonari's Cruyff turn and curled finish was enough to see off Ron Atkinson's Forest, it would be a rare highlight in a final seven games which produced an astonishingly poor eight points. Winnable home matches against Southampton and Coventry produced goalless draws, while confidence-sapping losses at West Ham and Arsenal would allow the chasing pack to turn a potential finish of sixth into a drop to eighth.

A late-season addition of Mikkel Beck would prove disastrous too, the forward voted as the worst-ever Rams signing in some quarters. 'He came in wearing a hairband and Jim just said, "Oh my God, what have we got here?" laughs one member of the coaching staff. Beck's signing would be the worst move of his career, but it wasn't the only poor call in the final weeks as Smith opted to allow Lee Carsley to leave for just under £4m to Blackburn Rovers.

In the quest for Europe and the ultimate disappointment to fall short again, one of the brightest hopes did come in the form of the increasingly reliable Rory Delap. Focus in the latter years of Smith's tenure came in finding youngsters to progress either from the club's youth system or the lower divisions, and Delap's signing from Carlisle for £200,000 in the spring of 1998 was the piece of business which gave hope that no major rebuild would be needed. It posed a problem for the press team though. Having worked from the opening of Pride Park in the communications department, Rams fan Kerry Ganly assumed she'd recognise any and all of the first-team squad, but came up short with Delap: 'I was working a matchday when Derby signed Rory, and he was young and fresh-faced. He popped into the press office just to say hello really and I didn't realise who he was; I thought he'd just come to help out. And bless him, he came in the press office and was like, "Hi, I'm Rory." So I said, "Oh I'd really like a cup of tea," so he became the teaboy and I had no idea at the time … although he made a really nice cup of tea.'

Delap had become the poster boy for quickfire evolution into the first-team squad, but it was behind him in the reserves and the youth system where – even amid stuttering runs of form – excitement grew. Because even while Smith would look to bring in his internationals, it wasn't his sole focus. Presented with a remit from the board to develop a backup side which was primarily British, Smith would work closely with Steve Round, Steve Taylor and Billy McEwan to blend a reserve team that would be immediately ready to make the transition to Premier League football when the time came.

'It was really before the academy was set up,' admits Neil Sillett. 'We just had the 16s and the 18s. Jim went about signing a second team, which came a little later in his tenure, but that was Andy Oakes, Richard Jackson, Paul Boertien, Riggs [Chris Riggott], Steve Elliott, Ian Evatt, Malcolm Christie. Steve Elliott was very outgoing and lively so he made him captain of that group. And Steve made one of the best [first-team] starts I've ever seen. He played against Asprilla and Shearer [Elliott's Rams debut had been in a goalless draw at Newcastle United in

December 1997] in his first game. And he was brilliant against them. The first-team players took to those guys and they were able to give the senior players a bit of grief because they were brought in as a group rather than one at a time. They integrated really quickly and really well.

'Delap was slightly older but came as a young buck out of Carlisle and was a massive success for the club. He could play anywhere really and Eranio would say, "He's a freak! Delap can play centre-forward, centre-half, right-back, right wing." Against Chelsea he played up front and got two goals at Pride Park [in October 1999]. It was not just their banter though, and the only bit of credit I'd ever give myself there is I was always encouraged by Jim to get them gelling and to say what they wanted to say. They'd never say anything in front of Jim, but they'd say it to me and Steve Round and Billy McEwan. They were just a young group of kids who were delighted to be there. And I brought a sports therapist from Portsmouth who had come out of the navy, a guy called John McKeown. He's now a sports scientist at Everton and he is like a comedian. Jim just let him loose on the squad and that helped.'

* * *

Focus is rightly heavy on internationalism within Smith's side, but having been given the remit to build homegrown talent as well, there was a crucial development that again placed Derby ahead of most others in the top division. The move from the Baseball Ground was difficult to accept for many, but it didn't necessarily mean the end for supporters when it came to visiting the old home. Still used as a training facility, it was what the reserve side would do on the remarkably replenished turf that gave the stadium a new lease of life – and silverware – in its final years before demolition.

For chronological transparency, the success of Derby County's reserve sides during the Bald Eagle years doesn't happen at this point in 1999. Premier Reserve League South success would come at the back end of the following two seasons, but unfortunately during that time so did quite a lot else.

Much is rightly made of the importance of academies and youth systems today. The Rams side at the time of writing is made almost exclusively of those who progressed through the Moor Farm factory, something which is successfully guiding the club through the necessity of actually being able to field an 11 for the time being. It's a development which has led to the growth of training facilities across the world of football, but during the 1990s, youth progression for Derby County took a different turn.

Raynesway's all-encompassing nature (for all-encompassing nature, read 'it was small') meant that the distance between first-teamers and those plying their trade through apprenticeships was slimmer than the modern day, with training facilities shared and youngsters called upon as bodies for Smith to test his new tactics on. Future Rams young player of the year Steve Elliott laughs at the thought: 'We were training with the first team where they would be setting their team up, and we would be the opposition and be pretty passive because you didn't want to get players injured. We got promoted in my second year as an apprentice and had a lot of players coming in, and the gaffer and Steve McClaren were just like, "You don't even go near them if you can help it. If you foul someone and they're out for Saturday, you're fined a week's wages."'

And though the fear of God would be put into some – not least when they were presented with Jim Smith for the first time – the inclusion in first-team training acted as an early insight of what life could potentially look like. Because for those deemed worthy, not only would they train with the first team, they'd also have the opportunity to play alongside some as part of a reserve team headed up by Steve Round, Steve Taylor and Billy McEwan.

One man they would find themselves aside was record signing Lee Morris, who struggled for fitness and form during Smith's tenure. His drop down to the reserves might have been perceived as a demotion, but he saw it as more of an opportunity to enjoy football again: 'A lot of people would look at it like, "Oh shit

I'm in the reserves," but I used to just like playing. It was an interesting time because I was in the crossover of first-team and reserve-team squads. I was getting 20–30 minutes for the first team and playing every reserve game, and the reserves was a hell of an atmosphere. You turn up and you realise it could be worse, you get excited to be there, get your pads on, start playing a game. The atmosphere around the reserve team was good and we would bring a good amount of tempo to the practices and stuff because we were all young and pretty confident. We used to go out there and have a good go. We had a good laugh, but the first team was a lot more serious, and it was a different atmosphere. [But] we used to fancy ourselves that we could beat the first team a lot of the time just because we were smashing teams and the first team were struggling.'

And with fluidity that saw the likes of Georgi Kinkladze and fellow first-teamers appear on an ad-hoc basis within the second string, it brought individuals closer together while bridging that gap. But perhaps more importantly for the success of that young group, it created a true squad unity below sides who would begin to struggle at senior level.

Come their second success in the 2000/01 campaign, it was Billy McEwan who would be charged with heading up the reserves, overseeing a side which saw a large majority make at least some form of an impression in the first team during their Derby days. Whether it be external captures such as Lee Morris, Youl Mawéné and captain Richard Jackson, or the likes of Elliott and Lee Grant who progressed through the youth system, Smith's task of building a young English side capable of progression to the main stage was an undeniable success. And with a coaching team consisting of a now Arsenal assistant manager, those medals seem a little less surprising.

'I actually remember sitting with Steve Round and talking through things then,' Marvin Robinson, one of the men to make it into the senior team, reflects. 'We had Tottenham in the first game I think. We already had the team sheet through and they had Sol Campbell, Ruel Fox, Justin Edinburgh. And we were a young core of Chris Riggott, Steve Elliot, Richard Jackson, Paul Boertien, Adam Murray, Malcolm Christie, myself. Then maybe someone like Kevin Harper or Danny Porter. We were young and they had the stars out. And then that psychology of Steve Round and how he presented it as an opportunity to show that you are of a level, because myself, you're playing against Sol Campbell who is at that point the best young defender in England. It's not long before he goes to Arsenal. So if you play to a certain level, then again you know you can do it.

'It sounds very simple but I always think about that particular game and why Steve did that. He made that game a lot more and it worked. We beat them, I scored two goals and I just think of psychologically what he did to me leading up to the game and then you think about it like brands or whatever. I'd just left school, I'm against Sol Campbell. Just the psychology of what that meant and that was the launchpad for all of us playing in the first team at some point, and for us to go and win that league. You've got people like Ashley Cole in that league, a lot of whom became top players. West Ham, their midfield was Gavin McCann, Michael Carrick and Joe Cole in a three. They were a star team and that winning of the Premier Reserve League, it's a shame a lot of [our] players didn't do more.'

But while Round, McEwan and Taylor were at the forefront, being able to rely on the coaches and sergeants of the first team was equally important. Elliott, a boyhood Rams fan who would cycle from Alvaston to the Baseball Ground for matches, found the likes of Gordon Guthrie as crucial in his development as anybody else: 'The regime ... was more military with the discipline side of it all, and some players just couldn't hack it and fell by the wayside. They just sort of couldn't hack the day-to-day of it all and it took a real strong character. Gordy was the main cause of it because he would try and break you, and some lads would be in bits. But he'd just say, "How are you gonna cope in front of 40–50,000 people if you break in front of me?" You 100 per cent would not get away with it today but it got us through and it sorted the men from the boys really.'

The double Premier Reserve League victory presented Derby at the height of both reserve- and youth-team football. Though the successes would come as the first team faltered, it would give an overview of what could save the club financially in the long run. The second championship during 2000/01 came with a nine-point gap, no mean feat considering opposition included Chelsea, Tottenham and Arsenal. Sadly by this point, they'd be looking to progress into a Derby side slowly losing their way and their status.

Still, good to celebrate something, isn't it?

12

ADJUSTING TO LOSS

IT'S DIFFICULT to fill a void. If you're reading this, you've been through something which leaves a hole in your heart and a gap in your life, and if you've not, you are quite frankly (and without meaning to be rude) a monster who has no feelings. Most deep voids come from significant life moments, such as a death or a heavy break-up. But the magic, or rather the curse, of life is that you tend not to know when loss is coming. It could come at your lowest ebb, could come at your greatest moment, or it could even come in the 99.99 per cent of the rest of your life. You don't get to choose when your life gets turned upside down, unfortunately.

The early months of 1999 were Derby County's void. For a club so consistent in delivering pain in the years before and since, the Bald Eagle's reign was an anomaly when it comes to painstaking occurrences. Fleeting love affairs with a Croatian duo would tug at the heartstrings, but there were replacements in place to ensure that those voids – the ones on the pitch – were filled, like a quickfire new relationship weeks after you find your significant other with someone else (I'm aware this sounds worryingly realistic, but it's just a scenario and has no basis in reality, I promise).

Jim Smith was beloved, adored, and rightly so. Worshipped by fans, players, club management and the people closest to him in his life. But as has been made clear in this book and in what happened in the years following, Jim was part of a double act.

The overall management of the club, the recruitment of players, the ability to make the first-team changing room a positive and thriving place to be, three of the many assets he possessed. But what Jim didn't possess in the same way that others did – at least in the mid 1990s – was the tactical know-how to bring a Premier League side together.

Steve McClaren did though. From the very first days he would pour Smith a whisky or a wine in the managerial office at the Manor Ground, there was a clear synergy between the duo. Despite their significant age gap and the fact McClaren was very much on the rookie end of the coaching stick, Smith found that he was able to complement and fill that void in the parts of his management he was not so successful in. The coaching, the tactical analysis, engaging players when it came to football. McClaren was truly Smith's right arm.

'Steve was good cop, the gaffer was bad cop,' laughs Deon Burton. 'Anything the gaffer would say would be, "Oh do this and that," and then Steve would douse the fire and say, "Don't worry, keep your minds straight," and then take me through the tactical side of what he wanted me to do. They had a really good blend.'

Whether it came in the training, the analysis or calming situations with players post a Smith outburst, McClaren was more integral to the success of that side than most can ever truly realise. Smith may have been the manager in title, but McClaren was as close to head coach as the decade would allow. In truth, the McClaren who returned to that main role and that title in 2013 was effectively the same one who worked under Jim, albeit now in a position where he would report only to himself. It was a suitable elevation, even if it had come well over a decade later.

Budding young coach George Glover was given an exclusive insight into what made McClaren tick at the time: 'I used to go down during my holidays from university to watch them train. I'd watch McClaren doing his little tactics and moving people around and it was brilliant. When I first saw McClaren coach, I'll never forget it. It was on this big fat old TV, and it was when

Princess Diana had died on that Saturday night. I walked in and everyone was looking down at the floor, then I looked at the telly and I was reading the little thing across the bottom. But back then they would use the coaches as the dummies or the players to do the sessions because there weren't really academies back then. So I could go home and write everything down and keep a log, take what you can from it and create your own ideas based on that. And they were very good at putting on sessions and working on a local level.'

Within the innovation chapters earlier in this book is more of a comprehensive overview on McClaren, but everything up until this point had his fingerprints on it. And that's why, for so long, Smith and McClaren came very much as a duo. Within this, though, came a fear of just how important he was to the run from First Division also-rans to European competition chasers. And it was the fear of what life would be like after one of the two had gone that ultimately played a significant part in the turmoil which would come next.

* * *

'All of the things Jim wasn't good at were the things Steve McClaren complemented him on. It's why they were so good together.'

Jacob Laursen was just one of the players of the 1990s who easily identified what each man brought to the club. Another was academy graduate Steve Elliott: 'I couldn't have had a better upbringing at Derby with Steve coaching and Jim as your manager. You can't go wrong with a future England manager and one of the biggest characters in the game. It was just a match made in heaven and to be a young lad being part of that, coming through and them liking me and playing me, it's just surreal. Thinking back, and I think back quite a lot, there must be hundreds, thousands and millions of kids who would love to play in the Premier League, and I managed to do it and it was thanks to Jim Smith and Steve McClaren.'

Later in life and when analysing his first spell in full managerial charge at Pride Park, McClaren referenced the 'holy trinity' that came so close to working for him during the 2013/14 season. It comprised McClaren, Sam Rush and Chris Evans, and he testaments the resurgence during this campaign to the fact they had the three in place. There was no trinity during the Jim Smith years, such were the numerous major players. Keith Loring was pivotal, Lionel Pickering it goes without saying, while Peter Gadsby and Stuart Webb were both hugely significant. But it was the coaching duo who were most important.

'Jim did need good people around him and to bounce ideas,' admits Malcolm Christie, who would go on to play under McClaren at Middlesbrough. 'Steve McClaren was a good one for that because he had the youth and the exuberance, the fresh ideas and Jim had the old-school approach.'

McClaren almost kept Smith young. Having departed the game prior to his Derby days, it was his allegiance with the former Rams midfielder that sparked perhaps the greatest spell in his entire managerial career. And for the gratitude he had to McClaren, he knew it would almost be a matter of time before it would come to an end.

Effectively being groomed to take over from Smith in the near future, that was at least the intention of the manager, who knew he couldn't go on forever and wanted to leave Derby at the highest possible point before handing the power to McClaren. There was a sting in the tail though, and it came directly from Smith's friendships in the game.

How Alex Ferguson came to decide on McClaren was no mystery either. The friendship between Ferguson and Smith was no secret in football, the duo adoring the company of one another both in and out of football.

Having fallen out with Brian Kidd in the first months of 1999, attentions immediately turned to the brightest young coach in British football with Ferguson putting the feelers out on bringing McClaren to Old Trafford. As Smith recalled in *It's Only a Game*, the approach came directly from Ferguson to Smith, a sign of both the respect he had for him and the friendship they had developed over a series of years.

Neil Sillett remembers the process, 'Alex was very up front in the way he wanted to approach and speak to Steve, and he asked Jim first, which is the way he should have done it. He did go about it the right way.'

Ferguson himself wrote in *Leading*, 'In my 26 years, the most important interviews I ever did were for the role of my assistant. After Brian Kidd left in 1998 I got more serious about interviewing, and the process became meticulous. We looked at several people but narrowed it down to David Moyes and Steve McClaren. David was very tense ... Steve was the opposite. He was bright, breezy and enthusiastic. He was a voracious consumer of books and videos about football and the training techniques. At that point Steve had a lot more experience in the top flight than David, and that swung my decision.'

The approach may have been unsurprising considering McClaren's growth under Smith, but it panicked a boardroom who – having at first been reluctant to even hire an assistant – recognised the worth he had on the constantly improving fortunes. Peter Gadsby recalls, 'When it was announced he was going, we had McClaren for not a lot of money. Lionel goes to me, "McClaren is your mate, isn't he? Tell him he can't go. He's got to stay, we need him. Go and ring him." So I rang Steve, "Where are you? I've got Lionel asking me to ask you to turn round and stay." "Peter, I'm off for an interview with Alex. They're top of the league, quarter-finals of the Champions League, semi of the FA Cup." And I think he also said "I'm on a quarter of a million" ... so I took that as a no then.

'There's no doubt in my mind that the decline came when McClaren went. What I don't know is – if Alex Ferguson had asked Jim could he approach McClaren, and there is no doubt in my mind that if Jim said no, Alex Ferguson wouldn't have taken him. No doubt. Such was the respect.'

The decision was a dagger to Derby County and to Jim Smith himself. In the edition of *The Ram* which followed McClaren's departure, the boss wrote, 'I greeted the news with mixed emotions – I was thrilled that somebody I have worked with so closely for so long had been recognised for his coaching talents, but I was sorry to see him go because he has been a great friend and a major influence ... I'm very sad in lots of ways.'

But, and in a realisation that only further pushes home the good heart Smith possessed, he didn't *have* to let McClaren go. If he wanted to, he could quite easily have kept hold of him, moved aside soon after and allowed him to take his first solo managerial job. The fact he didn't do this proved detrimental to Derby in the long run, but his valuation of McClaren as a man and as a friend is the same as it was for all others he encountered in and out of sport. Aware that this was a truly once-in-a-lifetime opportunity to join a side on the brink of footballing history, Smith opened the door to his protégé to build on everything he had achieved by this stage with Derby.

And McClaren wasn't alone in having the door to better opportunities opened for him. Players such as Igor and Wanchope were allowed to move on, regardless of the reasoning. The same too for the likes of Ramm Mylvaganam and his Prozone initiative, which would follow McClaren to Manchester United. So would Bill Beswick, but he recalls his own tale on the kindness that meant McClaren could leave: 'He [Jim] was a very kind man, I think the same with letting Steve and me go. He had less control over me but he recognised that if that [Steve moving to Manchester United] could have happened to him when he was a younger coach, it would have been a marvellous move.

'[But] it's funny because Steve and I went out to an Italian in Derby on the Monday night, and we talked about which clubs Steve would go to. Which clubs had good ethos, good work habits, good stable platforms to coach on. We came up with nine clubs, and we didn't include Manchester United because it was beyond our dreams. On the Tuesday night we played them, and Steve had introduced some tactics which worked very, very well; Fergie was intrigued.

'On the Wednesday, Fergie ran Jim to ask if he could speak to Steve. Jim gave permission. And he met Steve at a cafe halfway between Manchester and Derby, and they did the deal. Steve left and I stayed at Derby, because I was happy at Derby and I loved Derby. But eventually Steve said, "I've spoken to Alex about you coming, and he's considering it." The next thing I knew was a phone call one evening from Alex Ferguson, asking me to come in in the morning to chat at 7am. So I went in and we did an interview of 15 minutes; I started on the following Monday. Jim was very good about letting me go, and very good about letting Steve go.'

It may seem that Smith was allowing all those closest to him to leave, and that is certainly true, but it came from a position of being willing to sacrifice himself for the lives and success of others. At the time it was often questioned why a Derby side so close to Europe had slipped so drastically down the table, and it came because everybody around Smith was departing. Smith and Derby County would almost be the victims of their own success, as the football world slowly began to realise just what was happening in quiet little Derbyshire.

'My time with Jim prepared me enormously,' reflects McClaren. 'If I could work with Jim and handle Jim, I felt I could work with anybody. Because he really wanted the best, everything to work. And so if I hadn't have been with Jim in that kind of environment, what I learnt from foreign players, what I learnt even in the board level. Because Jim was a damn good manager and his teams were all exciting. Some of the games we won, they were incredible and the football that we played ... I don't think I would have got on in the game and been able to handle those players at United [if I hadn't] handled Jim, and that was tough. It was a tough environment that we grew up on. And we always kept in touch after that. Times together in Spain. He was just like a second dad, grandad, however you'd like to call it.'

It would be no easy task to replace McClaren. In fact, it was nigh on impossible, as will be highlighted shortly. But for McClaren too, although he would work with perhaps the greatest manager in the history of British football, he knew it would be difficult to replace Smith from his life as well. Following his departure and as referenced in a copy of *The Ram* ahead of a February 1999 tie against Charlton, he wrote, 'It has been a phenomenal four years and I can't express how much I will miss the chairman, the manager, the players, the backroom boys – no one will be forgotten. I loved it here. Apart from the late Friday nights it has been great to work with Jim – absolutely magnificent, an education. But it's not just that, it's the man himself, the freedom he has given me, which has been second to none.'

Smith had him in a good place though. When McClaren asked Ferguson what he wanted from him on the first day of training, the managerial titan responded with, 'Whatever you did with Derby, do that. That's why I brought you here.'

No compensation could ever replace McClaren, in the view of Stuart Webb. Without the finest mind of his generation, Smith would slowly struggle to the ultimate end, which saw his removal as manager in 2001.

* * *

To fill the void of McClaren, Smith made his first error: he swapped youth for experience. The initial addition of Ray Harford did look wise on paper. Part of the 1995 Premier League-winning coaching team with Blackburn Rovers, his move into the main seat quickly went sour, sacked inside his second season. Roles at West Brom and Queens Park Rangers swiftly went the same way and, having been out of management for two years, his appointment to fill in was an eyebrow-raiser.

Gadsby remembers the appointment as the first warning sign of what was soon to come in a Derby County that would struggle to adjust without the tactical brain of McClaren: 'Jim was a big friend of Big Ron [Atkinson] and he was shafted [at Coventry].

Jim always said, "That's the trouble when you bring in these bloody people you can't trust," so he said he would never bring a number two in. He brought in Ray Harford who had been at Blackburn, was clearly on his way out. Nobody talks about him, he was a disaster. Jim's number two, he went from McClaren to this guy who was 15 years older. All the players said, eh? And he got rid of him.'

The appointment was made in mind of consolidation in the short term, but a duo of older coaches would never find the same blend as the one Smith and McClaren did, not least in the fact Harford couldn't maintain the coaching style despite initial hopes he would. And having been reluctant to make a permanent move up from London, it soon spelled the end for his temporary stay.

There was another short-term man in the form of Malcolm Crosby, who struggled even more to get the players onside. Upcoming striker Marvin Robinson remembers sessions descending into farce, simply listing Crosby as: 'A disaster. You'd got Malcolm Crosby, and then you've just got Seth Johnson and Rory Delap laughing at his coaching sessions, and I remember him saying, "You're only laughing because you cannae do it." But no, it was rubbish. It's really hard to be super detailed but it was just old school.

'Sometimes you don't know what you've got until it's gone and you don't realise how forward-thinking Steve McClaren and that staff were until it's not there. There is always this perception that everything is at the level you are at, but they were the level beyond that, which is why Derby were performing at that level. So when it's gone and you've got someone trying to coach a 4-4-2, it doesn't work. Because we didn't have a squad for 4-4-2. He [Crosby] had one for Sunderland but we didn't have it. Rory Delap wasn't an orthodox right-back, Seth wasn't an orthodox left-midfielder or central-midfielder. It was square pegs and round holes and, from Malcolm's perspective, 4-4-2 was probably the most basic, the most obvious, most trusted, most known system and method of playing. So he probably couldn't get his head around how we could not do it. But it's because our whole thing wasn't living in that era, that squad.

'Christian Dailly was an attacking midfielder but became a sweeper in a back three. Danny Higginbotham was bought as an orthodox left-back and ended up playing as a left-sided centre-half or wing-back. Lee Carsley became the player he did because he sat as that deep-lying six in the midfield three. We had the ten in Baiano, Stefano played everywhere. I remember Eranio in central midfield against Vieira and Petit and he was juggling it over their heads; that was my first-ever appearance [away at Arsenal in May 1999]. So it was that fluidity and forward-thinking and that cosmopolitan outlook that he just did not have. And some of the softer skills as well.

'Communication to the players, player psychology. He wasn't from that era and it didn't work. Jim was the traditionalist who would bark the orders, get the discipline but he would then let the coaches innovate. And he'd manage. And then it didn't work with Malcolm. It was more of a disaster because everything within that coaching circle was at such a high level but not recognised truly as being as high a level as it was. Yes he went to Man United did Steve, but I remember at the time people were a bit surprised by that. It was like going back in time so it reflected badly on Jim.'

Robinson would sense it, much like the rest of the squad, that times had changed. And as Smith struggled to find first the blend in styles and then struggled with his squad not respecting his coaches, squad attention turned towards what they had lost. 'I think that the professional side of it, it got worse,' confesses Lars Bohinen. 'The quality and the demands got lower, it was easier to get away with things and I think Jim probably got a bit more stressed. I just remember things deteriorated quite a lot towards the end of 1999 season, or up until Christmas then. It was important for Jim to have Steve there because Steve was a bit more modern, he had different views, he balanced out the bad sides of Jim.'

And with Crosby unable to get his ideas across, it meant that the usual office-dwelling Smith needed to swap his suit trousers for shorts and get directly involved in sessions on a day-to-day basis. But even with him on the pitch, it remained obvious to those closest to Smith – such as Dane Farrell – that something was truly amiss: 'Post-Steve, we all had to step up. There was a time where I was given the responsibility for taking the guys away to Holland for pre-season when Jim and the others would join when away. It was an honour they trusted that with me, but it was a huge change as we all had to step up in that role. We all did miss Steve at that stage because he was the go-between who would know how to work Jim, how to get the best out of Jim, how to get relationships from players to Jim going in the best way. It was a parting of the ways when Steve left and I think Jim missed him then.'

Results would reflect the uncertainty and confusion within Raynesway. The European hopes of 1997/98 and 1998/99 were quickly forgotten about, with the order of the day becoming worry around how Premier League safety would be maintained. Eventually it wouldn't be, but in the short term the club did manage to cling on to their status for the next two campaigns, often against the odds.

With McClaren and Beswick gone, as well as Harford and then Crosby failing to build on the almost unachievable heights their predecessor had set, attention would soon turn to another man who possessed the youth, drive and invention of McClaren: Steve Round. While the future Arsenal, Manchester United and Everton coach had slowly and impressively made his way from academy coaching into the first team, the struggles around McClaren's replacements meant his time would come sooner than perhaps even he thought.

Round said, 'At the end of the 1998/99 season Jim pulled me into the office and just said, "Look, Steve's going to Man United. I'm bringing in a senior coach but I've been really pleased with what you've been doing with the reserve team and I want you to step up. I still want you involved with the reserve team and linking, but I want you to support the new coach. Don't worry about your contract, don't worry about anything else, I'll sort all that out." It was supporting the teamwork and lots of individual bits. I was working a little bit closer with Jim because, as you trust each other, your relationship always grows. But it was just a natural progression.

'I had mentors everywhere. I had Jim to look up to to see how he handled the environment, the media, the arena, how he managed enough, how he dealt with discipline, how he worked with the players, with families of players and how he looked after them off the field, how he dealt with selection issues, dropping players, how he recruited and brought players over and convinced them to come and play. It was just a massive learning curve. And I've got Steve McClaren that was on the grass, to learn and watch him work and see how he was innovative with his tactical coaching, his technical work, the sessions that were put on, the learnings he would deliver, the presentations. I got Bill Beswick who I could tap into from a psychological aspect and look at the bigger-picture thinking. It was just a massive learning curve and was so influential in everything I do. At the time and I still do, I couldn't thank Jim enough for giving me an opportunity and for allowing me into that inner sanctum and helping me develop as a coach. He was really unselfish with all of that.'

Round would find sanctuary and appreciation in the first-team squad for a multitude of reasons, not least because it meant a return to a younger coaching style on the training ground. Players could now relate to the man with the whistle and engage on almost a friendship level, rather than the sergeant major style of Crosby. One man who benefitted from this was Danny Higginbotham, who went the other in making the switch to Derby from United in 2000: 'With Roundy, what he would do is he would set you goals and aims for the season of what he wanted you to do. He'd pull you to one side and just tell you about certain aspects of the game, and he was relatively young himself at the time.'

Jacob Laursen remembers it being the same, and even questions whether the good times could have come back had the duo been together for longer: 'If we had stayed together and Steve had one or two more seasons with that group of players, we could have built something again. That's also one of the things, we didn't get a chance. Steve showed he was a top coach afterwards, and him and Jim could have done something similar as McClaren and Smith did.'

The case of Round is almost a like-for-like of the McClaren situation in this sense. Having won the treble within months of his arrival in Manchester and then worked alongside world stars such as David Beckham – in addition to authoritarians of the ilk of Jaap Stam and Roy Keane – McClaren would finally make the big step into senior management at Middlesbrough. Over time, it truly became a Jim Bowen-esque 'look at what you could have won'. Similar-sized club, a carbon copy of a stadium and a side built around surprise overseas additions, McClaren would lead them to League Cup success in 2004 and the UEFA Cup Final two years later. In the meantime, Derby lost Smith, lost Pickering, lost hope and almost lost their entire club in the process.

But though McClaren would move on from Derby, his decision to bring in Round to his Boro coaching staff showed he never forgot. And Smith's decision to let Round leave showed the same empathic nature as he had for his former assistant: 'It was gold dust [being allowed to move on by Jim]. If he had said to me, "I need you here and I want you to stay," I'd have stayed. That was my loyalty to him and to the club, because it is my club. It's my hometown, it's who I supported from as early as I can possibly remember, and I'd trained every day since I was nine or ten, played for them, coached for, I'd done every single job there apart from the manager job. So it was such a heavy decision to actually go, but inside me I knew there was something that said I had to try something new and step out of this and go for this.

'He called me in and said, "Look, we've had this approach from Steve. I don't know how long I've got left here at Derby because things are changing at ownership level, the club is going in a different direction. I don't want to lose you, I want you to stay and I'd be glad to give you a new contract, I'll look after you. But if you want my own personal opinion, this is a great chance for you to branch out, to further your career and take a step into the unknown and really go for it. I don't want to lose you, but my advice would be to seriously consider it." It was such an unselfish act to be able to say that and advise me from a personal career point of view, rather than a selfish point of view. I thought it was just what he was all about to be honest. It was all about doing the right thing, not necessarily what was maybe right for him. I'd never been out of Derby for work, I had lived there all my life, and so it was really brave and unselfish advice from him, and it was the right thing to say and the right thing to do. But I was very grateful for Jim's honesty, his integrity and it showed you everything that the man is about really.'

There was one more significant appointment that Jim would make to his coaching staff in the shape of Rams legend Colin Todd. But we'll get to that.

13

DOWNFALL

JIM SMITH is the greatest Rams manager in my lifetime. It's not a close competition. Smith was the first Derby leader I witnessed and, since then, the pickings have been relatively slim despite going through 17 men who have managed a minimum of ten games. The closest would be Steve McClaren himself during his original reign, while George Burley and Billy Davies can both be put in contention. For building togetherness, Golden Generation duo Frank Lampard and Wayne Rooney would enter the conversation too. But there is nobody who gets within the first syllable of a sentence without rightly being stopped.

It's why the end to this book is so difficult to comprehend as both a writer and presumably as an unsuspecting reader too. While focusing on the good and the great of the 1990s, what concludes shouldn't be how this book ends. Derby were on the brink of Europe, they were at the forefront of a changing game. A new stadium, a world-class coaching team, a phenomenal bank of international talent at their disposal. And then it all stopped. From 1995 to the summer of 1999, the club were the envy of others, threatening to break the mould, with no end in sight on what might be possible. But from the beginning of 1999 until relegation in April 2002, Derby descended.

There is a reason three seasons have been condensed into one chapter, and that is because the demise should not detract from what happened before. As addressed in the previous chapter, it did all begin with the departure of McClaren, but perhaps equally impressive is the fact Smith was able to keep the club in the Premier League for the next two seasons. This is the story of how that came to be.

* * *

In 1999, everything changed for Smith and Lionel Pickering. The year that the Pride Park dream began to unravel and thoughts of hopping on a British Midland flight for a midweek European tie became concerns of whether they would be heading to Gillingham this time next season. Having missed out on qualification for European competition by only a handful of points, vultures circled the eagle for his key assets. And without pointing the finger at one man, Rams fan and former director Don Amott played an unfortunate part in the process.

'In those days, my best friend was a bloke called Terry Brown, who was the chairman of West Ham,' laughs the ever-jovial King of Caravans. 'Terry owned caravan parks and I met him in Skegness once and said, "What you doing up here? You're a Londoner!" He told me a story about West Ham. And if you go back, he used to ring me every week: "Don, have you got any good players?" and I remember telling him, "Hey, I'm not qualified, I'm a fan! I can't do that." But he said, "Don you are. If you've got any players the fans love, I want to know about them." And you look in the history books, Igor and Wanchope went, Christian Dailly. A lot went to West Ham through my phone calls to Terry!'

It was an accidental assist from Amott, and one he didn't realise he was playing a part in at the time. But as accidental as it might have been, those weekly conversations would capitalise on a Derby side that garnered significant interest. And the first to find interest would be Paulo Wanchope. 'I had a great time but it was the right time for me to move on,' sighs the Costa Rican. 'I had two great seasons over there but it was good for the club financially and for me; I wanted to explore something new and move on. I left great friends over there and the good thing is that I can go over there to Derby and there would be no problems.'

Wanchope was the first departure that would not be significantly replaced. As things continued to get heated between the forward and Smith and with a bad feeling simmering between them, the manager was willing to accept a fee of around £3.5m. Though Wanchope would continue across the Premier League with first West Ham and then Manchester City, he would rarely find the same form he had in a Derby shirt. Although in saying that, he did enjoy his returns home.

Rams physio Neil Sillett grew close to Wanchope and remains friends with him to this very day: 'Paulo became certainly not arrogant in any way, but he became very good very quickly and became a name very quickly. Getting off at Man United, you can't get any quicker. We played at Liverpool and won 2-1, and he was awesome in that game. Paulo would admit he was still young, and the impetuosity at times. But he scored another against Liverpool at home where he was like a basketball player and there must be a picture because his legs were the height of my head, and Liverpool said to us, "He's better than Heskey, you can't beat that." And so they wouldn't be the only ones thinking that, then it gets into his head at 24 and wants to earn the sort of money which he did end up earning, and it's difficult then to keep them.

'But Jim loved him. I'll never forget when Harry [Redknapp] came back with West Ham, and Paulo hadn't played for maybe about a month. I took the team into the referee with the captain, came back and Choppy's name was on their team sheet. Jim looked at me and went, "He's playing isn't he?" I think he got both goals for them. And you couldn't stop him that day. But to score 45 goals in 73 internationals is some feat, two goals against Germany in the World Cup. Brazil as well, he was some player.'

And inevitably with a player of Wanchope's quality, replacing him would be a significant challenge. With overseas success the flavour of Derby's late-1990s dealings, Smith and his specially selected agents felt there was little need for change and turned their attentions south. As south as Argentina, for a forward unknown in the English game. The same had worked with Wanchope, with Smith opting to take a similar strategy. What ensued was, to all intents and purposes, one of the most ludicrous captures in British football: Esteban Fuertes.

* * *

'It's not a quick story,' sighed the late Keith Loring when the name was prompted his way. Charged with seeing this deal over the line, Loring took the same approach as he did to all other captures that Smith put on his desk. Fuertes was a contract like no other though, with ramifications which would cement Derby's place in pub quiz answers for years to come. 'We flew out [for a pre-season game], and in the hotel at Denver this agent arrives. My first impression of him was that he was a nightmare, but we signed the player in the room on the reception desk, and the deal was quite good money-wise. The player arrives and does his normal things, but there is no passport … He had a passport, he came in with his international but he didn't have his Italian bit, that was the one he needed.'

Due to arrive in England thanks to an Italian passport he was entitled to through his grandparents, Fuertes would eventually hunt his document down. Or *a* passport, at least. Loring said, 'I'm chasing him up, drove him to a game. I was over him like a rash. Eventually he brought his passport, and he bought it via a foreign player who I think played at Fulham. He came out of the airport, met a close friend of mine in London, got the passport and drove it to Derby. All we had to do was photocopy and fax it, then we were finished.'

Signed, sealed, delivered via a random Fulham player, the door was opened and there looked to be no issues in what should have been a standard transfer process. That's how it proved to be, with Fuertes appearing eight times for Jim Smith. While failing to ignite sparks on the pitch (one Premier League goal, one red card), he was a man to stick with, as his goal record at Los

Andes and Colón indicated. With the side as a whole faltering, an international break adventure to Portugal was on the cards to bring the ever-changing squad a little closer together.

It did the opposite. Relaxing with friends on a Saturday evening without a game, Loring was first made aware of the crisis when picking up a call from an unnamed first-team coach. '"We've just got booked into a hotel, and they've taken Fuertes' passport because it was dodgy." I don't know if he knew he had a dodgy one, but he showed it and they threw it out. It was a copy. I'm saying to the guy, "Are you taking the piss? Leave me alone, don't wind me up."'

Sillett adds, 'We got back to the airport and they wouldn't let him back into England. They said, "This isn't his passport, this page is false." We were all on the bus and Jim was going, "Where is he? Is he at duty-free?" Billy McEwan went back in and we couldn't even get him.' Fuertes would never be seen in person by his team-mates again, with his forged passport blocking entry to the UK and beginning an international incident.

It was only the latest development in a signing which caused headaches and sleepless nightmares for the dealmakers for weeks. Prior to Fuertes' signing, uncertainty over who actually owned the man arose. Much like the Carlos Tevez incident with West Ham during the 2006/07 campaign, the truth came out that the transfer wasn't to be made from Colón, where he was only on loan. Fuertes would actually be owned by two clubs and a separate management company. To appease, the initial £1.3m of the fee would be paid to the Argentinian FA.

But to the passport debacle, where rumours and conspiracies flew. Smith wrote, 'The immigration officials chose to scrutinise every detail of every passport, even down to using infra-red. It seemed clear to us that somebody knew about the fake passport and had tipped off the authorities.'

Whether that was the case is hearsay, but what was the case was that Derby had an asset they could not use and their summer plans had been destroyed. 'We played three or four games with him by then, so I was waiting to lose points on him which luckily we didn't,' Loring reflected. 'But we got an interest quickly in selling him to a team in France, Lens. What they did out there, the agents would all meet in Paris, so I got a flight out to meet them at 8am.

'The Lens guys all turned up for a meeting, and the Argentinians, they were all trying to lower the money. It got us out of jail because it was my whole life. I went home to go on holiday on the Saturday, and on the Monday morning I'm meeting Jimmy for lunch in Spain. And just before the end of the day he said, "By the way, Esteban scored last night for this Argentinian team, not Lens!" The Argentinian FA had a deal whereby because this player was in a bad position, they passed a deal so he could do something there as well. I lived an awful life for a year because of it, an awful year. The thing is if you deal with the FA here you know what you're doing. But with a foreign country, you have no idea what the rules are. We got out of prison there because the bottom line was nobody ever asked anybody for a proper passport. Sometimes you learn the hard way.'

The Fuertes incident saw the rules changed across English football, with passports needing to be ratified by the FA from that deal on. Still though, Fuertes did score a winner against Everton, so it wasn't all bad.

* * *

Beyond the forward line though, Smith had lost in the summer arguably his most important signing in his entire Derby reign. While Igor had begun to pick up injuries and saw his outings reduced season on season, he had found himself growing increasingly disgruntled in Derby and made the move to West Ham: 'I decided to choose London. I had three or four options but London was attractive, West Ham was a great club who were similar to Derby, a very familiar club and they treated people well. They had many homegrown boys, they trusted good players and brought in a good mixture. Harry and Jim were the best on the market to recognise players. It's easy to find a way to talk to them and agree with them.'

But although growing disillusioned at the direction of the club even before the sale of Wanchope and Igor himself, his disappointment came from a position of knowing exactly where Derby could have gone: 'We stopped doing logical moves in the market. For years, Jim and his staff were the best on the market in regard to spending and bringing in quality. Asanović for £800,000, Eranio on a free transfer, Wanchope as an unknown player who nobody had heard of ... it was amazing. And then you are saving more, building a new stadium, building a good team. And suddenly you decide to spend all you earned on three or four young players? No logic. I couldn't see logic in that.'

But for his disappointment in the direction Derby were heading in, Štimac isn't shy in continuing to declare his admiration for the club that introduced him to British football: 'Derby is my home ... it's my home. When you mention Derby County, the first word which comes to my mind is home. I'm not there but it's my home. Simple as that. I was approached to take the manager's job there but I was the national team coach at that time, and I love loyalty. It's the most important thing for me in life. You cannot mix things. I was approached by Sam Rush and he knew I had a job and commitments, and he put me in a situation to do both jobs at the same time, and then after the 2014 World Cup committing myself to Derby only. But it was not possible for me to accept it. I couldn't in that way be able to commit myself 100 per cent to both sides.

'Seeing so many managers doing a bad job there, you don't feel good. They've chosen flashy names instead of someone who can bring back passion and commitment and loyalty and honesty. We went wrong there the last seven years. Most of the managers used Derby County as a step to go somewhere else, to a better place. And that's wrong. You need someone to commit themselves to the club, the city, the supporters. Not for one year, not for six months. We were wrong there, definitely. Our time there, no players were leaving Derby. And Jim was there all the time, the only guy who left was Steve but OK, it's to Man United. Even I can't not justify that! He was a young assistant coach who was ambitious and all that, but we were all there, nobody was talking about changing their shirt. That dressing room was healthy and safe, protected, we felt good with the club and the supporters. Why think about change? But now it is a different time. Nobody appreciates or shows loyalty. Many players kiss a shirt, then another shirt. How do you explain that?'

Štimac's departure at the time felt bitter on both sides. With murmurs that his focus was elsewhere and questions over his fitness, a feeling of bad blood slowly rose to the surface. And while the break-up wasn't messy, there were certainly regrets on both sides at what had gone so historically well was coming to a premature end. And while Štimac maintains his desire to stay, across Sillett's time in the game he was able to observe what an unhappy player looks like across the training pitch: 'Body language tells you an awful lot, when they're walking around the training ground and are not involved. And they'll come and tell you as well, "Can't wait to get out of this place." But nobody really hides it very well and in the modern game and even at that time they would say to their agent, "Get me out of here, I've had enough." Jim was one of the better managers at seeing that and working with the player just to say, "Give me everything you've got for six months and then you can go." He worked things very cleverly like that and, even if a player was desperate to go, Jim would wait for the club's benefit for it to happen. That's a difficult skill.

'Now they just leave players out but we didn't have a big enough squad in quality and depth to do that at that time. They become difficult to handle and you know they could train, but you can't make them; a brave man makes them get out there and train with all of the protection they have now.'

With Igor and Wanchope both gone, Derby would falter from the summer of 1999. Though Horacio Carbonari (brought in a season prior) would thrive in the side, losing the players who had placed Derby on the Premier League map meant something felt amiss. And it showed in the early weeks of the 1999/00 campaign as the Rams struggled for any form of consistency. Immediately it became clear that a rot was setting in.

* * *

Derby starting a season slowly under Jim Smith was nothing new. In his four seasons at the helm heading into the millennium campaign, he had never won one of his first two games. But even by that underwhelming standard, what begun the 1999/00 campaign would have had him concerned by what was to come. Despite an opening-day draw at Leeds, three straight defeats afterwards were a cause for concern. Failing to click without talismanic figures at the front and back of the side, Smith found himself looking to adapt with new additions to the team.

Fuertes has been covered, but during the summer and in those early months of the campaign, the starting 11 took on a new look, persona and even style of play. Perhaps most notably for that latter change was the introduction of Seth Johnson, a menace of a young man who was as far removed from the Asanović central mould as one could imagine.

'I commuted from Crewe to Derby for a couple of months; I didn't know what I was doing,' begins Johnson. 'I'd just turned 20, I didn't have a car, not even passed my test. So Dario Gradi [Crewe manager] took me down for my initial talks with Jim, and then the first couple of weeks I passed my test and didn't get a car sorted until a few weeks into pre-season, so I borrowed my mate's Renault Clio. I was driving that in from Crewe every day; probably not even insured! I didn't even think about it in them days. I was clueless to everything. Getting a house, didn't know anything about mortgages or nothing, but I had an agent who looked after that side of it.'

Johnson, who delayed his switch to Derby in order to ensure Crewe's survival in the First Division the previous season (they stayed up by a single point) was one of the hottest young properties in the Football League system. Liverpool made no secret of their interest in the England under-21 international but it was the lure of Jim Smith that drew Johnson to Derby: 'I liked Jim instantly because he just had that personality that he was a likeable character. Just infectious, that's how I'd describe him, and it's exactly how he was with me, just made me feel really welcome and he was upbeat, bubbly, humorous and just a great character that you could spot instantly.'

The same can be said of Johnson himself. Never one to be shy across Raynesway, the one-time England international brought a bite to the team. Flexible and able to play across the midfield, the bulldog of a youth perfectly complemented the workmanship of the always underappreciated Darryl Powell next to him. Johnson said, 'I'd want to get on the ball earlier and get playing. I normally would get a feeling in the warm-up how I would feel physically. Sometimes you'd be in the warm-up and, no matter what you do or what the preparation is, you don't feel at it and you can start a game like that. But other times you feel good about yourself and buzzing a bit, and you start the game well. [For me] it was a case of letting them know you're there; I just played the way I played whether it was first or last minute. Obviously I'd have to be careful if you've been booked but it's how I tend to play my game.

'I knew I wasn't as gifted as Stefano [Eranio] but I knew he couldn't get around the pitch like me and get after people and be aggressive. We had different games. Powelly was good at that as well, he was a nuisance to play against and he knew what he was good at. So I just played to my strengths really. I used to give away needless fouls and free kicks, but there were parts of my game like the pressing and chasing back, which is what I enjoyed.'

Where Johnson most came into his own, however, was off the field, where his exuberance and being 'an oddball' (as Sillett succinctly describes it) kept life at Raynesway as unpredictable as they had once been inspiring. Forming a group with Rory Delap, later signing Danny Higginbotham and incorporating Steve Elliott, the youngsters caused havoc across the Ramarena for staff, coaches and most notably team-mates. Mart Poom recalls being the victim of several incidents: 'At Raynesway we had two dressing rooms because we couldn't get all in one. The other one was the youngsters. I came to England with these really light jeans, like these *Miami Vice* jeans, and one day after training I came back and they were cut to pieces.' Poom laughs, but the pain no doubt remains.

Another victim of the Raynesway rascals was Branko Strupar, the Belgian forward signed a few months after the Fuertes fiasco. Coming to England without knowledge of the language, the Croatian-born hitman made the fateful error in his opening weeks of finding refuge in a corner with Seth, who recalls, 'With Branko, I'd teach him the wrong swear words, so he'd be calling people a wonka and things like that. It was just daft things like that which he'd come out with. But he was good with mucking in with the English language, he was a good laugh.'

Strupar himself remembers the process of English lessons with Johnson: 'I would ask, "How can I say this in English?" and Seth would always say bad words. So when I said them, everyone would laugh at me, so I knew something was wrong! That was funny because "fuck", every second word was fuck this or fucking. In the dressing room, I didn't have a problem but I tried, and with the years it got better. I used to say, and they would laugh at me every time, I would say to Mart Poom, "You are the big rat." If you ask Mart, "Poomy, what did Branko say to you?" he will always say, "Big rat!" And he would laugh every time. "What you stupid big rat?"'

Over time the camaraderie across Raynesway would be needed as results worsened and morale threatened to deteriorate. But with Johnson, Delap, Higginbotham and Elliott on hand, spirits remained strong even amid confidence-sapping relegation battles. For the staff too they found light in taking their mind away from football and being terrorised. 'We wouldn't dare do Jim,' laughs Elliott, 'although we used to get Peter Melville, the physio. We used to cut holes in his pants all the time and he just stopped coming in pants in the end.

'I remember making Rory put the Thames machine, which was a physiotherapy machine, on his cheeks. We turned it up and it melted his filling and he was in agony. Literally, it either melted his filling or blew it out and he was in agony, and I thought, 'Oh my God, this has gone too far now!' He had to go to the dentist, he's got a game on Saturday. We used to mess about quite a bit with Powelly as well. He was always getting massages and all that so we'd mess about with his gear and put deep heat in the massage oil so he'd start burning.'

There were plenty more incidents, some of which are severely unprintable. A couple that are fine for publication come first from Higginbotham, who remembers, 'One afternoon, we finished training and we were having lunch. They all used to sit round and have a laugh with Jim at dinner, and it was myself, Rory, Stevie and Seth. We just decided we were going to go to the physio's room and completely empty it. And I mean empty to the point where we took every single machine out, every single bed out, we took all the bandages, anything in there went. We took everything. Then you've got Sill and Jon [Davidson] saying, "OK, let's go and do the treatment lads, come in." So we hid round the corner, they opened the door and there is just nothing in there. No machines, no beds, just this huge empty room. They know who it's going to be, so we had to think that if we were going to do something to them, it had to be something that can be quite a decent thing to do, because they were going to come back and do something even worse.'

And that playground fun became more important as time went by and results failed to materialise. Lacking the depth in the defence that he had at his disposal in previous years, Smith saw his side leak goals with a worrying frequency, without the capability to counteract them at the other end thanks to a striker shortage. That was where he hoped that Strupar would become pivotal to his rebuild. Had it not been for injuries, he would have done.

Following the Fuertes situation, Strupar would be identified as the latest man to lead the line alongside one of Dean Sturridge or

Deon Burton, or occasionally even both, with Francesco Baiano allowed to return to Italy. Strupar's capture would be much-needed too, particularly after a bid for Eiður Guðjohnsen was rejected. With only three wins from the first 17 games, Derby found themselves in the mire. Stuck in the drop zone and having failed to score in eight of those matches, an increasingly disgruntled – and worried – Smith went above and beyond. Aware of Strupar, at the time boasting a phenomenal goalscoring record at Belgian champions Genk of 61 in 110 league matches, Smith embarked on a solo mission to recruit the man he pinned his safety hopes on. He wouldn't even wait until the end of a match he was overseeing to do so.

Sillett recalls, 'We'd watched a video of him and Jim said he'd get goals. And he was playing on a Saturday night in Genk, and the chairman put on a plane for Jim. To get there in time, he had to leave East Midlands at 5.45pm, and we were playing Burnley in the FA Cup. And we were awful. He turned around and said, "I'm going to the airport, I can't watch this anymore. I'll come back with a striker." And he did!' Despite Smith witnessing Strupar miss a penalty and get sent off, what he had seen on video and in the flesh was enough to convince him to push for Pickering to pledge £3m for his capture. It reaped an instant reward with two goals in his second start, at home to Watford on 3 January 2000.

Though some form had been captured, primarily aided by Powell's looped ball into the box which somehow evaded Leicester's Tim Flowers for a 1-0 win at Filbert Street the previous month, the Rams headed into the millennium desperately attempting to clutch their way out of the drop zone. Strupar would set them on their way in his first Pride Park appearance. Whether the arrival of 300 Genk fans spurred him on is hard to say (Strupar was at the time the Belgian David Beckham), but they were not disappointed by a performance they had seen all too often over the previous seasons. Becoming the first scorer in English football of the new millennium is one feat which can't be taken away, but it's the overall day which means more to Branko. 'It meant everything. I remember I had a little bother with my calf, so on 31 December '99 with Neil Sillett, I came to Pride Park, just us. I was running up and down the stairs, up and down, up and down. It was foggy and a very scary atmosphere at Pride Park, but after that session it was only me and Neil, he wanted to check how I felt, and I said I couldn't feel any pain. So he told the gaffer, who started me the next day. But after that game I almost cried with how happy I was.

'The first goal was funny. It was a free kick from 25 yards, and I used to take all in Belgium. When the position was there, Darryl, Seth, Craig Burley were all there. I came and just managed to say, "I do." "What the fuck do you want?" said Craig. "No, let me do!" They were just looking at each other like, what the fuck does he want? And the ref blew the whistle, I just shot from 25 yards over the wall, very nice goal into the top corner. That was unbelievable. I couldn't say anything in English, just "me, me, me". And they just looked at me and said, "What the fuck, fuck off, go away, get in the box." We won 2-0 and then we got out of the bottom three. A very special day; probably the most important for me. I went to the dressing room and they said, "Branko, you have to go out one more time," and I got a standing ovation from the stadium, and then there were about 300 people from Belgium as well! It was just special, very special. I always played with emotions because that's the special game is football. And at that point, that moment, I was over the moon. It's a good saying, that, yes? Over the moon?'

It was a good saying, and a suitable one. Because for the adoration big Branko had in a Rams shirt, days like this were few and far between due to a series of recurring injuries which left the man in a state of despair. When fit, Strupar boasted the best goal-to-game ratio of any Rams player in the Premier League: 36 games brought a phenomenal return of 15 goals. It was clear that the difference between a relegation-threatened Derby and a mid-table team rested solely on whether he would be on the treatment table or not. More often than not, he was.

* * *

'Did you hear the story about when Jim told him he had a gun in his office?' It's not your average conversation-starter, but then Craig Burley doesn't do things by average. Signed around the same time as Strupar for £3m, the duo would be part of a mini-resurgence which proved pivotal in keeping the side in the Premier League. And they shared a lot in common too. Both were experienced in the game, particularly Burley with Chelsea and Celtic, and both would later in their Derby life be frozen out by a later regime. But back to the gun.

Burley continues, 'I mean, obviously he wasn't going to shoot him, but Branko had the most horrendous injury issues with his abductor and he couldn't get fit. He had operations and tried everything. Jim was desperate, Jim was struggling to survive, we were struggling, he knew his head was on the chopping block so we needed a striker. Branko couldn't get fit and it wasn't for a lack of trying. I don't know how long this was going on but after the umpteenth time Branko broke down in training, the physio told Jim that Branko had broken down again. He was sat in the cafeteria at Raynesway and his chin was on the table, he didn't know where to turn, he might never play again. Jim came out of his office having just been told that his star striker is still not fit, he shouted to Branko, "Branko, come in my office. I've got a gun." Branko just went, "Fuck off."'

It's another example of Smith's ability to find light in any given situation presented to him, and though insinuating Strupar bore a lot of similarities to an injured horse, his approach was designed to soften a gloomy outlook. And while Smith was as reliable as ever to bring some joy to his squad on an individual basis, Burley entered a Rams side in the doldrums: 'The fact we stayed up for a couple of years was a bit of a miracle because I remember arriving at Celtic, training and thinking, "Oh … this is going to be difficult." You can tell when somebody who has been in the camp at Chelsea or Celtic with Henrik Larsson or Paul Lambert or Mark Viduka, then you come into Derby and you know it's going to be a struggle. I used to say this to him [Smith], I used to say after we stayed up in the first year, "We're not gonna be able to keep doing this. The trap door is gonna open." But it wasn't him, it was the finances. And he knew. We couldn't keep staving it off, going round getting people by the scruff of the neck to try and drag that extra ten per cent out of them. That was the only disappointing thing as I would have liked to have played for him where it wasn't an absolute bun fight every Saturday for survival. That had to wear him down as well. He would brush it off and be this character who was larger than life; it had to have been affecting him as well. I know it was affecting the players because there was no enjoyment being fourth bottom, looking at the fixtures. It had to have affected him as well and it was getting him down, though he never displayed that in front of us.'

Working with Smith remains one of Burley's proudest memories though, particularly as he could sense the respect the manager had for him, even if he did have an abstract way of displaying it: 'I remember in my second or third game at Filbert Street, I went for a pee five minutes before the game. Jim came in and had a go at me. I'd only just signed and he said, "Craig, I brought you in to score goals, you've not had a shot yet!" He just couldn't help himself. I remember one thing Eric Steele said to me once: "Did you see what the gaffer said about you in the paper? He said pound for pound, one of the best signings I've ever made." And on the Monday he came up to me, said, "Did you see what I said? I was lying, you're the fucking worst!"'

Burley would become a statesman for the side, almost a mini-manager when things became too much for Smith. Brought in to add experience and steel to a Rams side which couldn't find form, he would play a significant part in what would eventually become a rather against-the-odds escape from relegation. Finishing the campaign two places and five points above 18th-placed Wimbledon, it represented the first brush with relegation for the side in the Premier League. But it also represented a campaign of heavy spending for a club that didn't possess the funds to compete with mid-table outfits. Strupar and Burley arrived for a combined £6m, which could be looked at as counteracted by the sales of Wanchope and later Fuertes. But adding in the outlay on Johnson, a record signing of Lee Morris and the full-time summer acquisition of Georgi Kinkladze, and things were less than rosy. Smith had even tried to bring in other names, with a move at the same £3m cost for Scottish defender Colin Hendry falling through. The tactic of signing unknowns on low wages and seeing them emerge into gems had been replaced by a heavy spending approach that didn't match the balance of the Rams' board.

'We went off to buy three players,' Keith Loring remembered, 'and we spent £20m. It may not seem a lot, but it was an awful lot to us. We bought Kinkladze for £3m. Craig Burley for £3m. Branko Strupar for £3m. Then wages, you can see where £20m goes. Now that was going to save our lives. We spent £20m to try and get out of trouble there. So along the line Jimmy had to make other decisions to replace that. It was a huge deal for us spending £20m.'

Morris and Kinkladze haven't been covered, but for differing reasons deserve to be. Kinky, as we will refer to him from hereon out, was, without pushing the limits of exaggeration, a genius. Famed in the Premier League for his wizardry at Manchester City, he arrived in Derbyshire on loan from Dutch giants Ajax after a nightmare time that saw him barely reach double figures in appearances. And though he could be as frustrating as he was enigmatic, the Georgian represented a need for flair to fill the gap left by the likes of Asanović, Baiano and Wanchope.

'A lot of players don't enjoy that side of it, the dirty side,' admits Johnson. 'Kinkladze definitely didn't, he just wanted you to give him the ball all the time. He certainly wasn't interested in getting after anyone. He literally would take the ball off your feet and go and play.' Alongside Eranio, Kinky would provide a secondary outlet that ensured Derby weren't just set up as a consolidatory side. And though *The Ram* may have slightly over-egged him upon his full signing by declaring him 'one of the world's most exciting players', his permanent capture indicated a desire to rebuild into the attacking 11 Smith had routinely looked to deliver.

That was clear too with the addition of another permanent signing, young Lee Morris. Long pursued by Smith, Morris passed up the opportunity to join Arsenal in order to make the short switch from Sheffield United in a deal which surpassed any other in the history of the club. It would be money which would ultimately leave the manager in a position of weakness when it came to what was available to him going forward.

Morris himself, who today spends his days coaching SC United Bantams in South Carolina, recognises that from the moment he broke his foot his value to Smith would be reduced: 'I remember him telling me in the office on day one, "You can't get injured. We're doing all this medical to make sure you're 100 per cent, you can't get injured." And then I broke my foot and was out of the season. It must have put a hell of a lot of pressure on him after all the money he spent being his record signing. Coming back the next pre-season having missed the whole of the last season, I didn't hit the ground running. It took me a while to get sharp, get fit, and the next pre-season we went to Holland and I remember him being on the sideline and this was five minutes into a game, yelling, "If you don't liven up, I'll sub you off," just shouting so loud and spitting and his head had gone really red. Stefan Schnoor was on the bench saying, "Gaffer, leave him alone, he's a young guy!" and little things like that stick in my mind now. I think he wanted me to do better for him than I did and he could see me being a problem to him from his higher-ups. You don't want to be spending your record amount of money on a player who isn't going to work out for you, and he could see that happening with me.'

The money spent was enough for Derby to survive though – just. Emerging talent from the academy such as Steve Elliott and Chris Riggott would prove significant, as would the progress of young forward Malcolm Christie – who had more of an impact the following season – but 1999/2000 represented the first real sign that problems were afoot at the club, both on and off the field.

* * *

It could again be argued that I should probably have made this chapter into at least two different ones, but at this point I've started it so we persevere. If you need a break from the despair, that paragraph above would be a good point to do so. Because it doesn't get any lighter from here.

Saying that, now seems as good a place as any to bring a bit of joy. Though it might not seem so long ago, the world of professional football is unrecognisable to the one this era covers. We've evaluated the changes in training techniques, the integration of players together, pranks and many other signs of the 1990s. But one thing that the modern footballer doesn't enjoy the same freedom in is the pre- and mid-season tour.

Derby, and particularly Jim Smith, loved them. Tours of Portugal, Spain, Netherlands, United States. When looking to build squad unity away from their standard seasonal base, Smith and his merry men would board the first possible flight at East Midlands Airport, heading for sun, sea and second-rate opposition to play for morale-boosting wins. Esteban Fuertes would first link up with Derby at one over in the US, and it would be a mid-season break in Portugal that would be his undoing upon return. But it was a rare – if well publicised – blip in what would be the diamond-encrusted start to a Premier League season.

Take a club trip to Amsterdam, for instance, midway through the 1999/00 season. 'On tours, you'd barely see the manager. I'm not saying what he was doing in Amsterdam at the time because God knows what he was up to, but pre-seasons are always good!' Spencer Prior laughs when reflecting on all that came before, and the hazy memories of a Derby County off the leash (and on the lash) in the true capital of Europe. Less a training camp and more of a glorified stag do for nobody in particular, Amsterdam was just one of the many tours the hierarchy found a reason to plan.

As you might expect, Seth Johnson enjoyed it, 'I'd just been away with the England under-21s and I got caught out drinking; me, Lee Hendrie and Matt Jansen. We played two games, I got booked in both so I was suspended for the last. We were in Slovakia and we just ended up having a night out in some random nightclub where there wasn't one person in there, but we were all in our England shorts and T-shirt, these luminous green. It was just us three and then the next day we went in to train and Matt didn't make training because he was hungover and he told them what had happened. So, we got banned for three months from international football. So Amsterdam was my first one away [after that] so I was trying to keep my head down. The lads went out the first night and I didn't even bother going out. I stayed in and then went out after that, but we ended up going all around the red light area and all that! I'd never been before so it was a bit of an experience. They were always good trips. It was crazy when we went. We saw all the shows and that!'

Ahead of and even during long, torturous campaigns where Saturday afternoons became even more difficult, those trips would grow in importance and keep a squad united. But they'd also at times provide Jim Smith with an opportunity to look at his latest additions. For an Amsterdam trip, that included Bjørn-Otto Bragstad, a defensive addition from Rosenborg. Craig Burley was on that trip and remembers an incident which would epitomise the Norwegian's Rams career: 'Sill [Neil Sillett] told me that 11 minutes into Bragstad's debut in pre-season away in Holland, Jim was in the stands, and he phoned Sill. "We've made a right fuck-up here." And Sill went, "What do you mean?" "Bragstad! He's fucking useless! No, no, no, we've made a right fuck-up!" And when Sill told me, I couldn't believe it, but I could believe it. He knew straight away and that was his way. He knew a player, but we were signing players based off recommendations. Bragstad was a lovely guy but he really had a hard time and Jim spotted it straight away.'

Bragstad would arrive in the summer for £1.5m, make 12 appearances and leave. Two more summer signings had more luck, though, in the shapes of Danny Higginbotham and young French defender Youl Mawéné. The former, a capture from Smith's old friend Alex Ferguson, would go on to be heralded in a Rams shirt, but found the initial switch a cause for anxiety. Burley remembers, 'Danny was really nervous when he first came in. I remember him saying to me, "Craig, how do you think the Derby fans will take to me?" So I said, "Well if you fucking kick the ball out the field every time you get it, not very well." He was really nervous at the start, had a couple of poor games and I can remember Jim saying, "Fucking Higginbotham, fucking Fergie has done me!" He phoned Fergie for a favour, has he got any young guys he could take. And when Danny had a couple of bad games, he was going round saying, "Fergie's done me!"'

Higginbotham would recover quickly, though, and counts his time with the club as the making of the defender he would go on to become across the Premier League. 'It was a big shock to my system … the first six or seven months of my time at Derby were just a nightmare. It was me adapting to a different side of things because when you're at United, whether you're playing for the under-13s or the B team or being involved with the first team, you spend most of your time attacking. And I remember after one pre-season session, we'd done this test and I had never ever done it before. And afterwards I'm just lay on the bowling green with my eyes shut because I'm just thinking, "I'm gonna be sick here at any point." This shadow just came over me and it was Roundy, and he just looked down at me and was like, "Just let me give you a bit of advice. You've come from a club that spent 80 per cent of time with the ball, we spend 80 per cent of the time without the ball. And your fitness levels have to be really high."

'After my first three games I got dropped after my third. I got taken off at half-time against Everton. I think it was Niclas Alexandersson and he just took me to the cleaners, and I needed to be taken out of it just for my own good. And it took me time to adjust but Jim stood by me and eventually I started playing as a centre-back, one of three centre-backs, and I just felt as though that really suited me in the system that Jim wanted to play. But everybody at the club was great with me and stood by me. To come out the other end on a personal note and to be doing a lot better was great, but it was a huge learning curve for me.'

But after £20m spent over the previous season, plus the new additions in the back line and Finnish midfielder Simo Valakari, the beginning to 2000/01 was a catastrophe. With that earlier stat about Derby not winning often in the early weeks of the seasons under Smith, they took things considerably too far by not registering a win before 18 November this time around. Sinking to the very foot of the table and conceding 29 times in the opening 11 games, Smith needed to shuffle again, just as he had the previous season. Two additions – one on and one off the pitch – gave the club a reprieve.

* * *

Colin Todd is a football genius. It's a slight adaptation of what Rams fans would attribute to Darryl Powell, but it's applicable. A Rams legend from the double championship-winning side, his name even today is synonymous with the Baseball Ground, with defensive solidity and with the people of Derby. But Smith's decision to bring him to Pride Park wasn't one covered in nostalgia. Todd in his own right had built up a managerial career across the divisions, most notably guiding Bolton Wanderers to promotion a year after Smith had taken Derby there.

And despite being in charge at Swindon, when Smith approached him to take over as his new assistant, he couldn't jump at the gardening leave quickly enough. Speaking for *Pride*, Todd remembered, 'Jim knew me, but he knew what my capabilities were. Steve Round was still there but he wanted a bit more experience. So I got the phone call and he just tried to suss out if I was interested. Even though I was a manager at Swindon, I decided to go back to Derby [because] I loved my time as a player there and had a lot of success. It was the right thing to do and it was a phone call from Jim that made it happen.'

Brought in with a particular focus on working with the defensive unit to plug the gap in front of Mart Poom, Todd's appointment had an almost instant impact as, almost overnight, Derby found a way to simply not concede goals. West Ham at home on 6 November saw the first Premier League clean sheet in a goalless draw, followed by another at Highbury in the performance of the campaign thus far. And while they set the foundations, what showed the side were truly learning from their defensive frailties came at home to Bradford City in the first win of the season, albeit at attempt 14.

Shortly before the corner began to be turned, and with a fight against relegation already under way, the ever-comedic Smith found light in the darkness. Craig Burley laughs at a story Sillett relayed to him: 'We played Norwich in the League Cup, [from the] league below us. We battered Norwich, it was not even a game. As we went 3-0 up, Jim turned to Neil and went, "Sill, we'll come straight back up next year! Look at the shit in the Championship!"'

Todd was instrumental in the sealing of what was an open safe in the back line, but whether he was the most important factor has question marks over it due to one other addition, whose impending arrival was revealed during that victory over Norwich as he sat watching on from the Pride Park stands: Taribo West.

A lot can and has been written about the *Championship Manager* icon, with most of it not even taking into account the world of football. Taribo's introduction to English football was another masterstroke from Smith, who plucked the Nigerian great on a loan spell from AC Milan. 'It's an assignment to be here,' he curiously said in his opening remarks in front of the media. 'All the clubs I have been with I have been an instrument of inspiration to the players and I am here to accomplish a mission. I believe in God and I believe my mission will be accomplished in the name of God. I believe in what God can do and I know that, from Saturday, Derby will be on a different level.'

For the laughter and confusion Taribo could often draw from people across the world of football, God had blessed him with the capabilities to lead Derby through a battle. Making his debut in the home win against Bradford, West would appear only 18 times for Derby yet stands out as maybe the key difference between the top flight and relegation.

A maverick (or 'nutcase' as Seth Johnson put it), West may have been sent by God to complete his mission, but throughout the course of the campaign he'd return to Milan to meet him at his own church. 'I did that deal,' Keith Loring recalled. 'Jimmy said, "Keith, we've got no chance here. They want this, want that." I believe it was £25,000 a month or week or something. So I went for broke and said to them, "Guys, we can't afford that. So I wish you all the luck in the world. If you had £5,000 on a three-month contract, then I could probably get it through." And to cut a long story short, we got the deal. Taribo West was an amazing guy because when you hear stories of defenders saying, "You do that again sunshine and I'm going to fucking kill you," he meant it.'

Returning to Milan on a weekly basis and only tending to appear on matchdays, the deal West had in place was akin to an overseas player in club cricket. Not a peep, then he'd *probably* turn up on matchday. Diane Wootton was responsible for arranging where he would be at any given day, and charged with getting him to matches: 'I had to do the flights and he had this chapel in Milan. So he had to get on this six o'clock flight on a Saturday to go to Milan, which wasn't a problem if you played a London club. But if he was playing Newcastle, he couldn't understand that there was no way I could get him to the airport for the flight. But he'd go every weekend and then on a Monday morning I'd get a phone call from Jim: "Di, get me bloody Taribo!" because he used to go AWOL. We'd have a game on the Tuesday night but couldn't find Taribo. Jim would call and say, "Have you found him?"'

When West was on site, he'd leave those around him speechless. Chef Mark Smith describes him as 'one of the strangest people I've ever met in my life. He was very, very strange. He was polite but when he talked to you he would always go back to God and bring it back to saying, "You are welcomed, come to pray with me." And one day he offered us all to be flown over to Milan to his church. He used to drag around his bag on wheels, where he had his Bibles and everything like that. Everywhere. It might be 30 degrees outside but Taribo would turn up in a big, black trench coat.'

With a prayer mat in the changing room and one or two unholy items in his Mickleover Court room, West would be treated with caution in the dressing room because nobody quite knew what they were dealing with. Holier-than-thou yet terrifying and unpredictable in equal measure, West instantly became a dressing room leader and a voice of power on the pitch. 'He saved us that season,' admits Neil Sillett. 'We were dead and couldn't stop conceding goals. He was a gamble, he wasn't match fit, but he was mentally fit. And he came in and was such a powerful influence. Some of the things he did was crazy, but he stopped players from going out of position on the pitch, with his instructions and sometimes even physically. We kept eight clean sheets in I think his first 12 games, and it turned the season around.'

A lesser manager wouldn't have put up with West, but Smith had been around long enough to know how to deal with perhaps the strangest footballer he'd ever had in his possession. Willing to find flexibility in his setup to accommodate the man who more than likely kept him in a job over the course of the campaign, it did mean he would be left frustrated at times.

Defensive partner Chris Riggott was in awe: 'I remember him saying a prayer against Arsenal I think it was. Jim left the team talk to him and he got us in a big circle, interlinked with arms around each other and he was giving it the "Our Father". He started preaching at us and 90 seconds into the game the ball goes into the channel and Taribo tries to shepherd it out of play, someone bumped him over the advertising hoardings, fell into the ditch and the guy squared it and scored. Jim said, "That's the last time I let Taribo take the pre-match prayer." We had a game away where he just didn't turn up. He showed up just before kick-off and the club got him some random gear. He had black slip-on leather shoes with a tracksuit, it was ridiculous. But he had just gone AWOL.

'He would show up sometimes, then he wouldn't. He'd have five or six Bibles stacked up and he'd be on his phone, back when not everybody did the whole phone thing, it was still quite new. But he'd be on the phone preaching to his church in Milan. On the way to big games, Jim would walk down and say, "Taribo come on, it's time to focus," and he'd be there preaching the word of God, not even in English, but he was so passionate. It had been drilled into professionalism in the game but here was Taribo, totally off the cuff and off his rocker.'

Lee Morris adds to Riggott, saying, 'Taribo and Colin came in at the same time and everyone thought Colin was this defensive guru and solved our problems, but as soon as Taribo came in we had pace, power, aggression. For that few months he never got the credit he deserved, but he solved all our problems and was so good. But then he did things like just not turn up. Charlton away, nobody knew where he was and he just didn't show up.' Even Stefano Eranio found West bizarre and mentioned a chance meeting years later in which West didn't elaborate on where he eventually disappeared to.

By the time safety had been secured at the backend of the campaign and after the extension of his deal until the end of the campaign, Smith had reached exhaustion, simply stating, 'I don't know what's happening with Taribo,' and fining him two weeks' wages. By that point his job was done though.

Today, Taribo is a pastor in Nigeria.

* * *

Derby's survival came in very similar circumstances to the previous campaign. A woeful start, a mid-season resurgence sparked by new faces and a panicked end. As results started to pick up, an unlikely survival was in Derby's hands from Christmas onwards as victories over Ipswich, Coventry and Newcastle built on the Bradford win. Tending to keep a five-point gap between themselves and the chasing pack of Bradford, Coventry and Manchester City, but for six games which warranted only three points in March and April, the Rams could even have been looking ahead rather than below.

But Derby do nothing simple, do they? That's why by the time they got to the penultimate match of the season, they still needed three points to guarantee safety. The only issue with that was that it came at the home of the champions, Manchester United.

'Alex [Ferguson] came to the hotel for dinner with me and Jim the night before,' Sillett looks back, 'and we were accused of this, that and the other by Coventry who went down as a result. But he said, "Look, I've got to put out the best team." But they'd won the league, it wasn't like they needed to win a game. Then Scholes didn't play, which was a big plus for us. But they still had something like 30 efforts on goal that day, so they had a fair few!

'The night before we had a lot of injuries going into that game, and we were struggling for a team really. We had plenty of wine with Alex, and then Darryl Powell called me on the morning, and he'd said to me in the five-a-side on the Friday evening, "I'm struggling a wee bit with my knee." He came to me and said, "I can't play." Jesus. "I've got to go to Jim and tell him, with a hangover, that you ain't gonna play!" And Jim went nuts. "I don't wanna see him in the hotel, tell him to get a taxi back to Derby, I don't want him at the ground." So I was due to go down and find out Alex's team and have a bit of lunch with Alex, and Jim said to me and Roundy, "You two, come outside with me." He went to walk through this sash window and it cut his head! He sat outside with a napkin on his head. And he went "What are we gonna do? I don't know what to do."

'And these ducks walked past. They were shaped like a diamond, and he started laughing because he was nearly crying before that, saying, "We're gonna go down!" So he started putting names on the ducks, and it was a mishmash of a team really. Carbonari, Riggott and Higginbotham at the back. Mawéné at right-back, who'd never played there in his life. Delap and Eranio in midfield, Boertien at left wing-back. Georgi in the ten position,

Lee Morris and Malcolm Christie who had never played together. Seth was on the bench, and he couldn't even run, that's how bad we were.'

But there's one more man who had a drink the night before – Steve McClaren. While Sillett and Round would share a drink with Smith that evening, his former assistant would too. McClaren said, 'We'd won the league already, but Jim was fighting relegation. And I told Alex, "Oh I'm going to see Jim for a glass of wine on Friday night; any messages?" "Yeah, tell him not to worry tomorrow, we're playing a younger team anyway. If Jim wants to know the team, I can't tell him who it is, but we're putting some youngsters in for experience." And Jim had that relationship with everyone. Jim wouldn't sleep on Friday nights before going to Old Trafford, so Alex just said, "OK, we're putting some youngsters in, so tell him he can sleep."'

Whether Smith slept or not is unknown (the alcohol may have helped at least), but what is clear is that his afternoon of work at the Theatre of Dreams would have been enough to clear even the strongest of hangovers. Because while the side he set out with was as far from what he imagined as it could possibly be, Smith had at his disposal a man who thrived when faced with United. A man who thus far has been overlooked but deserves a considerable mention.

Malcolm Christie rose from non-league obscurity to truly make it in the English game. Plucked from Nuneaton Borough (via shelf-stacking at a supermarket), he'd first begun to make his name during the 1999/2000 campaign, particularly with an expertly struck double at Middlesbrough on his first start in January 2000. And the months that followed, with the regular injuries to Strupar, Fuertes never returning, the lack of goalscoring prowess of Mikkel Beck, and Dean Sturridge falling out of favour, responsibility worked its way down to the £55,000 signing. 'I was on a big barren spell,' Christie reminisces. 'I'd not scored for 18 games [since a goal at home to Coventry in December 2000] so I look back and just thank Jim for being able to give me the opportunity to stop the run, to be fair. In many respects we were suffering from a lot of injuries as well, but as you are aware by the results, it's not like somebody else was taking the mantle of scoring loads of goals, so it was probably better the devil you know in all fairness.'

Christie would find himself partnered by Lee Morris in a move which surprised even the record signing, but the duo would strike a chord on an afternoon where things simply worked. Mawéné laughs: 'I saw the 12-minute highlights from the game. And I looked at those 12 minutes and at first I thought, "Fucking hell, we look decent here!" It actually surprised me; I looked all right you know! But that game, I remember Jim had his game plan spot on. His speech, he nailed that game. We fought to stay up and for those last few points, and United had just won the league the weekend before. And I remember throughout the week, Jim set out his tactical card of a 3-5-2. Eranio as a free and Kinkladze behind Malcolm. The rest of us, you defend, you defend. When you have the ball, just give it to them as quick as you can to Kinkladze and Eranio, let them do their thing. And it went exactly as planned.'

Christie's first-half strike was a long time coming – five months to be exact – but it would be enough to consolidate the most important three points of the season as safety was once again secured. And for him, it proved to be the highlight of a career later impacted by injuries: 'I never thought I'd be in a changing room at Old Trafford thinking we could beat them, but it's what everyone was talking about before the game – so that helped. We rode our luck at times, but we never got absolutely battered. We set up really well, we were adventurous, with Stefano and Georgi we were set up to get a result and get a win, which we ultimately did. It was a sweet moment for us all and after the game it was all about the team. I can look back and think what a great moment it was for me personally, but it was never about that, it was just relief after such a poor season that we were able to save it in a place like that.

'I got brought off with ten minutes to go and ended up sitting behind Jim, hoping and praying they weren't going to equalise because I'd missed an absolute golden chance to kill the game dead. I do sometimes replay it in my head and think of the times you could have gone on. But we were applauded off by the United fans, and that was the arena I always dreamt of playing on. So, to walk off the pitch having saved the season there, scored the winning goal and being applauded off by the United fans and Derby fans, I don't think it gets much better, without being in front of our own fans. But you had the whole corner packed out with our fans, and I'm sure there were a lot more Derby fans in the United end. I do now get the odd message from Derby fans saying they couldn't get a ticket for the Derby end, so I was in United end. But it's nice because, even though my career there is the negative side which dovetailed off horrendously, it's nice that I have got those memories and Derby fans have certain memories of myself which I can hold on to forever.'

While the corner celebrated long into the Manchester night and United's trophy collection was marred, Smith sniffed an opportunity to sneak away, beat the traffic and begin the relief-fuelled celebrations back in Derby. But, as Sillett remembers, it didn't go according to the Bald Eagle's plan: 'So afterwards, Alex said, "You two are going nowhere." But Jim had this brainwave that if all the fans are staying, we can get out before the traffic starts. So he rounded the lads up in the dressing room – and Alex had put this great big tub, one of those big ice cream electric tubs, full of beer in our dressing room – and said, "Bollocks to that, get them on the bus as quick as we can!" We got underneath the far side and it was like these ants coming down. We'd timed it two minutes too late, and they immobilised the bus, we were sat there for about an hour underneath the stand, and the United fans were all over it.'

On the bus was team chef Mark Smith, 'We came out of Old Trafford and I had to have two bottles of Rioja opened and ready for him. He'd come on the bus with a big cigar, blow it in Dane's [Farrell] face every time. So the bus pulls off and I'm standing up working on there. Pete the driver took the wrong turning and we ended up surrounded by thousands of Man United fans. They were all jeering at the bus and stuff, then the next minute Jim says, "Pete, you've took the wrong fucking turning, get the police! Get the police to get us out of here!"

'The next minute, United fans hit the emergency button on the side of the bus, the doors come open and Craig Burley is sitting on the front seat, and you've got United fans on the front bus step and halfway up the middle step! And Jim is going, "Get us fucking out of here!" He sat there with his Rioja and his cigar still going, but we had to call in for a police escort out. Every away game we had to have two Rioja, two bottles of Sauvignon white, 21 cans of small lager. The Rioja was just for Jim, nobody dared touch that. Even if you were only going down the A52 he'd manage to get through one!'

The journey back was sweet, and the last truly positive day for Smith at Derby. It would also be the last big win for Derby in the Premier League, in a torrid couple of decades which stretches to the present day. Derby were safe again, by hook and very much by crook. But it would be for the final time.

14

THE HARDEST GOODBYE

IN MY infancy, I can remember the exact time and location when I was sure Jim Smith had struck the mother lode again for his side. Playing in a garden scarce of greenery after one too many sessions of backyard cricket, the news had just come through of Smith's newest – and maybe even most exciting – acquisition. Floating around the garden, playing football very much alone (the perks of being an only child) I only wanted to play the part of one man. Derby County's newest star, the internationally acclaimed Rivaldo.

It was only days later the news would dawn on me that there was more than one international with an R and a V in their name, and the one who was finding the net with an accuracy which would have had local scouts purring (still available for professional contract; please tweet me) was not Rivaldo. It was a man called Fabrizio Ravanelli.

In an era where foreign forwards were dominating the scoring charts, Ravanelli had threatened to stand alone. Derby themselves had suffered at his feet, conceding a hat-trick in a demolition job during the 1996/97 campaign on his way to 17 Premier League goals and more than 30 in all competitions in his sole full season with Middlesbrough. And though the 'White Feather' had significantly fallen out of favour and form back in Italy and then France, Ravanelli was a welcomed addition to a side struggling to fill the post-Wanchope and Sturridge gaps in the frontline.

He would effectively become the final nail in Smith's tenure, though. And in time his capture would even threaten the existence of a club on the fine line between top flight rewards and financial annihilation.

* * *

The relationship between Smith and Lionel Pickering was one that both men had been searching for most of their careers in football for. Smith, whose boardroom-level relationship over his time in the game was very much a 50/50 split, found solace in a man of a similar age, with similar tastes and perhaps, most importantly, his own tavern. Pickering too, still very much a novice in the world of football ownership, first employed Smith based off a drink the two shared in earlier seasons. And though their friendship was far from a drinking buddy type of alignment, it helped. But in the same way that alcohol causes turmoil and arguments, it can also be the cause of many a bad decision. One such decision, which was the catalyst in bringing this working relationship to an end, happened at Lionel's Yew Tree.

'We went to Breadsall Priory, Keith [Loring] and I,' begins Peter Gadsby. Having learnt of Ravanelli's desire for a return to England in the summer of 2001, Gadsby and Loring met with the Italian and his agent, Gianni Paladini, to discuss how a deal could be done. Though there could be little dispute over what he could bring in front of goal, a Derby on a shoestring went in solely with the purpose of a one-year contract. Agreeing to terms including the receiving of a Mercedes and an astronomic £38,000 per week (making him one of the highest-paid players in the Premier League), Gadsby shook hands on a deal and returned home. 'I put the radio on in the morning … 'Ravanelli has signed for Derby County on a two-year contract'. They took him straight up to the pub,' he said.

A slightly more upbeat Loring remembers, 'He's one of the players that sustains you [and Jim] signed one every year. I didn't do the deal or the contract for Ravanelli [but] Jim wanted him. Andrew Mackenzie [financial director] got involved on the money and Jimmy said, "I don't want any other players, just this one deal." So in the end Lionel decided to back him.'

But having succumbed to the charm of Ravanelli and his agent, Pickering's agreement to pay £38,000 for the next 104 weeks was akin to signing both his and Smith's own resignation letters. A dumbstruck Malcolm Christie struggled to soak in the numbers, saying, 'Ravanelli came in with his own admissions of his best years behind him. When I saw how much money he was earning a week, I thought, "Oh my God, I didn't know that at the time!" I probably wouldn't have liked playing with him to be fair! He was probably earning ten times the amount I was.'

If the numbers are correct, Ravanelli's wage would have sat in a similar column to the entire squad – combined. Had Derby had the financial might that a sustained Premier League club does today, no issue would have been posed. But coming at a time when rewards were on the lower spectrum and television deals didn't reap the same numbers as they do today, the eye-watering figure spelled doom, not least because the squad was actually weakened over the summer.

A more fondly remembered Italian, Stefano Eranio, made the decision to leave the club during the 2000/01 campaign, departing Derbyshire following the final-day draw at home to George Burley's Ipswich side. The decision, sparked by both a desire to bring his time at Pride Park to a successful close and an incident which left his daughter needing urgent care in Italy, saw the loss of a man who could perform astonishingly well across the midfield and at full-back would cause significant issues in not only playing style but also off the field too. He did perform a U-turn, first holidaying with Ravanelli and then being part of the official kit launch after being persuaded to stay on, but ultimately opted to leave when Smith would, having never appeared again because of injury.

Add to this the departures at different times of two vastly underappreciated individuals in Seth Johnson and Rory Delap, and not only do you lose experience and flair, but also the reliability of two of the finest young talents in the game at the time. Delap would go on to build a long-term career in the top flight, while Johnson made a well-publicised move to Leeds, cost them £7m, and ultimately returned to Derby in 2005 on a free transfer. Good lad, Seth.

An increasing cause for concern was the amount of time and responsibility Smith was needing to take on away from football. While Smith was no stranger to the overall management of a football club over the course of his career, personal reasons saw Pickering begin to take a back seat, particularly after the loss of his wife, Marcia. It's perhaps a reasoning as to why decisions would begin to wander between curious and disastrous. 'If I'm honest,' admits Neil Sillett, 'by the end I don't think Jim was making great decisions. The board were pulling in different ways. Lionel wanted to go one way, Peter Gadsby and [John] Kirkland the other. Maybe Jim's head was being scrambled by being pulled in all the directions. Most importantly, and I'm keen for this to be said, but Jim was being pulled because he just wanted to do the best for the club.

'Maybe he felt if he was left to his own thing he could [do best for the club], but he was trying to appease people too much at that time rather than doing his own thing. Some of the board weren't just happy with staying in the Premier League, they wanted to be sixth and seventh and it's been proven that it takes years and years. They were trying to run before they walked, and one or two of those signings prove that wasn't maybe the way to go about it.'

Jim was losing not only players, but coaches and friends too. Sillett would opt to leave in the summer, while goalkeeping coach Eric Steele went to Aston Villa. A new first-team coach in John Trewick would enter, but the core that Smith found so successful had been ripped away. He'd lost his confidant, his goalkeeping coach, his psychologist and his assistant in quick succession.

And while Smith would take up more responsibilities off the field, in the boardroom things were beginning to unravel, as Gadsby recalls: 'I wouldn't say Lionel had lost interest but he was finding it extremely difficult to continue. Cash was getting difficult and Jim, he was old-school. Jim once said to me, "Mr Gadsby, if you sell a player and the money goes to the club and you don't have a player in, the crowd will ask for you to be sacked. So what's the point of selling players?" Probably true, but you know.

'One example of that was that we were struggling for cash and we had a boardroom meeting. Lionel tended to leave the finances to me and he said on one occasion, "You're always on about cashflow you are, bloody cashflow." And I said, "You haven't got a cashflow problem, Lionel, because it's all going out." And he just said, "Jim'll sort it, he's coming later."'

There were opportunities to redirect that flow, but Pickering's reluctance put paid to efforts to turn around a worrying financial stance. Gadsby said, 'Christie was scoring goals for fun and so the board had decided that, if they got an offer for him, he would help alleviate the problem. So Jim came in and Lionel said, "Tell him Jim. Mr Gadsby here wants to sell players." So Jim just said, "Oh, do the fans know?" "Well the fans don't see the balance sheets, Jim." Faced with a £7m offer from Boro and their now manager Steve McClaren, the financial decision-makers took an unguarded risk. Lionel said [to Jim], "Tell him what you told me last night. Tell him. Tell him what you told me in the pub." We were all looking round, so Jim just said, "Well he's 22 and he's quick, he gets around the back, he can put a ball in the net, Ferguson likes him," and Lionel went, "That's it, Ferguson wants him. If Alex Ferguson wants him, he's worth a lot of money; £10m, £10m and not a penny less." Jim went, "Is that it then?" and went out. We never got that bid, Christie didn't go, things went downhill and he went for £700,000 a year later.'

* * *

For all the arguments which can be and have been pointed at Ravanelli in the two decades since his disastrous capture, a fully fit White Feather would have been the difference again between safety and demise. Because – as shown during the opening-day victory at home to Blackburn – his quality remained. In a 2-1 win, his beautiful free kick had supporters, media and his own coach salivating at what they could have on their hands. That day's programme notes saw Smith write, 'I can't recall this kind of interest in a Derby County player and it's testament to his stature in the game that the club was making sporting headlines around the world this summer.'

There had been a reason for Ravanelli's sporadic appearances over recent seasons, however. Past 30 and nursing a collection of knocks, he wasn't a man whose fitness could be relied on. More accustomed to title challenges and the slower style of Serie A, a physical Premier League at his age always had the potential to go heavily wrong. And while he started his Derby career in fine form, he was very much a solo performer as the club plummeted back to the depths of the division.

Always with intentions to pass the reins down when he felt his time was closing in on him, Smith had lost his initial plan once Steve McClaren had left him in 1999. It no doubt made handing over a more difficult task without a clear successor in place. Yet while any end would have been a hard one to stomach for man and supporters, Jim Smith's departure was unnecessarily bitter.

Depending on who you get the opinion of, different stories arise. Some would point towards Colin Todd being a natural successor, with managerial experience and an affinity to the club which doesn't need delving into considering how common knowledge it is. But for others, the way the situation came about with Todd taking control was unnecessarily bitter.

Keith Loring remembered the bones of the situation as it happened: 'He got to the September international break in 2001, so I decided to sod off. I used to go away in June and we were there together with some other friends from Derby, but this time I just went myself. That was on the Sunday. On the Tuesday I got a phone call from another director, and he was the guy who lent us the £10m to finance the company which kept us going and helped pay for the stadium. He phoned me to say, "Keith, you need to know that we've made a decision today and we're going to promote Jimmy to top man and bring in Colin Todd as manager." So they said I must not say anything about it because they were going to tell Jim on Wednesday.' Loring, who was told 24 hours in advance, respected Smith too much to listen to those around him: 'I went home, sat Jimmy in the bathroom and just told him the truth. "And the reason I'm telling you Jimmy, is for one reason. Just deal with it, handle it and don't go storming away."'

Gadsby would be left to pick up the pieces. 'I remember Jim's words, "Pick somebody that wants your job and they'll have your job." But he thought with that he would never replace McClaren like for like. That was also a downturn. And the demise from Jim was very sad. He'd been to see Lionel. Jim rang me and said, "You don't know, do you? You're the effing vice-chairman and you don't know what's going on. I'm being sacked." He'd been up to see Lionel and you couldn't get him before 12, but Lionel told he was going to be the footballing man and Toddy was taking over. So Jim was on his way down to Todd. He got to the ground and Todd said, "I don't want you. Don't want you Jim." Jim was absolutely … it finished him. It just did him.'

* * *

The loss of Jim Smith was the loss of any form of identity for Derby. Under first Todd and subsequently the disastrous (and financially catastrophic) reign of John Gregory, Derby would lose any vision, isolate half of their squad in due course and ultimately, drop into the Football League for the first time in seven seasons. They have spent a solitary one in the Premier League since; the worst top-flight season of any English club, ever.

'We go on about managers now having to have these different licences and certificates,' Danny Higginbotham looks back, 'but what Jim – which you cannot write down on a piece of paper and you can't give someone a certificate for it – had is his man-management skills. He is one of the only managers, and even when

I'm speaking about him my hairs just stand on end because I just remember him so fondly, he was a manager that could come into the dressing room after the game and rip you to pieces. Absolutely rip you to pieces. Within five minutes, he's giving you a massive air hug and a massive kiss and everything is forgotten about. You can't teach that. You either have it or you don't.

'Forget the management side of things, forget the tactical side and all those elements, just as a human being he had this know-how of when a player needed a kick up the backside, and he would give it to you. He knew when a player was struggling a bit and he'd take you in the office. He would always ask how you were and things like that, and he was just unbelievable. He'd join in with crossing and finishing at times. There was one club, maybe Halifax, where he was a top goalscorer, and he'd come and he'd join in, he'd come in with his flat cap, he'd have these long shorts on and have his ankle socks pulled right up, and he'd join in. And I used to say the same about Sir Alex Ferguson, but you knew he was nearby without even seeing or hearing him. He just had this aura about him and very few people that you meet in life have that.

'You know how well he was respected in the football world, and at his funeral just listening to people talk about him and the people there, he was just an incredible individual that is greatly missed by a lot of people. An unbelievable individual and a great family man.'

Higginbotham is one voice picked out in isolation, because anybody else who spoke for this book echoed the sentiments. And for those who were at the club in the days of his departure, the loss of the great man was inconceivable. Branko Strupar says, 'I was very, very sad. We had a special relationship and when I came to the club he was like my second father. And I was very, very, very, very sad when I heard that Jimmy had passed away. Mart Poom told me. He phoned me and said. I knew how old he was when he died, but really, when you lose someone who you have a lot of respect for, it was a very sad day for me. I know he meant to me a lot. And a sad day for English football as well.'

Craig Burley adds, 'Without Jim it was different. Nobody with the jokes or ribbing people or shouting, it was a completely different place. But I never get involved in the politics, ever. All I know is I kept saying to him for a long, long time, "We need to sign players." Not once did he disagree, he knew. He never ever got them though, it was working with what we had at the time. But we made the most of what we could have done when he was there. From my time when I arrived to when Jim left, there is not much more he could have got out of what we had. I know he was frustrated with it because he would still be going on about it Monday morning but there was a realisation. Staving off relegation was about as much or more than we thought we were gonna get. We never saw it as an achievement but in some senses it was, and in a way as much as getting that team with Igor and the other guys playing the way they did, because there was a lot less to work with. The achievement was staying up. It was a minor miracle.'

That's what Jim Smith worked at Derby County. The miracle to win promotion automatically, which he is still the last man to do. The miracle to consolidate the club in the Premier League. The miracle to make supporters dream again.

'Oh, we could have gone all the way. Why not? At that time Man United and Arsenal were strong, some others were challenging, but we could beat anyone and we were doing so. We were winning at Old Trafford, beating Arsenal, Liverpool, Chelsea regularly. The most important thing is we continuously played attractive and amazing football. If you go back to that time and remember the goals we were scoring, how many passes before scoring the goal, how long we could keep the ball, it was amazing. We had people who could score goals, people who could overrun, we had enough speed and intelligence, we had everything. We could have gone all the way.'

So says Igor.

15

BONUS CHAPTER: PLAY THE BBC ATHLETICS THEME TUNE

'LEGENDARY' IS very much an over-used term and one of those ones which invokes a bit of a shudder. I've read the intro to this paragraph countless times now and it still makes me uneasy, which I think is the point I'm trying to get across. Beans on toast can be described as legendary. Your old maths teacher? Legendary. It's a word that almost has no meaning anymore, another four syllables lost due to over-saturation in everyday language. But in rare instances, legendary retains exactly the power it should. Defined by Oxford Dictionaries as 'remarkable enough to be famous; very well known' (or 'described in or based on legends' if you prefer to go for the first answer on Google), it's a term which should have almost have a cap on it for those instances, those moments, those people who truly deserve to have it adorned to them.

To Derby County followers across three decades, the word is justified when used in reference to Graham Richards. A district judge by trade, Richards became the voice of football almost by chance and transformed not only local media, but he played his part in the progression of sport on a national scale.

With that gruff voice recognisable in a millisecond and a turn of phrase the like of which has never caressed local airwaves before or since, Richards became the voice of Derby County much before the era this book delves into. Not that it matters. Because for the role he played, his story deserves to be told. Not that it is only his story. Alongside Graham for every commentary and every road trip across almost 30 years at the microphone was Colin Gibson.

A man taken for granted by supporters, Gibson is the one staple of the club since the 1980s. Whether stitching things together at BBC Radio Derby or later in life being a core part of the RamsTV team at the club, Gibson lives and breathes Derby County, even if he wouldn't say it quite so crassly. Together, the duo – alongside vital components such as broadcaster Ian Hall and the former managing editor of the station, Brian Harris, offered a new way to absorb football.

Today in his 80s, Richards warned in advance of a meeting at Stoke-on-Trent just after Christmas 2021, 'By dint of age, I have forgotten much of what went on!' He needn't have mentioned. For within five minutes, a bygone era of football had returned to the forefront of his encyclopaedic mind. 'I'm not a journalist, I was a barrister who was very keen on football,' begins Richards. 'I went to America to friends of mine who I had known since I was a student, I went to Philadelphia. Their close friends owned the Phillies baseball team. I saw a baseball game on my third night in America and, well, I fell in love with the game and it has remained with me. Because I knew the owners, one wet afternoon in New York they needed something to do so they talked to me about cricket on air and the similarities between the games. I've never met an American who understands cricket at all – not at all. They can't conceive of the fact you can score from behind the bat, because every American stands behind the net and if the ball goes back there it's a foul. So I thought when broadcasting, "I really like this," and I came back.

'I had been a Derby supporter since I moved up here in 1965 and I was listening to commentary on Radio Nottingham and I thought, "I can do better than these chumps." They were bone idle. So I went down to Tom Beasley who managed Radio Nottingham and I said, "Give me a shot." So I had two trials off air, then I was on and I finished the season as Forest's commentator. And I was better than the other two silly buggers, because if I hadn't been, I'd have poisoned myself.' His sharp tongue remains.

'I moved in 1977 for a home game at Sunderland and from then on it was pretty well straightforward. I had worked with Mike Ingham who of course is a well-known commentator and became the BBC's football correspondent. Well there we are, he moved on to Sky Television. Then Colin came in with enthusiasm and youth and the desire to push it on, and we did, didn't we. We were front runners in commentary on a Saturday afternoon at local radio. Colin got the rights and we broadcast from a match at Bury, and that's it. Things straightened out and we went through Stuart Webb, on to the Maxwells, which I was very much involved in, they might be my best stories, and here we are today. Anything else you want to know on that topic?'

That would prove enough on the intro. It's been now 20 years since Richards departed from the main microphone and, as time wanes, he has become a footnote in a time many no longer remember or simply were not alive for. That's why this chapter is dedicated away from football and instead on Graham and Colin. Because without the duo, the way we consume sports media may just be different.

* * *

A graduate of the National Broadcasting School, Gibson was picked up by the BBC as a behind-the-scenes operator at a time where sport was an almost forbidden word. 'A guy called Alex Trelinski came in as sports producer, but the bizarre thing was he wasn't really interested in covering Derby,' begins Gibson. 'So I thought it might be an opportunity for me to move in because he was also reluctant to go and do interviews with Derby. So I said, "Look, I'll always go and do them." And it was an awkward time with the club because they weren't doing very well. Then we had a new managing editor who came into Radio Derby, a guy called Brian Harris who wanted to give the station a fresh sound. So I said, "How about we have a lead-in programme to the sports programme and we'll call it *Pop Side*? For home games I'll present it live from the Baseball Ground and we'll get interviews and features, supporters' news and so on." So we did that. Then it was when Graham and I started working together because I would stay on in the sports programme to help Graham out. We didn't do commentaries to start off with because you weren't allowed to and for away games I did effectively what I was doing at Derby County over the last few years, with things like *RamsTV Meets*.

'And then the rules changed that local radio could start to use commentaries more freely. So that was where Graham said, "OK, let's make this work. We know the audience is there so why give them only six score flashes in 90 minutes, when we could do commentary?" So the manager backed it and we started travelling the country. The first one was Bury away. One-all draw at Gigg Lane and for a quarter-past-three game, it still finished before five o'clock, and we were off and running. Although the club were going through a difficult time we actually built up a good relationship with them that they would allow us to do home commentaries, which were just unheard of. But we could only do the second half and we couldn't advertise we were doing commentary beforehand. There were really tight regulations back in the day but Derby were prepared to bend the rules a little bit and that's how it started. But again we had to be careful to not be too close because the club was going through all sorts of turmoil. So there was always the news element of reporting on the football club and not being seen to be too close. But I think we got it pretty well right.'

Right they did. From being able to broadcast nothing to then being able to broadcast the second 45 minutes of a game, the natural next step was full match rights at a time where local media simply did not have this. That restriction was in place due to, well, I'll let Graham explain.

'The Football League thought if you have broadcast then there would be nobody in the ground, but exactly the opposite was going to happen. If you've got a good product, the more you can get it advertised the more you'll sell, and they couldn't see that. We had absolute Neanderthals like Jack Dunnett at Notts County and a chap with my own name, Richards at Barnsley. Neanderthals. I don't think he'd drawn breath since 1856, he was an absolute oaf. The people who run football are still oafs but they're not as bad as they were. And it was a huge push because the whole concept of local radio was unknown. There was no competition, the BBC had no competition and did the same thing all the time and it was a bit depressing, even then. But we pioneered it, Colin and I. We followed up with the Monday night chat show, which we were pioneers of as well. It was a different world.'

With BBC Derby's stock rising as supporters clamoured to get their fix of sporting action across the 1980s, it was during *Sportscene Talk-In* – the Monday night phone-in – that Gibson and co. took their next step. Still a staple of the output today, the often-christened 'moan-in' remains an opportunity for disgruntled fans to have their voice heard. And there was no time that drew more noise than during the infamous run of Robert Maxwell. Now 30 years since one of the most explosive episodes of the long-running soap opera that is the phone-in, one January evening in 1991 brought Richards into his own.

Aghast at the reception given to him on one of his fleeting visits to the Baseball Ground, Robert Maxwell's loathing of his own business was only exacerbated when it affected his Mirror Group empire, courtesy of Richards. 'That winter we went to Newcastle and lost a cup tie in a huge game. We had the wind behind us in the first half and had done nothing, second half they got one goal. Colin and I had great trouble getting back, the gales in Yorkshire were ferocious. And on the Monday night we came in to do the show, and it was packed. There were hundreds waiting to come on and we ran for an extra hour and the tone was, "What are we going to do about it?" And I was saying, "Well I can't do anything; I've not got the money. If you're going to complain to me, don't complain like this. Complain to Maxwell! We'll get his number for you." So, we gave them the number of the *Daily Mirror*. We didn't have Maxwell's home phone number, though I had been to his house.

'They phoned in en masse and I'm told there were at least 4,000 calls which went into the *Mirror* and they couldn't handle it. Maxwell is sitting back in New York on his boat, *Lady Ghislaine*, and he can't get through to the *Mirror* to know what the print run is going to be and those sort of things. So he makes enquiries and he discovers he has people trying to get in and the reason is Radio Derby. He'd never give us a moment of consideration but he researched it with his lawyers, demanded a tape which he was legally entitled to, listened to the programme and then he issued a writ against me for defamation. The BBC as the second party, they stood behind me to the hilt and that was the start of the end.

'He banned me from the ground spectacularly one Sunday afternoon against Tottenham. Gary Lineker scored the winning goal and actually he had been bought by Robert Maxwell's money – he'd loaned it to Tottenham. And two of our best players, Mark Wright and Dean Saunders, were sold. Combined value of £7m, but that money never came to Derby County. I was banned for a long time, the rest of that season and a bit of the next. And I can tell you with some authority that I have never read 27 pages of more garbage in my life, and I've read some garbage. And the only two real accusations were that I had given a number out, which actually isn't defamation at all and cannot be. And secondly that I was a Nottingham Forest supporter, which I considered as defamatory on his part! That was part of the defence that BBC filed for me, one was that he had defamed me! Nothing ever happened. When he died I discovered that at least a quarter of the writs in the Queen's Bench had been issued by Robert Maxwell to try and get rid of these and those people.'

Months later, Maxwell would die at sea, going overboard from *Lady Ghislaine*. On Maxwell and his time at the club, head back to the beginning of this book. For more on Maxwell and his general life, just search 'Robert Maxwell pension funds' to get an understanding of the type of man running Derby County.

* * *

Away from courting controversy and delivering timeless lines, Richards and Gibson continued their knack for transformation of local media and paid particular interest in the progression of the listening experience for Rams fans. Already boasting a relationship with the club that local media across Britain is unable to access today, further opportunities became available. At half-time, Gibson was able to grab 30 seconds with Steve McClaren to get his immediate reaction. Extended shows were created as demand and hunger grew for Derby content. And the team they would operate with expanded, as then budding journalist Ross Fletcher can attest to, 'I couldn't have had a better mentor than Colin Gibson. He took me under his wing and he didn't have to at all, but he really showed me the ropes. I have so much respect for Colin because of the amount of time and effort he poured into me. And the faith he showed in me; I became interwoven into the relationship between Colin, Graham and Ian [Hall]. In a lot of those Premier League days I was able to be a pitchside reporter too, which was magnificent. I always remember standing just inside the tunnel at Pride Park, you go in on the right-hand side where there was a tiny little interview station. You would just wait for Jim Smith to come out. There was always that moment of adrenaline and even when times were tough towards the end of his tenure he would come and front up and always give you a very honest interview. To get that from a Premier League manager is just fantastic.

'But there was more and more appetite for content around Derby County because they were doing well. We did a show on home game mornings from 9 to 12 from Pride Park. It was basically nine-to-six wall-to-wall Derby County. So I felt like BBC Radio Derby was so firmly interwoven into the fabric of the club itself. I would occasionally do road games as well, which was an education. I didn't talk much, it would be Colin, Graham and Ian sharing stories from days gone by and it was just a great education for me to learn from some terrific broadcasters and they are memories I will treasure from those and I have lessons learnt from those days.'

Fletcher is one of countless people influenced by the team during what many consider to be a heyday of Derby County. When pressed for what he learnt from his peers, no hesitation was taken: 'From Colin I learnt to always be firm in your conviction. When interviewing it can sometimes be adversarial and Colin always taught me to be firm but fair. Colin was a master of that art. I don't think to this day I have ever seen a more consummate interviewer than Colin. He just had a terrific way about him and he taught me that. Almost by osmosis, I would look up to him and see the way he would interview players, managers, celebrities and I would just be in awe of his ability to do that. From Graham being the commentator, the biggest thing I learnt from him was turn of phrase. He just had the most magical, golden turn of phrase and he had that instinctive ability to come up with the right words at the right moment. Nothing was scripted for the big moment, he is a supremely intelligent man. And he had the right pitch, the right tone in those big moments, the highlight reel moments. I learnt from him the way to stand out is to have that turn of phrase, something to just lift the moment off the page, and Graham really had that. And for Ian Hall, he was a sage. He was a really deep thinker about the game, and he would educate me about the game, particularly on those road trips where we would sit in the car, or we would be at the Little Chef halfway to Southampton on the A34. The way he talked about the game and thought about tactics was something I never deeply thought about in my early years as a sports broadcaster. He really made me think about the game in a deeper way. Each of them were incredibly valuable.'

Among the paragraph above, one sentence stands out above all others. 'He [Graham] just had the most magical, golden turn of phrase.' If 'They think it's all over, it is now' is written firmly into English footballing folklore, think of what a BBC Radio Derby book could like. For a man untrained in the art of broadcast journalism, Richards' ability to utter anomalous lines must be something garnered from either the courtrooms or a natural given talent. To choose one to input into this book would be doing the rest an injustice, so here are some personal highlights:

- *On Dean Saunders' goal vs Nottingham Forest, 1990,* 'Micklewhite thumps it over, early ball, up goes Saunders …goal! Goal! Goal! Dig that one out of the net, Mark Crossley! Not a chance!'

- *That Paulo Wanchope goal at Old Trafford, 1997,* 'Wanchope comes into the Manchester United half, dribbles on, finds some space, goes into the box, shoots and it's in! What a run. Wanchope took them on down the middle and as Schmeichel came out, he picked his spot and United looked absolutely second rate! He beat four players, they just couldn't take the ball off him and Schmeichel looked mesmerised! Wanchope treated Manchester United's defence with absolute contempt!'

- *On Horacio Carbonari's goal against Nottingham Forest, 1998,* 'Horacio from Rosario!'

- *Describing the opening goal in the play-off tie at Millwall's New Den, on the night the BBC Radio Derby car got trashed by home supporters,* 'Gabbiadini! Seventeen minutes and Millwall dealt a solar plexus blow!'

- *Describing Steve Emery's goal in the 4-1 win over Nottingham Forest, 1979,* 'Forest are in absolute ruins and manager Brian Clough, I have never seen such an expression of disgust on his face!'

- *When describing Jacob Laursen's goal vs Manchester United, 1996,* 'It's in! Twenty-seven yards and Peter Schmeichel never smelt it! One of the best goalkeepers in the world just waved it goodbye!'

* * *

For the remainder of this chapter, I wanted to be able to bring you, the person reading this, into the conversation. Being able to meet with and listen to both Graham and Colin together was a privilege and a transformation back to my own childhood. Like many of you, I spent countless Saturday afternoons listening to the BBC Radio Derby team. Although we met outside of footballing circumstances – Stoke-on-Trent station to be exact – seeing the duo reminisce on days gone by was a joy. So, enjoy the conversation, you fly on the wall.

* * *

Graham Richards (GR): I think those were the fun days. I don't see this as much fun at all. It's business and TV runs it. The expenses are so huge that only TV can run it really. I don't think any of us could see the enormous interest in the Premier League from abroad and the money coming in from China, India, wherever, it isn't something we ever really threw into the formula. And it's when the game has gone away from ordinary people.

I can't see how Radio Derby's listenership is as big now as it was in our day. If you wanted to follow Derby County, it was Colin and I on a Saturday afternoon. You are the umpteenth person who has said to me, 'I used to listen to you when I was a boy.' People remember me. Now if I meet people when I go to Derby, I am always spotted and they say, 'I used to listen to you every Saturday on Radio Derby.' I was in court actually and a bloke said to me, 'Do you know, you sound just like a commentator at Radio Derby.' He couldn't quite understand the bloke on the bench was a commentator. And he said, 'Well, I live in Skegness and I used to lean out of my bedroom window with the radio to pick up East Midlands radio.'

But it's gone back enormously, especially for anyone outside of the top six. Because the locality has been lost. But here's a story, bang up to date. In October of this year, I was at Southport vs Altrincham, FA Cup [a fourth qualifying round tie in 2021/22].

I got on a train at Southport and had to change at Crewe to come back here. I got on the train and Derby County were at Preston that afternoon. Five hundred at least Derby County fans piled off the train and got on the Crewe to Stoke to Derby, and I'm sitting there. And in a few minutes of coming on, some bloke of about 50, says, 'Hey, it's Graham Richards! Have you enjoyed the match?' And immediately all of them, 500 of them on this two-car train, so I was with them all the way down to Stoke. At least half of them were all pissed up and they had a terrific bonhomie about it. I was saying to them, 'The club's in terrible trouble, it might close down.' 'Best season ever,' they say. 'We'll beat the bastards!' And an old chap towards my age said it's the best season supporting Derby he had ever had.

Colin Gibson (CG): But the media has changed beyond belief. I've seen it from the other side having worked at the club for five or six years. The Premier League changed everything and I don't think anybody could believe how much it would change football. It's all about the Premier League and it's a massive business. Therefore, the clubs are very protective of their brand, as they would call it.

The job was to protect the brand from outside media, and to promote the brand which is all about Derby, and that was the basis of being head of communications. I took the view when I was at Derby that it was still about Radio Derby and *Derby Telegraph*. Sky you have to deal with and the national papers it was keep them at a distance and we'll give them interviews when we see fit. Because they're not really interested in Derby. Yes we had Steve McClaren and then Paul Clement so there was a national presence there, so there was an interest there. And clubs like Derby, whether they're in the Premier League, Championship, wherever, they need their local media and they need to service their local media. And actually I think they need to service their local media better than they do.

GR: Do you know who came to Derby with that idea first of all? Brian Clough. Brian Clough was very pro-local when he came.

CG: So we've got close to going to the Premier League on a few occasions and, in the February of each year, the Premier League would send representatives to come to Pride Park and to look at the facilities – is it Premier League-ready? But actually, what TV and broadcasters and the league demand is huge. And you know that if you get into the Premier League, Radio Derby go from being the first or second interview post-match, they're going to drop down the pecking order. As somebody who works in local radio I don't want that to happen, but I've no choice in the matter because Sky and foreign broadcasters pay hundreds of millions of pounds a year and money talks. So they'll come in and inspect the facilities and tell you that at the end of the game you will make two players available immediately and we will tell you which players we're going to be talking to one minute after the final whistle. Then within 20 minutes of the final whistle, the manager has got to come out and do Sky, *Match of the Day*, Premier League Productions and maybe one of the foreign broadcasters. And then there's club TV, and oh there's Radio Derby. So you automatically as a local broadcaster fall down the pecking order.

However much attention you give to the club, and Radio Derby and the *Telegraph* give massive amounts, once you get into the Premier League it's effectively taken out of your hands as a football club. So there is a forced change because that's the way the Premier League is. In the Championship, it's still the case of 10, 15 minutes after the final whistle the manager comes out and to my mind, he should still speak to Radio Derby first, but of course he won't. If you're in the Premier League, you deal with all those rights holders, then club TV, then to your local radio station. But in the Championship and lower, it should be that the final whistle goes, and who is live broadcasting? The local radio station. So they should go to local radio first, then to your club TV because it's not live.

I'm arguing against myself here because everything was about the club's media and making sure we got things first, and working with the local media because I worked it and I understood it as well. But I'm afraid it's changed massively and the emergence of club media has again lessened the influence of your local media. And they will control it because it's promote and protect. I still struggle with this now that BBC outlets will put out club material, which goes against BBC broadcast guidelines because you don't control the editorial output. You are taking something taken by a third party and that is wrong.

We mentioned earlier about falling out with managers, and we're pretty good at that because they don't like the criticism that we've given out over the years. We will not be Radio Derby County. Nigel Clough and I had a big falling out and one close season he decided he wasn't going to speak to Radio Derby at all. He'd give us nothing. So I said to my managing editor, this is the situation and unless I get the stories through a journalist, we're not running Derby. And he absolutely backed me 100 per cent.

So pre-season, there are stories starting to come out about Kris Commons running his contract down and eventually leaving. I got a phone call from a BBC colleague who said he had an interview with Kris Commons. Great, send it over. The interview comes over and it's the Derby County head of media doing the interview. So I phone them back and say, 'Where's the question about his future and his contract? Not how wonderful life is. I'm not running this, it goes against BBC guidelines and there is no editorial control over it.' So I just dismissed it and it's that sort of thing that has gradually been whittled away. Sky are the worst for it. They started to whittle that separation away. Courtesy of Chelsea TV, courtesy of MUTV. Where's your editorial?

GR: It's something that's guided you all your career. You were good but this is where you were very good. You asked the penetrating questions, something like, 'Is that consistent with your policy?' or whatever the point it was. And I think Radio Derby through you were leaders in that sphere. But players' wages, everything, it's gone through the roof. And local radio doesn't have that sort of money, so to me it was our golden era. I'd say to you as a 27-year-old, enjoy it. Because you'll certainly only see it when it's finished.

CG: I was 16 and 19 when Derby won the league and thought this is it, this is my football club, this is what we do. We win Football Leagues. And then we go to an FA Cup semi-final and from that moment on the golden era is gone, and nine years later we are in the Third Division.

GR: The year before any of us were born, we were in the top two of the First Division three times in the 1930s and then in 1948 we were in the Second Division.

CG: It's like Graham says, you have to just enjoy those moments because unfortunately they are fleeting.

GR: They [Jim Smith and Lionel Pickering] were people you knew, you knew where they lived. They'd often but not always been on the terraces as kids, they'd certainly claim they were even if they weren't.

CG: One of the things we actually lost between the Baseball Ground and Pride Park was the intimacy of the Baseball Ground. There was nowhere else to go. There was the stands, bits you'd built on but the corridor with the manager's office, the dressing room, the directors' lounge at the far end, there was nowhere else to go. So the geography of where the press room was, the players had to go past you to come in and leave the ground, so you would bump into them. I'd go along to a training ground on Thursday and there was no press officer to tell me who I could or couldn't talk to. I just turned up and grab them. 'Bobby Davison, will you do an interview for Radio Derby?' and he'd say yes or no. If he said no, I'd ask somebody else because this bloke [Graham] had upset them their previous week.

GR: Haha!

CG: And then I'd go to the Baseball Ground on a Friday for a more formal interview and it would be just myself and Gerald Mortimer, and it was very low-key. The introduction of the press officer to co-ordinate everything was a good thing in a way but also it was a blockage put in the way of me doing my job. So I didn't have to have an invite to Raynesway, I'd just invite myself along and if the manager said 'sling your hook' then fine, but you could push the boundaries in those days.

GR: It was a game. It wasn't a brand, it wasn't money. It was a game.

Ryan Hills *(RH – the person writing this book)*: I spoke to Marian McMinn last week.

GR: Who? I don't know her.

CG: You'd have known her as Marian Taylor, she was Arthur's PA.

GR: Did she marry Ted McMinn? I didn't know that.

CG: Well they are yeah, only about 20 odd years.

GR: Oh I missed it!

RH: I spoke with Marian last week and she also spoke about in between the time moving from the Baseball Ground to Pride Park, the entire Derby staff grew massively as well.

CG: But that was inevitable though, because you were moving into the 21st century effectively and a club like Derby with the Baseball Ground, it was very limited use. You'd got the directors' lounge, the thing they built between the Pop Side and the Normanton End. But when you got Pride Park, it has to become a seven-day-a-week organisation. It's about corporate facilities and it's how you move on to that stadium and you've got to make them pay and you've got to have people to run it.

At the Baseball Ground you had the chairman, the chief executive, the secretary, three or four administrative staff and that was it. They basically ran the club. There was a commercial manager but it wasn't that big a deal. You go to Pride Park and you've got to sell that stadium, sell those facilities. You've got to service all the corporate facilities, all the meals, all the conferencing, all the corporate hospitality, it all has to be serviced and operated. That's why I said you lost that intimacy and the only way you could get around the Baseball Ground was to walk up and down the corridor. Pride Park, you get nowhere near the players tunnel because there were other ways of doing it geographically.

GR: I'd go out and rebuild the Baseball Ground now. What a place. Knock Pride Park down.

CG: It was of its time. A complete side issue to this, I went down to Southampton last week and the satnav starts to take me to avoid the main motorway. Suddenly I'm driving and I thought, 'This is Archers Road,' and sure enough, this is Milton Street on the corner and it was where The Dell used to be. That's all houses now. I thought, 'Oh that's why it's brought me up here, for a journey down memory lane.' I said to [wife] Julie, 'This is where The Dell used to be!' and sure enough it took us out.

GR: That was a very similar ground to the Baseball Ground. Not as good.

CG: And suddenly my mind went back to a Monday night FA Cup replay at The Dell, winning 2-1. Ted McMinn and Nigel Callaghan with the winning goal in extra time, and us getting back to Derby at about half past three in the morning.

GR: I'd got an interview with the Lord Chancellor on the next morning. And the police stopped us coming off the motorway at Loughborough. There was four of us in there. 'Where have you guys been then?'

CG: 'Southampton,' which was obviously not the reply he was expecting.

GR: 'Hey, there will be no cheek.' Never went to bed at all, but we won the match though.

CG: And no waiting ten days for the game to be replayed. Drew 2-2 at the Baseball Ground on the Saturday and replayed on the Monday night.

GR: You and I used to have a commentary position on the roof at Southampton.

CG: Talking about the facilities changing and the broadcast and written media, at The Dell you were behind glass and the broadcasters were all at one end of this press box, behind glass. There would be us commentating, Radio Solent, probably somebody from Radio 5 there as well, all these voices going against each other. And the wonderful thing about The Dell was they used to pass a tray of sandwiches down as the half went on. By the time it got to the broadcasters you'd got the scrag end of sandwiches left because the written boys had nicked it all.

GR: The written boys always smoked too. We couldn't because we were on air. It was Gerald there with his fag on. I remember Cambridge was like that. There were eight seats, we were all in a glass box and Gerald would be next smoking all afternoon.

RH: What about the catering at the Baseball Ground?

GR: None. The Baseball Ground, none.

CG: There was a hot urn and you'd get a cup of tea, but there were no sandwiches.

GR: The press box, there were no facilities whatsoever.

CG: Media catering again is something of the Premier League era.

GR: We always stopped at Little Chef, didn't we. Never ate at the ground.

RH: Did you have any away grounds that you particularly loved?

CG: Arsenal's old ground, Highbury.

GR: The new ground is fabulous too, but I loathe the Arsenal. They are the one team, they're just repulsive. They're so privileged. Their backstage directors' box is beautiful, but it's like a nightclub. Chelsea is the same. Tottenham is another smashing ground, the old White Hart Lane. It was low down. Gascoigne takes a free kick 30 yards out, inside right channel and I say, 'Well he's too far out to score anyway, isn't he. Shilton's there, he can't beat Shilton from 30 yards.' Up he steps and BANG. And later in the same game, McMinn squares one at the bottom end and it goes through, and I think it's gone in the net because I'm so low down I can't tell. But I've announced an equalising goal which never, ever happened! You saw it or you missed it then. Let's do the grounds we hate. Nottingham Forest because we loathe them anyway.

CG: Plough Lane at Wimbledon.

GR: I was coming to that, Wimbledon. Horrible place. We had an incident at Wimbledon in the Jim Smith era. When we get to the seats there was a seat between us and a great big bloody bloke in a motorcycle helmet.

CG: It was the Arthur Cox era, not Jim.

GR: Was it? Anyway, we say, 'Would you mind moving?' 'I'm not leaving, I've been watching from here since 1922,' and he sat there resolutely whilst Colin and I commentated with this gonk between us! Dear me, awful place. No sandwiches at Wimbledon.

RH: What about Millwall?

GR: Oh, oh dear me. We were commentating at The Den and I said on commentary, 'I think that was Derby County's throw-in there, the ref has given it to Millwall.' And a bloke stood up and said, 'You fucking biased Midlands bastard!' It reminds me of another match at Forest, where there was a mutual loathing. The chap knew who I was because I'd been on Radio Nottingham before it anyway. The middle of the second half we're commentating on a very tight game and this steward comes up to me, right in front of me and says, 'Can I see your ticket please?' I'm broadcasting and I had to say excuse me listeners, I'm just being asked for my ticket.' What else … We used to like going to Plymouth and places like that.

CG: Portsmouth, climbing up the ladder to get to the press box.

GR: Colin always arrived early you see. Commando early. We'd got to be out of the Midlands by dawn at the latest, so we'd get to Portsmouth by about nine o'clock. Not even the caretaker's at Fratton Park. And Colin finds this ladder and we climb it.

CG: Once at Port Vale, Radio Stoke and the visiting commentary were garden sheds on top of the stand roof. We got there and Radio Stoke hadn't arrived and we were on air half an hour later. So I got a screwdriver out of the vehicle we'd got and was taking the doors off this garden shed, so we could get in to plug in the ISDN so we could actually get on air.

GR: Another cup tie at Hartlepool, we're in a shed and there are no windows, but a thing you drop down and look through. Well it was locked and the kick-off time comes closer and closer, and the only thing I can see is a wooden shed.

CG: About ten to three they eventually opened it so we could see the pitch.

GR: And then at Liverpool once, Colin is up in the gantry at the top of the far side, 150 feet above the terraces. Colin's broadcasting and this git comes up and says, 'Right, I'm taking the plug out.' I said, 'We're still broadcasting!' 'It don't matter, I'm going home.' And he was reaching for this thing with Colin on air, and he pushed me and I could have easily dropped 150 feet on to the terraces! 'Don't you touch my equipment!'

GR: People always say to me, with my legal stories I should write a book. I don't think I could. I don't think I could start! I can't spell so that's that. Here's one man who always wanted to have a book written didn't you? And I've always been the killjoy.

CG: Yes, yes. Maybe too late to do it now.

GR: It's history now, you'd have to do it in papyrus.

RH: It's never too late, I'm sure you've both got some very interesting stories to tell.

Here's hoping that book will come soon.

16

REMEMBERING JIM

HARRY REDKNAPP

Footballing legend and long-time friend who worked
with Jim Smith at Portsmouth

Jim was a great character. I was always going to Derby when Jim was there. I'd go in his office and most times in them days Dave Mackay would be there. Dave for me was just the best player ever to play for Tottenham. He was just an incredible footballer and what he achieved when he went to Derby as a player, and Dave would always be in Jim's office when we went to play there. We would always see Dave and have a little chat because he was an amazing man. But win or lose, you'd always go in Jim's office after and have a drink; he'd always have a full office with loads of friends there, a good atmosphere. It was the most welcoming office in the country without a doubt.

He'd always have a cigar on him and a glass of wine for sure. But Jim was just a great character. [I remember] going to Lilleshall with Jim for the managers' talks every year, and it was a great big thing where every manager and coach would be. Jim was just the life and soul of it. I remember Charles Hughes stood up and started talking about how he'd been to South America studying the Brazilians and why they were so good. He said, 'I've realised the reason they are so good is because the play on the beach and it's where they hone their skills. The uneven bounce of the ball on the beach. That's why they're the best in the world because they have the beaches there.' And Jim said, 'In that case, why ain't Torquay, Brighton and Bournemouth top of the effing league?' That was Jim. It was a full house, and you can imagine everyone just laughing. I don't think Charles was best pleased.

Managing against Jim was no different really. I'd be having rows with other managers during the games anyway but once the game started you just want to win for your life. Friendship goes completely out the window during the game but, win or lose, you'd go and have a drink with Jim in his office. And he was great fun. Playing golf with him when he came to Portsmouth with me, we'd go and play and have a laugh. Jim's golf, when he used to hit the ball, he didn't say 'fore', he shouted another word that I can't repeat! He used to shout that at nearly every hole with his bad shots. I can see his golf swing now; it wasn't a pretty sight!

I took over at Portsmouth and I took it when they'd been struggling for three or four years in the bottom six [of the First Division]. I thought, 'I've got no real chance here,' but we had Milan Mandarić, and my first signing and my most important signing was Jim. He was the best signing I made. I knew that he was loved at the club when he was there before, I knew he could come in and work with me and I thought who better to bring in and get a good feeling back to the club than Jim? He knew the game, he knew the players and he was great for me.

Our first game of the season, on the Friday morning we lost our centre-forward before we played Notts Forest on the first game. We hadn't got a forward on our books, so Jim said, 'What about Deon Burton?' He rang Derby, got him on loan that morning because you could sign them up to five o'clock that time or whatever, we got it done. He didn't train with us, stuck him straight in on the Saturday and he hit the ground running and did great for us. That was Jim. He knew where we could get somebody and, from day one, the crowd used to sing 'Harry and Jim, Harry and Jim'. Non-stop. They loved it and it was great times. We never had a single down when we were together. We won the league in the first year, we stayed up [in the Premier League], there was never a down for us. It was just a big shame that we left for Southampton and then he decided not to go back to Portsmouth. He said, 'I've had enough, Harry, I'm gonna call it a day,' so he didn't come back with me a second time. But we were still close.

But Jim just knew the game, he understood the game. There was no fannying with Jim. None of this silly jargon that I keep hearing now where a manager comes out after they're beaten 5-0 and you hear, 'There were lots of positives, ya' know.' Jim would tell you how it was. If you were bad, he wouldn't try to hide it because he knew that people aren't stupid, and he spoke the language of the fans really. He just told it as it was; Jim was a straight shooter.

It was just fun, you just enjoyed seeing him and we would have a laugh. We'd talk football, we were successful together and it was great. We had Kevin Bond, Joe Jordan. I remember Jim telling Teddy Sheringham one day, he's playing head tennis with Teddy, and he said to him, 'I got 120 goals once in one season.' And we went, 'What? Shut up Jim! Who for?' And he said, 'It was in the Sheffield League!'

* * *

ANDY DAWSON

Jim's son-in-law and former commercial manager at Derby County

My home was always Oxford, which is where I met Fiona [Jim's youngest daughter] back in 1989. Jim was at Newcastle whereas Fiona was living in Oxford. The first time I met Jim was when he invited Fiona and I up to his place in Tynemouth where him and Yvonne were staying, when I was about 20 years old. I was a big Oxford United fan and still am, it's my adopted team, so I followed them as a fan during the years when Jim was successful. He took them from the old Third Division, Second Division up to the First Division, so it was a bit bizarre because he was a bit of a hero of mine growing up. So being confronted and introduced to him as Fiona's dad, it was a bit bizarre and a bit intimidating at the very start. But he and Yvonne made me feel very welcome.

He was very much a family man. It was football and family and that was it. But the things intertwined because it is a 24/7 job. He would always make time for his family, so they were always coming up from Oxford, he always made time for us and the grandchildren. Obviously, there were ups and downs with results and that can always spill out. When things weren't going well it would not be the same as when things were going well, but that's the up and down of football. And he would always talk about football, stories, things that were going on, so he never completely separated it.

But he had a huge amount of support and love for his family as well. From day one to when he passed away, he was full of stories from way back when. From times when all the managers were really close, during those Midlands years when he was manager at Birmingham and Ron Atkinson was at West Brom. There was a real tight unit. And he was obviously close friends with Sir Alex Ferguson, so those managers had a very close unit that there doesn't seem to be now. But there were just so many fantastic stories. He was always good to be around, he was always holding court and he filled the room when he entered it.

* * *

HOWARD WILKINSON

Managerial titan and close friends with Jim

I was about 16 and I was at grammar school. Through that, the two Sheffield clubs became aware of me. One of the lads who played with me in Nether Edge Grammar School, later to become Abbeydale, was actually training at Sheffield United. The coach who was taking that group was talking to him one day and he said, 'Well we've got another good player in our team, in fact he's captain.' So through that, despite the fact I was a Wednesdayite, I was asked if I would like to go and train. And as a result of that I got picked for what was then the Yorkshire League side.

So the first time I went there was when I met Jim. And I played a couple of games in the Yorkshire League with Jim, but because of that we formed a friendship which then was picked up again when he was at Boston United and I was at Brighton. I'd seen Jim at a game, I can't remember which. He was sat in the stand and he was manager at Boston United. And we got talking, kept in touch. So he mentioned to me, 'Do you fancy coming to Boston as my assistant? Player-coach?' That's the story of how and that friendship just lasted then in the sense that I went to Boston; after 14 months he left and I took over the team but we kept in touch. Like me he was interested in this new-fangled idea called coach education and then all of a sudden there was a science behind football.

Although Jim might not give off this impression, he was a very intelligent bloke and was interested in that and saw the benefits of it. He left Boston and that was me starting my career on the ladder. It was a link that we maintained over the years. Obviously the basis of that was football but, at the same time, it was more than an interest because we were both coaches. We knew about each other and family. And the fact we were both from Sheffield with similar backgrounds ... he was always great. If you forget the football, after a game when you've played each other or you meet him at a function, or at a coaches get-together, he was so funny. He was *so* funny. It was his boundless enthusiasm, which at times bubbled over and with Jim what you saw was what you got.

When I was at Notts County, I joined them at Christmas of the following season. In my first season, we played Birmingham at the end of the season away, and they were going to get promoted. The game eventually finishes 3-3 but there were moments when we were winning. After the game, Jim came over, shook my hand and at times in the game he had gone. He was throwing the sponge down on the ground, kicking the bucket. And he said, and only Jim could do this, he said, 'I thought you were my fucking friend!' And I went 'Errr ...' and after about two seconds he went, 'Ahh, I'm only fucking joking,' and he put his arms round me.

Sometimes Jim was very good at creating something that you believed in. And he was always very enthusiastic, very honest and he would always pick the phone up for something not connected to football. The League Managers' Association, he was very briefly CEO of. We started in 1992/93, Graham [Taylor] and I started it. That weren't a job for Jim. We both knew it. The main thing regarding that was that I knew him and could trust him. That's what we had. And I got to know his family without really meeting them, apart from Yvonne. We actually stayed with him out in Spain, Sam and I. We went to Trevor Francis's son's wedding and stayed with Jim and Yvonne. And at dinners, Jim was Jim.

We had an LMA committee, it combined the LMA and the committee and we were lucky enough to get a vineyard out in France. We'd come here, have a look around because we had one or two wine lovers, notably Sir Alex Ferguson. That night we had dinner in this place and, as things did then, at the end of the dinner there was nice wine and everything. Somebody said, 'Let's go round the table and you've got to say which manager you dislike most.' And it comes to Jim who is sat next to me and next to Alex. Jim's got the cigar on and basically he said, 'I'll tell you the manager I fucking dislike the most … fucking hate him … it's you!' and he's saying it to Alex! Jim was laughing and saying, 'Because you fucking win everything!'

He was serious about being fit, serious about individuals giving 100 per cent for themselves but mostly for the team. He'd have a short fuse but it wouldn't last long and generally there would be a joke at some point in that. And I think from a manager to player point of view, and even from player to player, what people recognised was respect, authenticity, they recognised humility. They recognised someone who talks about we, not me. And they recognised someone for whom football is a love and a passion, above anything else. That's what was at the core of that person. That's what he expected of everybody and it's what his teams generally had.

I only coached one and a bit seasons with him when he said, 'I'm leaving. I've had a word with Mr Malkinson and I've told him what I think should happen – you should take charge of the team.' We were able [at Boston] to run the show properly. And he [Mr Malkinson] would sanction an overnight stay if you said to him on this occasion to give us the best chance. But there was no board, no committee. A great way to run a football club. And because of that, you didn't take advantage of it and try to be somebody he wasn't. So he didn't try to be, he didn't want to talk about who was playing, and again Jim got a very good first club because he'd got a very, very good and ideal chairman. These days they get called all sorts of things, but that link between that person and the one above him is very similar to what you want between a coach and players, and then between the players and the players. So what you saw was what you got and what you got was always 100 per cent. Good or bad.

It's a Sheffield saying I think, but he was good at acting daft. If he was your friend, you were guaranteed a good evening. Sam and I and Yvonne, one time we were in Portugal. We had a very enjoyable social side of that small amount of time together. We stayed with him in Spain, and he loved it there. We'd had a night and he appeared the next morning and said, 'Morning everybody. Welcome to another day in fucking paradise,' and then walked out, bearing in mind we'd had a long night, he walked four yards and straight in the pool.

I knew Jim from 27, 28, so we knew each other as managers, coaches involved in football for a long, long time. And I can't remember one incident, one moment. You knew that, if necessary, Jim would have your back. And if you were in his cluster, because in football you meet a lot of people, you get on with a lot of people but not many of those are what you would call friends. Put it this way, the Jim Smith I met when I was 27 years old was the Jim Smith before he died. From start to then. There were a lot of ups and downs, but he was always the same bloke. If you're rating him as a performer in his chosen profession, you have to say it was a very, very successful career.

* * *

STEVE McCLAREN

Derby County coach who went on to manage England and achieve
international success with Manchester United

I don't think I would have got on in the game and been able to handle them players at United [without Jim]. Because I handled Jim and the foreign players and that was tough. It was a tough environment that we grew up on and, personally, the amount of bottles of wine we drank together, we were bound to get on socially as well.

And we always kept in touch. After that I had a little bit of a bad time but the times we had in Spain, what he used to do, his initiatives like taking the wives and the players to La Manga for pre-season. He was ahead of the game. Everywhere we went he was loved. Recognised, loved by managers, chairmen. He was a well-respected football man and everybody loved him. Everywhere you went, that was the beauty of working with him, and I went everywhere with him and saw the love and affection that everybody gave him.

And he was like a second dad personally too.

* * *

NEIL SILLETT

Long-time friend of Jim's and his former physio at
Derby County and Portsmouth

It was in 1985 [when I first met Jim]. I was working with my dad [John Sillett] at Coventry. I was playing for Coventry then and my dad was with Colin Dobson, the youth coach. I played up front in a reserve game at Birmingham and my old man lost his head and told me to go around like a lunatic. And how I didn't get a red card, I don't know. But that game Jim was stood with my dad as manager of Birmingham telling me to calm down, and then they both had a beer afterwards, and he always called me a lunatic after that.

I was with him so much and I've always called him my second dad. He was such a big part of my life. But only smiles and laughter. I told stories to the family at the funeral – me and my wife were along with two ex-Pompey players invited for a private dinner afterwards, and I told them stories about Jim away from football that the grandkids wanted to hear because he was just great fun to be with. Some of the sayings that weren't proper English but made you fall over laughing. I'd said no twice to coming to Derby, and he was at me for about a year trying to get me. I'd said no twice because I'd just met my wife in Portsmouth in the mid-'90s, and he said, 'Listen, I know you love it down there but these two Italians, you will have never seen anything like these two play football. Come up tomorrow and have a look.' And they'd just lost against Newcastle in the League Cup but the two Italians were brilliant. I saw the stadium and, wow, this was fantastic.

We had a long night after the game and I agreed to it after that to work with him again. That night it was me, Jim, Alan Brazil, and Andy Gray in his office at three in the morning. We got a taxi back to the hotel where he'd put me up, and then he talked about the game until 5am. I woke up and thought, 'Do I *really* want to go back to that?!' but I said it to myself with a smile because it was going back to old times. And some of the performances were just fantastic. And he was right, the football side of me fell in love with the two Italians. Getting to know them and spending a lot of time with Eranio, we became very good friends and he made me the best tiramisu I've ever had. He brought it round to my family one Sunday. I used to ask him loads of questions about the Milan team and what they did in training, what he enjoyed about Derby, and he was a great mine of information for me.

My memories were of him enjoying that football and he loved the team that he built, and he was proud of it. It's different in Portsmouth because he came when we had a bunch of kids who weren't quite ready for the first team and he said, 'Fuck it, I'm gonna pick five of them tomorrow.' Jim, I haven't done the rooms yet! We played Darryl Powell, Darren Anderton, Kit Symons, Andy Awford and half of the team was just youth. He moulded them on a ride to the FA Cup semi-finals and how they never got to the Premier League; they got to 88 points and didn't go up. They lost out by scoring one goal less. Alan McLoughlin, Marc Chamberlain, Paul Walsh. People go on about all these modern methods, but Jim introduced football to Derby that hadn't been seen since Cloughie's day. And I'd argue it was more difficult to do it in Jim's day because the superpowers of Man United and Arsenal have arrived and Jim brought players from abroad.

Look at Portsmouth, what he did was unbelievable. That football was right on the doorstep of what he produced at Derby. We drew one game at Oxford with Portsmouth. We were 5-2 up and he had friends on the Oxford board, they leant down to me and said, 'This could be seven or eight in a minute. So he took a couple off and we ended up drawing 5-5. If we'd have won we'd have got promoted. He came in and kicked the skip, hurt his toe and he said to the lads, 'That will come back to haunt us.' But he said the next day, 'I've not seen football like that for ages,' but Jim could produce it. He liked attacking teams, he played different ways, different formations.

Some people go on about him and say he liked his red wine and he used to go mad. But look at what he brought to the game in terms of the players he introduced to the British game, and the systems he produced, he'd be fine managing now in the Premier League. He'd be right up there. I'm just proud of having my time with him. He treated me like a son, and I'd have to admit – a drinking partner! My wife had never seen me so upset as when I got the phone call from his daughter that he'd gone.

Everyone you speak to about him, he cared about them. I work in bits with the FA, and I always say that the players have to like the coach or head coach or manager. They won't play for them if they don't like them. Every day when you're with them, you don't see what happens on the training ground, but players must like Guardiola to play like that for him. Man United lads liked Sir Alex because he had a laugh with them and talked about racing. Now you have young coaches who come in and they want to change everything, and this is where I am, and one thing that drives me and it would drive Jim crazy, is when managers would do interviews and say 'my team'. It's the fans' team, it's the fans' players. You should always say 'our' and Jim always did that. It would always bug him. 'He must have given birth to all of them then!' he used to say, and he was right. He looked after players and cared about them and wanted them to do well and to be happy. It was important to him.

Me and my wife saw the other side to him a lot because we would eat out with them twice a week and we're still very close to Yvonne now. We saw what he was like following his retirement, and we went to stay with him and Yvonne in Spain. At Derby and at Portsmouth, he adapted to the modern player and, as they changed, he changed with that. Yes he would still lose his temper but he was so clever at making it right again. You hear these terms, but Jim really didn't hold a grudge with anyone and he was so good at that, whereas a lot of people now let things fester. You see it on social media now, people have a go and then they're enemies. But that never happened with Jim. He would still vent up until the day he died. I was with him three days before he died, and he was still Jim in hospital.

But we knew him so well, and when we speak about him, it just makes us smile. You just remember the happy stuff because he was such a funny guy. He had a lot of outside football loves as well. Jim loved his music, he loved his wine, walking and scenery. He liked his history as well. You'd be surprised what he liked! He liked his Tina Turner, she was a favourite. Frank Sinatra, that sort of thing. He liked his clothes, he had his jackets and would often wear a handkerchief in his top pocket. And he always pretty smart as well. He did have his stuff away from football that he did like, but it would be wrong to say he could switch off because he never could. He was always thinking about the next opponent or the next day's training.

* * *

DEON BURTON

Former Derby County striker who played under Jim Smith

He was my second dad. I always said he was my second dad. He was a real father figure and just like your parents you never wanted to let Jim down. They're always there by your side, and yes, honest truth can sometimes hurt but you know they're doing it for the right reasons, and that's how Jim was. If he liked you, his methods might not have been standard, but if you knew him the way that I did, I knew he was doing it for the right reasons because he thought highly of me.

He had me at Portsmouth, then Derby and then Portsmouth again. That's what makes a good manager. The man-management comes first, because he would always be polite and know the names of your mum and dad off by heart, and you thought it was all personal. He'd ask what you did at the weekend: 'Did you go out again Deon? Yeah, I know you did!' The little things, but the man management was second to none and you never wanted to let him down because you thought so highly of him.

He gave me my start in the job I wanted to do, he gave me my start and saw something in me. To play for him at the first club you've ever played for is great, but to then have the honour of him seeing enough in me to take me to another club, and then again to a third club, it just means even more. Maybe I might have doubted myself sometimes and wondered, 'How good am I?' But he obviously saw something in me with his experience that appreciated and rated me more than I rated myself. You don't owe anyone anything unless they have an opinion of something that can help, and he did that for me. I'm always indebted to Jim for that.

* * *

STEVE ROUND

Former Derby County coach and current assistant manager
at Arsenal under Mikel Arteta

Jim was obviously super passionate about his football but I thought he was quite a well-balanced individual. He was very comfortable in a social setting, he loved to go out with the wives and have a meal, and just entertain. And when you got a few red wines down him, he was incredibly entertaining. Around that time you had Brian Clough, Sir Alex, Big Sam. Lots of different characters that were almost larger than life. Ron Atkinson was his very good friend. So, he was very comfortable in that setting. My wife used to love going out with his wife and all mixing together, and Steve's [McClaren] wife, and it was a real family atmosphere together, and he looked after you really well.

There is nobody that I hold in more regard in football. He gave me my opportunity, he supported me, he looked after me. You have to remember that when I was 24 years of age and he first came into the club, I was the lowest I have ever been in my life. I'd had this dream ever since I can remember that I would be a professional footballer and play for Derby County and win the Premier League, play for England, you name it. That was the dream. And unfortunately one bad injury and it was taken away. All your dreams are shattered. And then along comes this guy who says, 'OK, yeah. That's happened. You've got another life and you've got a real chance to be something. You've got to channel all of that into this new career. You can be a career coach, and you've played at the highest level so you can develop into something special as a coach, and I'm going to help you do it.' That was really special.

To take me from where I was personally and give that opportunity and support through it, it meant a lot to me. It really did.

* * *

YOUL MAWÉNÉ

Former Derby County defender who was brought to England by Jim

There will always be great coaches but Jim and those generation of coaches, I don't think you'll make them like that anymore. I look at it, and I'm a bit impartial because I'm fond of those times as well; yes it wasn't as monitored or scientific in the approach, but you'd compensate by building a relationship with someone. I say that, but at the time Jim was a father figure for all the young players, or a grandfather figure. It's like your old man because he has a moan at you but deep down he really cares and really has love for you. That was Jim. I do feel the way football worked in those days with the amount of money, now with the overcomplicated science and the complicated approach, there is an element of proximity that's lost. We used to go and eat, go out, we used to go to the town centre, to your local Chinese, local shops, and Derby was crazy. People would just talk to you about the game all the time. They loved the club so much and you had an exchange with the people.

In my first few days ahead of pre-season, we had the barbecue at the chairman's house and the dinner ladies were there, everyone was just treated the same. The families, the kids were running around, that proximity sometimes gets lost. When I look at Jim, his impact and how he connected with people and got close to managing people, I do feel there is an element of me where you have to get the balance right. People like Jim I just don't think you'll find in the game anymore. I look back and think, 'What would have happened if we had maybe kept Jim Smith in some capacity as a leader? And kept those younger players, surrounded them? What could have happened?' I know we went down and by that time there had been a lot of changes. But sometimes you do wonder, look back and think it could have been a different story.

BIBLIOGRAPHY

Books

- Davis, G., and Matthews, P., *Greatest Games: Derby County* (Pitch Publishing, 2013)
- Ellis, A., *Derby County Thirty Memorable Games from the Nineties* (DB Publishing, 2011)
- Ellis, A., *The Baseball Ground: Gone but Not Forgotten* (2020)
- Ferguson, A., *My Autobiography* (Hodder & Stoughton, 2013)
- Hall, I., *Journey Through a Season* (Breedon Books, 1997)
- Higginbotham, D., *Rise of the Underdog* (Trinity Mirror, 2015)
- Hills, R., *Pride: The Inside Story of Derby County* (Pitch Publishing, 2020)
- McGrath, P., *Back from the Brink* (Arrow, 2007)
- Mortimer G., *Derby County: The Complete Record* (Breedon Books, 2006)
- Mortimer G., *The Who's Who of Derby County* (Breedon Books, 2004)
- Parkin, D., and Fearn, J., *Pride Park: The Story of a Stadium* (1999)
- Redknapp, H., *Always Managing: My Autobiography* (Ebury Press, 2013)
- Smith, J., *It's Only a Game* (Andre Deutsch, 2002)

- Webb, S., *Clough, Maxwell & Me (North Bridge Publishing, 2016)*

Publications
- Goulden, R. et al., *Newspaper Coverage of Mental Illness in the UK, 1992–2008* (2011)
- Derby Telegraph
- Rampage
- The Ram
- Numerous matchday programmes from away matches

Digital
- BBC Derby
- BBC Sport
- The42.ie
- The Coaches' Voice
- And to the many amazing people I do not know who have uploaded classic Derby County footage on to their YouTube channels. You are doing God's work. Or Taribo's.

DERBY COUNTY:
THE JIM SMITH YEARS

1995/96

13 Aug 1995	Derby County v Port Vale	0-0	League Division 1
19 Aug 1995	Reading v Derby County	3-2	League Division 1
26 Aug 1995	Derby County v Grimsby Town	1-1	League Division 1
30 Aug 1995	Wolves v Derby County	3-0	League Division 1
02 Sep 1995	Luton Town v Derby County	1-2	League Division 1
10 Sep 1995	Derby County v Leicester City	0-1	League Division 1
13 Sep 1995	Derby County v Southend United	1-0	League Division 1
16 Sep 1995	Portsmouth v Derby County	2-2	League Division 1
19 Sep 1995	Shrewsbury v Derby County	1-3	League Cup
23 Sep 1995	Barnsley v Derby County	2-0	League Division 1
01 Oct 1995	Derby County v Millwall	2-2	League Division 1
04 Oct 1995	Derby County v Shrewsbury	1-1	League Cup
07 Oct 1995	Sheffield United v Derby County	0-2	League Division 1
14 Oct 1995	Derby County v Ipswich Town	1-1	League Division 1
22 Oct 1995	Stoke City v Derby County	1-1	League Division 1
25 Oct 1995	Derby County v Leeds United	0-1	League Cup
28 Oct 1995	Derby County v Oldham Athletic	2-1	League Division 1
04 Nov 1995	Tranmere Rovers v Derby County	5-1	League Division 1
11 Nov 1995	Derby County v West Brom	3-0	League Division 1
18 Nov 1995	Derby County v Charlton Athletic	2-0	League Division 1

21 Nov 1995	Birmingham City v Derby County	1-4	League Division 1
25 Nov 1995	Crystal Palace v Derby County	0-0	League Division 1
02 Dec 1995	Derby County v Sheffield United	4-2	League Division 1
09 Dec 1995	Derby County v Barnsley	4-1	League Division 1
16 Dec 1995	Millwall v Derby County	0-1	League Division 1
23 Dec 1995	Derby County v Sunderland	3-1	League Division 1
26 Dec 1995	Huddersfield v Derby County	0-1	League Division 1
01 Jan 1996	Derby County v Norwich City	2-1	League Division 1
07 Jan 1996	Derby County v Leeds United	2-4	FA Cup
13 Jan 1996	Derby County v Reading	3-0	League Division 1
20 Jan 1996	Port Vale v Derby County	1-1	League Division 1
03 Feb 1996	Grimsby Town v Derby County	1-1	League Division 1
10 Feb 1996	Derby County v Wolves	0-0	League Division 1
17 Feb 1996	Southend United v Derby County	1-2	League Division 1
21 Feb 1996	Derby County v Luton Town	1-1	League Division 1
24 Feb 1996	Derby County v Portsmouth	3-2	League Division 1
28 Feb 1996	Leicester City v Derby County	0-0	League Division 1
02 Mar 1996	Derby County v Huddersfield	3-2	League Division 1
05 Mar 1996	Watford v Derby County	0-0	League Division 1
09 Mar 1996	Sunderland v Derby County	3-0	League Division 1
16 Mar 1996	Derby County v Watford	1-1	League Division 1
23 Mar 1996	Norwich City v Derby County	1-0	League Division 1
30 Mar 1996	Derby County v Stoke City	3-1	League Division 1
02 Apr 1996	Ipswich Town v Derby County	1-0	League Division 1
06 Apr 1996	Oldham Athletic v Derby County	0-1	League Division 1
08 Apr 1996	Derby County v Tranmere Rovers	6-2	League Division 1
14 Apr 1996	Charlton Athletic v Derby County	0-0	League Division 1
20 Apr 1996	Derby County v Birmingham City	1-1	League Division 1
28 Apr 1996	Derby County v Crystal Palace	2-1	League Division 1
05 May 1996	West Brom v Derby County	3-2	League Division 1

1996/97

17 Aug 1996	Derby County v Leeds United	3-3	Premier League
21 Aug 1996	Tottenham v Derby County	1-1	Premier League
24 Aug 1996	Aston Villa v Derby County	2-0	Premier League
04 Sep 1996	Derby County v Manchester United	1-1	Premier League
09 Sep 1996	Blackburn Rovers v Derby County	1-2	Premier League
14 Sep 1996	Derby County v Sunderland	1-0	Premier League
17 Sep 1996	Luton Town v Derby County	1-0	League Cup
21 Sep 1996	Sheffield Weds v Derby County	0-0	Premier League
25 Sep 1996	Derby County v Luton Town	2-2	League Cup
28 Sep 1996	Derby County v Wimbledon	0-2	Premier League
12 Oct 1996	Derby County v Newcastle United	0-1	Premier League
19 Oct 1996	Nottingham Forest v Derby County	1-1	Premier League
27 Oct 1996	Liverpool v Derby County	2-1	Premier League
02 Nov 1996	Derby County v Leicester City	2-0	Premier League
17 Nov 1996	Derby County v Middlesbrough	2-1	Premier League
23 Nov 1996	West Ham United v Derby County	1-1	Premier League
30 Nov 1996	Derby County v Coventry City	2-1	Premier League
07 Dec 1996	Arsenal v Derby County	2-2	Premier League
16 Dec 1996	Derby County v Everton	0-1	Premier League
21 Dec 1996	Southampton v Derby County	3-1	Premier League
26 Dec 1996	Sunderland v Derby County	2-0	Premier League
28 Dec 1996	Derby County v Blackburn Rovers	0-0	Premier League
11 Jan 1997	Wimbledon v Derby County	1-1	Premier League
18 Jan 1997	Chelsea v Derby County	3-1	Premier League
21 Jan 1997	Gillingham v Derby County	0-2	FA Cup
25 Jan 1997	Derby County v Aston Villa	3-1	FA Cup
29 Jan 1997	Leeds United v Derby County	0-0	Premier League
01 Feb 1997	Derby County v Liverpool	0-1	Premier League
15 Feb 1997	Derby County v West Ham United	1-0	Premier League

19 Feb 1997	Derby County v Sheffield Weds	2-2	Premier League
22 Feb 1997	Leicester City v Derby County	4-2	Premier League
26 Feb 1997	Derby County v Coventry City	3-2	FA Cup
01 Mar 1997	Derby County v Chelsea	3-2	Premier League
05 Mar 1997	Middlesbrough v Derby County	6-1	Premier League
08 Mar 1997	Derby County v Middlesbrough	0-2	FA Cup
15 Mar 1997	Everton v Derby County	1-0	Premier League
22 Mar 1997	Derby County v Tottenham	4-2	Premier League
05 Apr 1997	Manchester United v Derby County	2-3	Premier League
09 Apr 1997	Derby County v Southampton	1-1	Premier League
12 Apr 1997	Derby County v Aston Villa	2-1	Premier League
19 Apr 1997	Newcastle United v Derby County	3-1	Premier League
23 Apr 1997	Derby County v Nottingham Forest	0-0	Premier League
03 May 1997	Coventry City v Derby County	1-2	Premier League
11 May 1997	Derby County v Arsenal	1-3	Premier League

1997/98

09 Aug 1997	Blackburn Rovers v Derby County	1-0	Premier League
23 Aug 1997	Tottenham v Derby County	1-0	Premier League
30 Aug 1997	Derby County v Barnsley	1-0	Premier League
13 Sep 1997	Derby County v Everton	3-1	Premier League
16 Sep 1997	Southend United v Derby County	0-1	League Cup
20 Sep 1997	Aston Villa v Derby County	2-1	Premier League
24 Sep 1997	Sheffield Weds v Derby County	2-5	Premier League
27 Sep 1997	Derby County v Southampton	4-0	Premier League
01 Oct 1997	Derby County v Southend United	5-0	League Cup
06 Oct 1997	Leicester City v Derby County	1-2	Premier League
15 Oct 1997	Tottenham v Derby County	1-2	League Cup
18 Oct 1997	Derby County v Manchester United	2-2	Premier League
22 Oct 1997	Derby County v Wimbledon	1-1	Premier League

25 Oct 1997	Liverpool v Derby County	4-0	Premier League
01 Nov 1997	Derby County v Arsenal	3-0	Premier League
08 Nov 1997	Leeds United v Derby County	4-3	Premier League
18 Nov 1997	Derby County v Newcastle United	0-1	League Cup
22 Nov 1997	Derby County v Coventry City	3-1	Premier League
29 Nov 1997	Chelsea v Derby County	4-0	Premier League
06 Dec 1997	Derby County v West Ham United	2-0	Premier League
14 Dec 1997	Bolton v Derby County	3-3	Premier League
17 Dec 1997	Newcastle v Derby County	0-0	Premier League
20 Dec 1997	Derby County v Crystal Palace	0-0	Premier League
26 Dec 1997	Derby County v Newcastle United	1-0	Premier League
28 Dec 1997	Barnsley v Derby County	1-0	Premier League
03 Jan 1998	Derby County v Southampton	2-0	FA Cup
11 Jan 1998	Derby County v Blackburn	3-1	Premier League
17 Jan 1998	Wimbledon v Derby County	0-0	Premier League
24 Jan 1998	Coventry City v Derby County	2-0	FA Cup
31 Jan 1998	Derby County v Tottenham	2-1	Premier League
07 Feb 1998	Derby County v Aston Villa	0-1	Premier League
14 Feb 1998	Everton v Derby County	1-2	Premier League
21 Feb 1998	Manchester United v Derby County	2-0	Premier League
28 Feb 1998	Derby County v Sheffield Weds	3-0	Premier League
15 Mar 1998	Derby County v Leeds United	0-5	Premier League
28 Mar 1998	Coventry City v Derby County	1-0	Premier League
05 Apr 1998	Derby County v Chelsea	0-1	Premier League
11 Apr 1998	West Ham v Derby County	0-0	Premier League
13 Apr 1998	Derby County v Bolton	4-0	Premier League
18 Apr 1998	Crystal Palace v Derby County	3-1	Premier League
26 Apr 1998	Derby County v Leicester City	0-4	Premier League
29 Apr 1998	Arsenal v Derby County	1-0	Premier League
02 May 1998	Southampton v Derby County	0-2	Premier League
10 May 1998	Derby County v Liverpool	1-0	Premier League

1998/99

15 Aug 1998	Blackburn Rovers v Derby County	0-0	Premier League
22 Aug 1998	Derby County v Wimbledon	0-0	Premier League
29 Aug 1998	Middlesbrough v Derby County	1-1	Premier League
09 Sep 1998	Derby County v Sheffield Weds	1-0	Premier League
12 Sep 1998	Charlton Athletic v Derby County	1-2	Premier League
16 Sep 1998	Derby County v Manchester City	1-1	League Cup
19 Sep 1998	Derby County v Leicester City	2-0	Premier League
23 Sep 1998	Manchester City v Derby County	0-1	League Cup
26 Sep 1998	Aston Villa v Derby County	1-0	Premier League
03 Oct 1998	Derby County v Tottenham	0-1	Premier League
17 Oct 1998	Newcastle United v Derby County	2-1	Premier League
24 Oct 1998	Derby County v Manchester United	1-1	Premier League
28 Oct 1998	Derby County v Arsenal	1-2	League Cup
31 Oct 1998	Derby County v Leeds United	2-2	Premier League
07 Nov 1998	Liverpool v Derby County	1-2	Premier League
16 Nov 1998	Nottingham Forest v Derby County	2-2	Premier League
22 Nov 1998	Derby County v West Ham United	0-2	Premier League
28 Nov 1998	Southampton v Derby County	0-1	Premier League
05 Dec 1998	Derby County v Arsenal	0-0	Premier League
12 Dec 1998	Derby County v Chelsea	2-2	Premier League
19 Dec 1998	Coventry City v Derby County	1-1	Premier League
26 Dec 1998	Everton v Derby County	0-0	Premier League
28 Dec 1998	Derby County v Middlesbrough	2-1	Premier League
02 Jan 1999	Plymouth Argyle v Derby County	0-3	FA Cup
09 Jan 1999	Wimbledon v Derby County	2-1	Premier League
16 Jan 1999	Derby County v Blackburn Rovers	1-0	Premier League
23 Jan 1999	Swansea City v Derby County	0-1	FA Cup
30 Jan 1999	Sheffield Weds v Derby County	0-1	Premier League
03 Feb 1999	Manchester United v Derby County	1-0	Premier League
07 Feb 1999	Derby County v Everton	2-1	Premier League

13 Feb 1999	Huddersfield v Derby County	2-2	FA Cup
20 Feb 1999	Derby County v Charlton Athletic	0-2	Premier League
24 Feb 1999	Derby County v Huddersfield	3-1	FA Cup
27 Feb 1999	Tottenham v Derby County	1-1	Premier League
06 Mar 1999	Arsenal v Derby County	1-0	FA Cup
10 Mar 1999	Derby County v Aston Villa	2-1	Premier League
13 Mar 1999	Derby County v Liverpool	3-2	Premier League
20 Mar 1999	Leeds United v Derby County	4-1	Premier League
03 Apr 1999	Derby County v Newcastle United	3-4	Premier League
10 Apr 1999	Derby County v Nottingham Forest	1-0	Premier League
17 Apr 1999	West Ham United v Derby County	5-1	Premier League
24 Apr 1999	Derby County v Southampton	0-0	Premier League
02 May 1999	Arsenal v Derby County	1-0	Premier League
05 May 1999	Leicester City v Derby County	1-2	Premier League
08 May 1999	Derby County v Coventry City	0-0	Premier League
16 May 1999	Chelsea v Derby County	2-1	Premier League

1999/00

07 Aug 1999	Leeds United v Derby County	0-0	Premier League
10 Aug 1999	Derby County v Arsenal	1-2	Premier League
14 Aug 1999	Derby County v Middlesbrough	1-3	Premier League
21 Aug 1999	Coventry City v Derby County	2-0	Premier League
25 Aug 1999	Sheffield Weds v Derby County	0-2	Premier League
28 Aug 1999	Derby County v Everton	1-0	Premier League
11 Sep 1999	Wimbledon v Derby County	2-2	Premier League
14 Sep 1999	Swansea City v Derby County	0-0	League Cup
18 Sep 1999	Derby County v Sunderland	0-5	Premier League
22 Sep 1999	Derby County v Swansea City	3-1	League Cup
25 Sep 1999	Derby County v Bradford City	0-1	Premier League
04 Oct 1999	Southampton v Derby County	3-3	Premier League

13 Oct 1999	Derby County v Bolton	1-2	League Cup
16 Oct 1999	Derby County v Tottenham	0-1	Premier League
25 Oct 1999	Newcastle United v Derby County	2-0	Premier League
30 Oct 1999	Derby County v Chelsea	3-1	Premier League
06 Nov 1999	Liverpool v Derby County	2-0	Premier League
20 Nov 1999	Derby County v Manchester United	1-2	Premier League
28 Nov 1999	Arsenal v Derby County	2-1	Premier League
05 Dec 1999	Derby County v Leeds United	0-1	Premier League
11 Dec 1999	Derby County v Burnley	0-1	FA Cup
18 Dec 1999	Leicester City v Derby County	0-1	Premier League
26 Dec 1999	Derby County v Aston Villa	0-2	Premier League
28 Dec 1999	West Ham United v Derby County	1-1	Premier League
03 Jan 2000	Derby County v Watford	2-0	Premier League
15 Jan 2000	Middlesbrough v Derby County	1-4	Premier League
22 Jan 2000	Derby County v Coventry City	0-0	Premier League
05 Feb 2000	Derby County v Sheffield Weds	3-3	Premier League
12 Feb 2000	Everton v Derby County	2-1	Premier League
26 Feb 2000	Sunderland v Derby County	1-1	Premier League
04 Mar 2000	Derby County v Wimbledon	4-0	Premier League
11 Mar 2000	Manchester United v Derby County	3-1	Premier League
18 Mar 2000	Derby County v Liverpool	0-2	Premier League
25 Mar 2000	Aston Villa v Derby County	2-0	Premier League
02 Apr 2000	Derby County v Leicester City	3-0	Premier League
08 Apr 2000	Watford v Derby County	0-0	Premier League
15 Apr 2000	Derby County v West Ham	1-2	Premier League
21 Apr 2000	Bradford City v Derby County	4-4	Premier League
24 Apr 2000	Derby County v Southampton	2-0	Premier League
29 Apr 2000	Tottenham v Derby County	1-1	Premier League
06 May 2000	Derby County v Newcastle United	0-0	Premier League
14 May 2000	Chelsea v Derby County	4-0	Premier League

2000/01

19 Aug 2000	Derby County v Southampton	2-2	Premier League
23 Aug 2000	Newcastle United v Derby County	3-2	Premier League
26 Aug 2000	Everton v Derby County	2-2	Premier League
06 Sep 2000	Derby County v Middlesbrough	3-3	Premier League
10 Sep 2000	Derby County v Charlton Athletic	2-2	Premier League
16 Sep 2000	Sunderland v Derby County	2-1	Premier League
19 Sep 2000	Derby County v West Brom	1-2	League Cup
23 Sep 2000	Derby County v Leeds United	1-1	Premier League
26 Sep 2000	West Brom v Derby County	2-4	League Cup
30 Sep 2000	Aston Villa v Derby County	4-1	Premier League
15 Oct 2000	Derby County v Liverpool	0-4	Premier League
21 Oct 2000	Tottenham v Derby County	3-1	Premier League
28 Oct 2000	Leicester City v Derby County	2-1	Premier League
01 Nov 2000	Derby County v Norwich City	3-0	League Cup
06 Nov 2000	Derby County v West Ham United	0-0	Premier League
11 Nov 2000	Arsenal v Derby County	0-0	Premier League
18 Nov 2000	Derby County v Bradford City	2-0	Premier League
25 Nov 2000	Derby County v Manchester United	0-3	Premier League
29 Nov 2000	Fulham v Derby County	3-2	League Cup
02 Dec 2000	Ipswich Town v Derby County	0-1	Premier League
09 Dec 2000	Chelsea v Derby County	4-1	Premier League
16 Dec 2000	Derby County v Coventry City	1-0	Premier League
23 Dec 2000	Derby County v Newcastle United	2-0	Premier League
26 Dec 2000	Manchester City v Derby County	0-0	Premier League
30 Dec 2000	Southampton v Derby County	1-0	Premier League
01 Jan 2001	Derby County v Everton	1-0	Premier League
06 Jan 2001	Derby County v West Brom	3-2	FA Cup
13 Jan 2001	Middlesbrough v Derby County	4-0	Premier League
20 Jan 2001	Derby County v Manchester City	1-1	Premier League
27 Jan 2001	Blackburn Rovers v Derby County	0-0	FA Cup

30 Jan 2001	Charlton Athletic v Derby County	2-1	Premier League
03 Feb 2001	Derby County v Sunderland	1-0	Premier League
07 Feb 2001	Derby County v Blackburn Rovers	2-5	FA Cup
10 Feb 2001	Leeds United v Derby County	0-0	Premier League
24 Feb 2001	Derby County v Aston Villa	1-0	Premier League
03 Mar 2001	Derby County v Tottenham	2-1	Premier League
18 Mar 2001	Liverpool v Derby County	1-1	Premier League
31 Mar 2001	Coventry City v Derby County	2-0	Premier League
07 Apr 2001	Derby County v Chelsea	0-4	Premier League
14 Apr 2001	West Ham United v Derby County	3-1	Premier League
16 Apr 2001	Derby County v Leicester City	2-0	Premier League
21 Apr 2001	Bradford City v Derby County	2-0	Premier League
28 Apr 2001	Derby County v Arsenal	1-2	Premier League
05 May 2001	Manchester United v Derby County	0-1	Premier League
19 May 2001	Derby County v Ipswich Town	1-1	Premier League

2001/02

18 Aug 2001	Derby County v Blackburn Rovers	2-1	Premier League
21 Aug 2001	Ipswich Town v Derby County	3-1	Premier League
25 Aug 2001	Fulham v Derby County	0-0	Premier League
08 Sep 2001	Derby County v West Ham United	0-0	Premier League
12 Sep 2001	Derby County v Hull City	3-0	League Cup
15 Sep 2001	Derby County v Leicester City	2-3	Premier League
23 Sep 2001	Leeds United v Derby County	3-0	Premier League
29 Sep 2001	Derby County v Arsenal	0-2	Premier League

FROM THE SAME AUTHOR

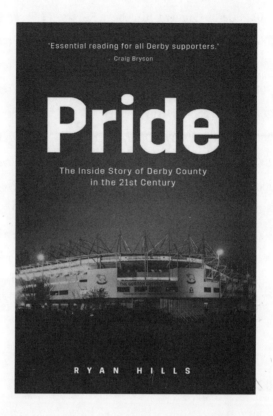

Pride: The Inside Story of Derby County in the 21st Century is the fascinating story of one of Britain's most tumultuous football teams, as told by the people at the heart of the club. Ryan Hills gained exclusive access to almost 50 former players, managers and board members to bring you the Rams' modern history. The move to Pride Park in 1997 was supposed to mark an exciting new chapter for the club. But despite initial success, things started to go wrong. Relegation from the Premier League caused huge financial strife, leading to the arrest of three board members. On the pitch, a single promotion brought the worst season in Derby's history and a 362-day wait for a win. Since that fateful season, the club have been on a cyclical and so far fruitless mission to return to the Premier League, while dressing-room turmoil, car crashes and a man named Bobby have stood in their way. Pride gives you the inside track on a football club that refuses to accept obscurity, as revealed by those who know it best.

Thank you, Jim.